Watching Sea Birds

Watching Sea Birds

RICHARD PERRY

ILLUSTRATED BY RICHARD RICHARDSON

TAPLINGER PUBLISHING COMPANY
NEW YORK

First published in the United States in 1975 by
TAPLINGER PUBLISHING CO., INC.
New York, New York.
Copyright © 1975 by Richard Perry
All rights reserved.
Printed in Great Britain

Library of Congress Catalog Card Number: 75-904
ISBN 0-8008-8047-1

CONTENTS

INTRODUCTION

This is an account of two springs and summers devoted exclusively to intensive watching of sea bird colonies. On Lundy my main studies were kittiwakes, puffins, razorbills and guillemots from 20 March to 7 August; and on Noss, in Shetland, great skuas, arctic skuas and gannets from 2 April to 18 September.

Northumberland 1974   Richard Perry

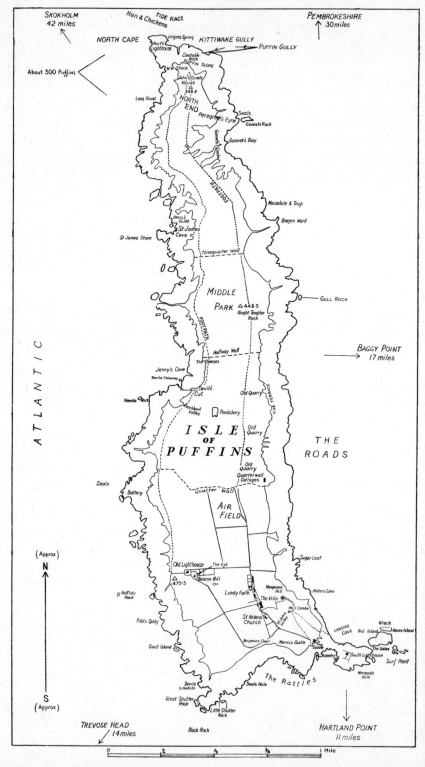

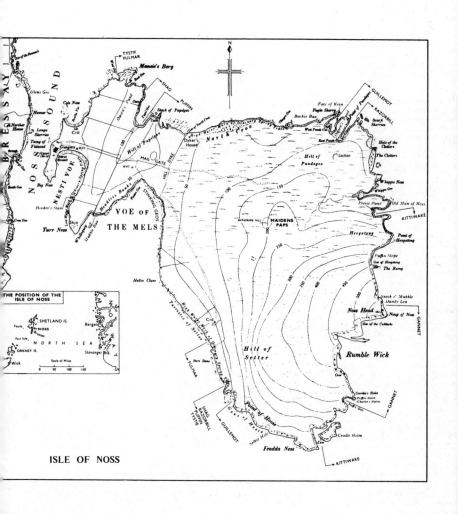

ISLE OF NOSS

I

HOME FROM SEA

Look west to the Atlantic from the steep headlands of North Devon. When the rain clouds are low there is a grey blur at the horizon, which becomes a long buttress of cliffs on clear days. The Norsemen, coming upon this colossal block of granite shearing out of the sea, named it Lunde, or Island of Puffins – *lundi* is still a puffin among the men of the Faroes. For hundreds of years this stronghold of pirates and smugglers and renegades has also been known as a fastness of nesting sea birds. Therefore, on a March morning, we shut up the cottage in the wooded Devon combe and flew over the green marshes of the Taw at a thousand feet, climbing another thousand feet into the brilliant sunshine over the sea. Twenty minutes of passaging from one enveloping wisp of cloud mist to another, and a 400-foot wall of cliff and green siding was swooping up at us. Swaying down over a huddle of farm buildings and a square-towered church at the southern end of the island, we banked round an old lighthouse, sped low over a stone dyke and came to rest on a rough sheep pasture. We stepped out into the clean cold air of an Atlantic wind. The sear winter grazing was white with gulls, and from on high sounded the deep bassoon notes of great black-backs, wheeling black and silver in the sun. All day and every day, especially on fine evenings, but also on stormy, the island's dominant sound was the antiphonal crying and sweet barking of the gulls.

Our dwelling would be a ruinous keeper's cottage beside an old lighthouse. Standing on Beacon Hill, the highest point of the island, the lantern of the Old Light was 570 feet above the breakers booming against the steep cliffs and sidings below. From its derelict gallery, ninety feet above the ground, we could look over the three mile length of the island : a table mountain, half a mile across, sheering up 400 feet from the sea on granite cliffs and shelving green sidings. Away to the north of the Old Light there was rough sheep grazing as far as Quarter Wall : a grey dyke straggling across the island from siding to siding. Beyond the dyke was a stretch of heather and tussocky bogs of scrub willow and waving cotton plumes. Between Halfway Wall and Three-quarter Wall were the old bracken-strewn pastures of Middle Park, which girdled the island with a green belt – *Inyswyre,* Isle of Hay, was an early name for the Island. Beyond Three-quarter Wall were more brown heather moors scarred with outcrops of weathered granite, and at the north end an arid plateau of grey, fire-scorched wastes of granite grit, red with stonecrop.

Three hundred feet below the grey and black shale and slate of the cliffs south-east of the Old Light was the quarter-moon bay of Landing Cove and its tiny beach of shingle and boulders, all grey. The shingle strewn with spars, rusted boats and derricks and huge bell lobster pots had silted up what was once a little rock harbour for the fishermen, before a concrete breakwater checked the natural sweeping of the tides. The mind drew an infinite tranquillity from the island's coves, with their black smuggling caverns and their deep narrow steps cut steeply into the face of the cliff, zigzagging up to the black and white South Light. In June the valerian on the edge of the grey road winding up from the beach was a blaze of carmine and red against the sombre slate cliffs. Above was the square grey ruin of Marisco Castle, sentinel this 800 years over Landing Cove, and high up in the green sidings the wooded cleft of Millcombe – *Lunde* can also mean a grove, either of trees or of worship – with its wild hyacinths and golden kingcups, its groves of oak and willow, ash and sycamore, beeches and conifers. Northwards from Landing Cove a hanging terrace wound high across the face of the sidings, under and over the jumbled trunks of ancient willows uprooted by easterly gales, past cavernous bushy grottoes and the ivied walls of old roofless cottages and derelict, overgrown quarry workings, from whose square-hewn sides hung great clusters of broom in globes of burnished gold.

At Halfway Wall the terrace lost itself in a maze of deer and goat tracks, beaten out in the crumbling mould through the belts of bracken that clothed the eastern side of the island with an almost impenetrable undergrowth from May onwards. The furled brown claws of the bracken shot up five, six or even seven feet from the mould, sweet-smelling with the bluebell fragrance of a thousand years.

Where the terrace ended, there was a great gathering of Knights Templar carved out of craggy outcrops from the sidings : six or seven giant figures sitting in effigy, mailed fists crossed on sword hilts between drawn-up knees – for which reason, no doubt, the Welsh knew the island as *Caersidi*, the Fortress of the Fairies. Further north a steep crag, Peregrine's Eyrie, hung over the Rock of Gannets. From the steep rounded summits of the Eyrie and adjacent granite crags one looked down and out a hundred feet or so to the flattish top of the Rock : a granite sphinx, bleached by the sun and whitened by the briny spray, rearing up 200 feet from the green Atlantic swell; no gannets have nested on the Rock this century, though known to have done so for hundreds of years previously. Instead, the ebbing wavelets lapping the base of the Rock echoed the moaning music of the great grey seals, whose sleek shining marbled bodies cruised lazily and sinuously through the clear green waters.

The tremendous cliffs, stacks and promontories of the island's north and Atlantic coasts were fretted by innumerable sea holes and coves and bays, and riven by stupendous chasms two or three hundred feet deep and seventy yards across. In autumn and early winter the multitudinous ledges and niches of these cliffs are usually deserted, save for an occasional pensive gull or a cormorant fishing in the deep waters below; but they will undoubtedly be visited by kittiwakes and guillemots from time to time during this offseason, for on cliffs as far apart as Cornwall and St Abb's Head kittiwakes are to be seen standing on old nest-drums early in October, while at St Abb's Head as many as a thousand guillemots may be massed on their nesting ledges on a fine day at the end of that month. So too, while some fulmars are visiting late-fledging young in the middle of September on the east and north coasts of Scotland, others are sitting up on the cliffs in the first week of October, and are in daily attendance at these by the end of November, although they will not lay eggs until the middle of the following May. However, shortly before Christmas kittiwakes begin to fish regularly in the Lundy tide race, and guillemots come in from sea to caw and jostle on the cliff ledges and platforms. It was these, the seventy thousand or so kittiwakes, guillemots, razorbills and puffins, that were to be my primary study.

Until incubation begins in May the attendance of guillemots at the cliffs is irregular, and the ledges and platforms are frequently deserted for days at a time; this is true also of razorbills which, though returning to Lundy waters late in December, do not alight on the cliffs and sidings until late in February, and of puffins returning from their winter fishing waters late in March. But once the old year is out the attraction of the island is always felt, and there are few calm days that do not bring some guillemots in to the cliffs. Individuals of these pelagic species frequent their nesting cliffs for seven or eight months of the twelve, for there are still a few guillemots on the cliffs late in August, and kittiwakes in September. Throughout the autumn and early winter there are always a few kittiwakes hovering over the lines of every north-east fishing coble in inshore waters, and packs of twenty-five or more white-faced guillemots bobbing on the swell. From their first coming in December until they lay their eggs in May the behaviour of the guillemots on their ledges undergoes little change. Like the fulmars, they are as noisily conscious of their cliff environment on the first day of their return as at the height of the nesting season. Yesterday they swam silently over the sea, diving and flapping their wings, as they had done daily for five months past : today, without any intermediate period of adjustment, they are noisy and quarrelsome on the cliffs!

Until May, attendance at their nesting territories of all three auks showed an almost one hundred per cent coincidence with calm weather and small seas : and absence a similar coincidence with stormy weather and big seas, and, to a small extent, with the thick fog which is usually associated with a heavy ground swell; while units lingered for a day after the breaking of the weather, or arrived the day before a storm had abated on the seas about Lundy. If we allow the usual day's or two day's latitude for the big Atlantic swell that presages tempest, and a similar period for the subsidence of the swell out at sea, it is clear that the comings and goings of the auks depended entirely on the state of the sea. We can then assign one of three reasons for their spasmodic periods of absence from the island : that heavy seas had driven them further afield for their fishing; that bad weather had rendered fishing so unprofitable as to necessitate a long stay at sea – for until incubation began few auks fished anywhere in the vicinity of the island, despite the ample supply of whitebait which the kittiwakes picked up in the tide race; or that good weather gave full rein to their reproductive impulses, with the consequent inclination to come to land. Total absences of guillemots might run to as much as eight days at a time, though three to five days was the usual period. Puffins and razorbills seldom stayed out for as long as four days, and their absence was never quite complete. Three days was the normal period of consecutive full attendance for all species. On such days they were on the sea and on the wing about the cliffs at the first light: little groups of auks continually whirring north, south, east and west through the thousands of kittiwakes fishing in the ebb tide round the North Cape, many apparently coming in from open sea and heading for the cliffs. But by two in the afternoon most of them had gone out to sea again, although by mid-April units were staying until dark : especially of guillemots which tended to stay later than the other two, and of which a few blocks would remain on the stacks all night late in April incessantly noisy.

R.A. Richardson

Puffins on a ledge.

II

PUFFINS – EIGHTEEN WEEKS ON A SIDING

1. *The Dancers*

It was on a morning late in March, with a chill mist blowing off the sea, that climbing over the south escarpment of Puffin Slope I chanced upon one of those scenes of which a naturalist dreams. Over the green siding circled an endless army of puffins and razorbills, and many hundreds more stood about in ones and twos on the boulders and on the grass plots between them. For hour after hour this astounding flighting continued, while I half sheltered behind a boulder. And the next day too, 30 March, the massed thousands were still circling across the slope into a tearing easterly gale.

While I sat for hours half hidden, an unbroken column of red-billed, red-webbed puffins hurtled with menacing directness at my boulder, swaying from side to side on the gale : radiating like streams of tracer bullets to their respective boulders seventy yards up and down the Slope. Sheering off easily, without shock, from my head, with a soft flutter-thud of keeling wings, the short black leaf points of their spread tails projected fanwise on either side of their scarlet or orange legs as they turned to plane down to the sea with great *élan*.

Hovering delicately on flickering wings, with rose-coloured paddles let down, some pitch neatly on to their boulders, bowed forward into the wind, with great bills uptilted and convex wings lifted for some seconds well above the level of their backs, before standing fair and square on their vermilion tarsi, so brilliant against the dull green and yellow lichen of the grey rock. But they soon take off again, drooping at head and stern, with perfect swallow dives, and quiver like black hawkmoths down the Slope : red webs clasped together, stretched out behind, delicately fluttering wings arched a little convexly – a most graceful, fragile motion. They circle swiftly out over the sea, often mounting to four or five hundred feet with quick-beating whirring wings, and rejoin the throng of their fellows flighting like a scattered swarm of starlings hawking winged ants.

Once in a while hundreds, sometimes thousands of puffins from both above and below ground, and often razorbills and kittiwakes from the gullies below, leave the Slope spontaneously and shoal out to sea : a black and silver cloud over the water. Though three or four thousand may alight on the sea, there is no apparent diminution in the number remaining on the boulders. Others wheel back to join the circle of flighters : perhaps to alight again on their boulders and run up their sheer sides with wings raised, beetlewise; or tumble on to the grassy terraces. Down these they run and hop very nimbly, with a comically cautious air of looking guardedly where they are going, for their great beaks are bowed to their breasts and their short wings bound tightly to their sides.

When the flighting dies, and a great many puffins are swimming on the sea below the Slope, there are still others popping out from burries and from below boulders for a long while after: already, on the first day of their return, they go in and out of their nesting burrows, often landing and scuttering, in almost one movement. Later still, when the jumbled scree of white-grey boulders seemed bare and strangely desolate of its former life and colour, I was suddenly aware of the white belly and gaily coloured beak of a puffin standing on a boulder seven feet from me, and then another, and another. A sudden soft thud of wings by my side or at my back and a puffin whirred past with scarlet paddles spread wide, gliding swifly seawards, with the fine rocketing plane of a partridge.

On the evening before this mass flighting, a single puffin – and he the first home from eight months at sea – had whirred over Puffin Slope, but had shortly vanished out to sea again. Normally the returning puffins frequent the seas about the North End for four or five days before coming in to visit their burrows on the sidings, but the calm weather and mist and damp of the morning following this particular homing presumably influenced them to land immediately : for it is always this type of weather that they favour for their landing.

In these early days, in contrast to the incessant mating antics of guillemots and affectionate nibbling of razorbills, the puffins displayed little excitement or even awareness of one another. During their first two days on the Slope I only once saw a puffin do as much as run at another and eject him from a point that was too close to the mouth of a burrow. Although in pairs, prolonged observation was often necessary before it could be confirmed that two little puffins standing or sitting side by side on a boulder were indeed a mated pair.

To sit among these thousands of puffins and razorbills continually alighting and taking off, standing or sitting, a dozen on a boulder, preening or asleep with heads tucked back into wings, has been one of the supreme experiences of my life as a naturalist. For once among birds I was not an object of fearful suspicion, but only of curiosity. These puffins were just in from the vast pathways of ocean. At midwinter I have come upon them in ones and twos out to the twelve-mile limit of the onshore fisherman : bounding resiliently from wave to wave off bright coral paddles stretched out behind them, flat and widely splayed : or bobbing up and down on the swell, sipping water nervously at the coble's approach. The thousands present on Puffin Slope had only recently been scattered over an enormous mileage of ocean in units and little packs. Yet here they were ringing round me confidently, a score or more in a seven-foot circle about me conducting their various little intimacies, indifferent to my presence, so suspect to most wild birds.

And what I had hoped for eventually happened. First two and then three puffins alighted on the boulder against which I was sitting and, not content with that, came pattering very easily up its far side with the aid of their tiny black claws, to examine me more closely from its apex. One, indeed, pattered down to its nearest edge and there squatted on its white belly without betraying any uneasiness at my small movements. And then, to crown it, another puffin settled by his side, and the two squatted facing me, their feathers intermingled, so close that I had only to stretch out my hand to touch them.

By his confidence and uniquely engaging ways the puffin was to make a stronger appeal to me and leave a deeper impression on my mind than any other bird – excepting, for different reasons, the remarkable guillemot. His every small mannerism and oddness of plumage is graven on the retina of my memory – the black pupil and sparkling red-brown iris of his eye set deeply in its bright terracotta orbital ring, within the embossed slate bars of its triangle : a tiny grey crease slanting up from its apex and another running back from it across the wide white sweep of his protuberant cheek with its pleasant smoky blush. Not a comical eye at all, but soft and limpid and startlingly alive and intelligent when contrasted with the cold hard eyes of adult gulls. In some lights the slate bars were an intense black, giving him that partly depraved, partly attractive makeup associated with a liberal use of eye-black! Most cock puffins displayed a greater expanse of white cheek and were altogether bigger in the head and plumper in the body than their mates, but it was not always easy to ascertain which was which if they were not together.

At the base of his smoke-grey bill, with its great carmine coulter-neb embossed with pale horn, is a soft, pale-peach rosette of folded skin : a bright disk of colour above his grey chin. His rusty-black mantle has a sealskin gloss in the sun, which, shining through the membranes of his webs, lights them up a glowing scarlet or orange. This is also the startling hue of his black-gartered tarsi.

After this first homing all but a stray bird or two went out to sea for a couple of days : to come in *en masse* with the first big landfall of razorbills on Puffin Slope on 2 April, and settle down to all those diverse antics that are necessary to a puffin's full enjoyment of the nesting cycle. One or two pairs 'kiss', in a manner peculiarly their own, with a violent shaking of heads and rapping of hard bills. This entails much mutual pattering around one another and nuzzling in of great bills : they get down to it like boxers, crouching and weaving, each pushing and rapping its bill right along the other's. Sometimes both bear in, at other times only one, the second retreating, with a more upright stance. And the brittle rapping is frequently broken off for a moment's reflection, only to be taken up again with renewed vigour at the advance of one or the other, for one bird is usually keener to prolong this pleasure than the other. Each bout of bill rapping is succeeded by a slight, thought perceptible, sippering of their scissor mandibles. It is probable, therefore, that, as in the case of so many other sea birds, a certain secretion is exuded during the rapping, pleasurable to the participants.

The return of the puffins was welcomed by the gulls, and it was a common sight to see a pair of great black-backs disembowelling an unfortunate puffin or razorbill, or even a shearwater, or waiting on an oiled puffin, finally plopping down on to it : only to leave it in dislike of the viscous oil. But this season the puffins were spared their deadliest persecutors, the peregrines : deadliest but not most destructive, for it is the insidious brown rat that works most havoc with their eggs and chicks.

After their first amorousness almost all the puffins deserted the sidings for another five days : though on the fourth day the sea below Puffin Slope was characteristically spattered with ones and twos and threes of twinkling white breasts and black mantles : grey and silver dots on the sun-stream at a quarter of a mile. Flotillas rode the waves in a continual communal bob on the Atlantic swell, which often spun them round, despite the alternate paddling of their tiny orange or scarlet webs, visible in the deep green water two hundred feet below and four hundred yards out. Some floated, idly circling, their bills rose-coloured in the pale morning sun : others spun around, their heads turned back into their wings. Ones and pairs and small units were continually flying forward, with square-spread paddles like tiny spurts of flame, to plunge into the water and up – for a puffin normally plumps into the sea with his whole body submerging, although alighting on dropped webs. Continually rising in the sea, they flapped their short wings and frequently sipped water – habits common to most sea birds. Occasionally one rocketed three or four hundred yards down to the sea from her burrow and alighted on the water by the side of what was presumably her mate, though from the moment she left the burrow her line of flight was as straight as an arrow.

On the fifth day, 8 April, there was a full house of puffins on the Slope, and many more than hitherto spreading thickly to the north over the thrift-cushioned slopes of Kittiwake Gully, and to the south over the bluff dividing Puffin Slope from the colony of lesser black-backed gulls. One or two pairs were even perched on the crags crowning the Slope, and there were other pairs east and north of the lighthouse and on the north-west slopes over the great guillemot colonies. Here, by 10 April, many scores were dotted about as far south as the great chasm of Long Roost, which was the home of some three thousand guillemots and fifteen hundred razorbills. Looking down the three hundred feet of Puffin Slope from the crags, the moraine-like jumble of great boulders swarmed with puffins and razorbills as with a plague of beetles. The grassy parts were dotted with puffins in ones and twos, standing or sitting, egg-like — so fat are their white bellies — at innumerable entrances to burrows, often half in. Rows of white bellies, bright in the morning sun, twinkled along the terraces all the way up the Slope : the sentinels retreating slowly, unsteadily and a little apprehensively backwards on their mates' speedy alighting in from sea. Delightful as they were on the turfy terraces and tumbled boulders of the Slope, their colours were even brighter on the sidings of thrift, where, seen from above, they stood sentinel in scarlet and black on the bright blue-green cushions of thrift.

I sat among them on the Slope for four hours, a more or less disregarded spectator of a scene like none other in the world of birds, watching with unbounded interest the gradual unfolding of this new terrestrial existence. From indeterminate directions sounded a continual bass sobbing *co-o-or-aa* : an elusive and very properly sepulchral groan, for it came mainly from those little birds grubbing about underground in turfy burrows or rock tunnels beneath the boulders. Under the fifty thousand square yards of the Slope was a world of subterranean activity. Occasionally an enquiring gaudy bill and white cheek appeared at the sunlit entrance to a dark burrow, over which a second puffin stood guard outside, the owner vanishing into the darkness again on seeing me. And from time to time a dishevelled puffin, her white belly stained with earth, would suddenly appear at the mouth of her burry, and stand outside it defiantly on widely planted legs, visibly panting from her exertions. Other puffins, both male and female, went in and out of burries with beakfuls of dead and fresh grasses, or having deposited one load, immediately came out again to collect another. This collecting might be undertaken alone or with mates standing by, and the amount taken into the burrow varied greatly from one bird to another, dead grasses being preferred. Although in this operation the enormous beak is slightly parted along the whole length of the mandibles, the grasses are actually picked up by a nibbling motion of that very hooked tip to the upper mandible, with which the puffin also nibbles his mate's cheeks affectionately. This enables him, incidentally, to go on picking up material long after his bill is apparently crammed full.

As yet, however, the coordination between impulse and purpose is characteristically incomplete. One collector shakes her bill violently and scatters her great bunch of grasses to the winds. Or first one little puffin patters out from a burrow with a beakful of stuff, and then, a few seconds or minutes later, another, much stained about the belly, both looking very bashful. For some minutes they stand at its entrance, turning their great heads alertly from side to side, before swallow-diving down to the sea, the male still holding his grasses. These he continues to grip while bobbing on the swell and during his circling athwart the Slope in the massed flight of his fellows. It is possible that more than mere nidificatory operations are conducted in the seclusion of the burrows, and these bashful goings in and comings out, one hard upon the other's shoulder, are not unconnected with more passionate pleasures. Their ingoings certainly interest other puffins in the vicinity, and the male of a nearby pair, on observing one such dual entry, takes a tentative step or two in the direction of the burrow: but returns to his mate. Later, however, his curiosity or desire is too strong for him, and he patters along the terrace and peers in at the burrow, but, as before, quickly returns to his mate. In the course of my investigations I sometimes chanced upon a solitary puffin standing in her burrow on the few grasses she had yet managed to collect, having a fine caw all to herself. A most despairing groan, this cawing, or a satirical guffaw, according to one's mood of the moment – a *haa-aa* . . . *aa-aa/aa-aa-aa* – but like many other things pertaining to the puffin, unique. Usually silent outside his burrow, in contrast to razorbills and guillemots, a puffin startled into flight from his boulder would occasionally give vent to his alarm with a short harsh *urrr*.

This acceleration of vocal expression coincided with greater physical excitement, and everywhere over the Slope might be seen the delightful and exclusively puffinesque spectacle of hundreds of little birds dancing. Shifting leisurely from one web to the other, padding slowly and impressively up and down, parrot-like, the comical little fellow paces slowly forward over the boulder, holding himself very erect, with short tail, and indeed his whole stern, perked up like a wren's and his huge bill drawn stiffly in to his breast. It soon became apparent that every puffin alighting on the Slope was likely to provoke another already *in situ* to a brief dancing, and that every bout of bill rapping was preceded and worked up to by one or both of the participants circling round with this dignified and bashful lifting of the webs.

The puffin is a quiet and pacific little fellow for the most part, rubbing shoulders with those neighbours who patter up and down outside the very entrance to his burrow, with very little of the aggressiveness of razorbills and guillemots. This equanimity is fortunate, for the back slope of Puffin Gully, for instance, fifteen yards square, was honeycombed with the burrows of seventy-five pairs of puffins : nor was this an exceptional density. Occasional desperate and prolonged combats are, however, waged over the actual holding of what must be a limited supply of desirable burrows. Two with bills locked fast somersault head over tail down the Slope, thudding heavily with great smacks from ledge to ledge of the cliffs below. When finally falling in mid air they break and whir seawards. Their tenacity is remarkable, and they fight always with grappling bills. Of two grimly grappling thus at the mouth of a burrow, one eventually pushes the other backwards down the siding with one red web hard up against his breast, and the two go rolling down to the sea, smashing heedlessly and terribly down the face of the cliff. Separating in their flight to the water, they come up twice again and fight outside the burrow. Despite their vigorous scrapping, other puffins in the vicinity ignore them, beyond pattering hastily out of the way of their somersault down the Slope. On the third and last of these they separate as usual in their flight to the water, but on this occasion, after swimming round and about for some seconds, they come together and renew their fighting, spinning around one another in a threshing circle.

Actual fighting is usually restricted to the occupation of nesting burrows. When it is merely a matter of standing room on a boulder the bellicose impulse is only momentarily dominant, and the combatants quickly and abruptly break off hostilities, to pad about their mates instead and rap bills with great ardour. The mere alighting of another puffin on the same terrace is sufficient to provoke a bout of bill rapping or, at the least, a measure of dancing from a pair already *in situ*. The only impulse which struck me as being very much more, and most amusingly, to the fore among all three auks than among most wild birds was that of curiosity. Sentinel puffins would turn their heads to watch their neighbours alight, and run nimbly to a boulder to observe their mates climbing up its opposite side; while those emerging from burrows would usually stand outside for several minutes, looking curiously about them and shaking their enormous bills.

By the third week in April many puffins were approaching their peak of emotional excitement : though this was not nearly so sustained or so intense as that of razorbills and guillemots. Increased excitement was, however, expressed by a new antic, in which the males would repeatedly cock up their closed bills. For this antic there was a good reason, since it was now that the puffin conducted his mating ceremony. This again, in marked contrast to the incessant mating of razorbills and guillemots, was rarely to be seen. If puffins do not mate in their burrows, and I have no actual evidence that they do, then their matings take place solely and infrequently on the sea. I saw only one attempt, and that unsuccessful, at a mating on a boulder : the hen puffin running around it, with the cock balancing precariously on her stern with wildly fanning wings. This was evidently an abnormal procedure, and the ceremony was normally to be observed among those afloat in packs of five hundred or so off the cliffs : but not, I think, after the month of April. Continually 'kissing' pairs twirled round and round on the swell. And as among packs of razorbills or, for that matter, teal or eider, there was a strained tension visible among the trios and little groups of the puffin packs : the hens constantly turning away from their attendant cock or cocks, with that suggestive attitude so common among wild birds of being uncomfortable at what the males' bill cocking might imply. To avoid their attentions they eventually dived, seeming to submerge a split second before opening their wings, and popped up again a few feet away. Should, however, the hen be well-disposed, the cock mounts her, after much bill cocking – when afloat he holds his head higher than she does – while she swims with head and breast high out of the water, and he flaps his wings vigorously. But even if he has got thus far, she may shortly dive to rid herself of him. Very occasionally, a cock puffin persuaded another cock's mate to a brief bill rapping with him before the other cock, suddenly aware of what was going on, drove off the seducer with swift and savage onslaught.

So here on Puffin Slope at the end of April were some five thousand puffins alighting with raised wings on the boulders and pattering up their sides : standing very erect on their summits or 'kissing' with a brittle rapping of horny bills; collecting grasses, going in and out of burrows to investigate nesting possibilities, and cawing in their dark chambers : a continual bass chorus under the boulder at my feet; running along terraces very swiftly, jumping from one to another with arched wings; dancing; sitting like eggs - one or two sitting back on the length of their shanks in the manner of razorbills; preening; sleeping with closed eyes or heads tucked back under wings; hopping from boulder to boulder; yawning with straight-edged scissor bills, or flapping wings; and finally swallow-diving down the Slope to the sea two hundred feet below and joining that army of their fellows endlessly circling over sea and slope.

To go out in the evening and find the Slope deserted and barren of all life but a stray gull or pipit or rabbit, was unreal. But until the second week in May it was so.

2. *Burrow Antics*

The morning of 8 May was fair after fog at night, and when I sat down on the south slope of tiny Puffin Gully I was aware of exceptional activity among the puffins thirty yards away on the opposite slope, and much sporadic collecting of grasses. One, pulling up an enormous billful of fresh grasses and weeds, continued, as ever, to pluck them long after his bill was apparently full ; but after standing about, often shaking the grasses tickling his head, he flew down to sea with his load in the familiar way. How and why does a puffin differentiate between dead and fresh grasses? For while a minority may pluck fresh grasses, the majority patter deliberately over fresh patches of a terrace to pluck the dead stuff at its edge. And, for the first time, why only now were puffins frequently to be seen standing on one leg scratching their heads? – an antic which required the steadying of a shuffled wing, and was even then a shaky business. Again, it had hitherto been exceptional to observe a puffin excrete while present on the Slope : indeed for some days after their initial return, the boulders remained unwhitened by either razorbills or puffins. Yet on this day puffins were continually turning their tails to the edges of boulders or turfy ledges, in characteristic sea-bird manner, and ejecting a powerful yellow stream very possibly on to the head of a fellow below.

The main activity of the day, however, had to do with the continual goings in and out of burrows, round the entrances to which there was unprecedented excitement. Even those puffins merely entering burrows were of interest to their neighbours, though there were only two or three instances of territorial aggressiveness : one puffin gripping another firmly by the nape, until the latter could free himself and escape down to the sea. Pairs of puffins were continually rapping bills, one in and one out of a burrow : other pairs peering at, or in to burrows with quaintly cocked heads. 'Kissing' in burrows stimulated an enormous amount of interest among other puffins in the vicinity, even among those several yards distant, who would come pattering up in their sheepish way, very upright of carriage with beaks bowed in to chins, and evidently full of curiosity. On one occasion no fewer than fourteen puffins were gathered round the entrance to a burrow, and three or four were actually in its entrance gully at the same time : though this was partly because the gully formed the entrance to two burrows. But after a strong suspicion that one of a pair 'kissing' in this gully had previously rapped bills with a mate inside one of the burrows, I saw him rap bills with two puffins outside, one after the other. Not only, therefore, did these bouts of 'kissing' arouse the close and deep interest of other puffins in the vicinity, but they so stimulated some that occasionally a third bird tried to join in. He, or she, was usually driven off by one of the 'kissers', but was often so worked up that he continued to wave his bill in the air, with no other bill to rap.

This double burrow continued to be a centre of interest for more than an hour : first one and then another puffin, and certainly more than the four residents, marched along its entrance gully, without apparently causing any territorial excitement. On one occasion three separate puffins entered the gully together : two rapped bills, and the third, trying to join in, was repulsed, but continued to lean down over the edge of the gully close to the 'kissers' until another puffin came over and cocked his bill at her, whereupon she moved away.

Almost every bout of bill rapping, in or out of burrows, attracted a group of highly interested observers anxious to join in, and those rapping would break off abruptly with a characteristic slow, strained tilting up sideways of their huge bills at the nearest intruder. The rapping was usually resumed after a long menacing glare, but should the intrusion be especially resented – should, that is, the kissers be sufficiently worked up, sexually or territorially, to feel strongly aggressive – this strained attitude was liable to develop into a new threat antic, not hitherto observable, in which the smooth white cheeks were swollen out and the great beak, being partially opened, was kept for some seconds in a curious yawning position – very similar to a threat antic of those pugnacious little passerines, blue and great tits. This gaping, common to both cock and hen puffin, revealed the short orange tongue, as fleshy as a parrot's, and the deep orange colour of the buccal cavity.

Coupled with this antic was another, partly sexual and partly bellicose. This was continually in evidence among the excited groups standing round the pairs of kissers, and took the form of a cocking of bills in unison of as many as five birds in seven : that same cocking that preceded their matings on the sea. The puffin's enormous bill appears to have a considerable threat significance.

All these bill rappings and diverse antics – there was not so much dancing as usual – were frequently interrupted by one or more of the participants hurrying off to their own burrows, for which their mates were in the meantime collecting grasses. Their arrival at their burrows necessitated further bouts of 'kissing' and more curiosity from neighbouring puffins : the focal point of excitement was continually shifting from one burrow to another. The double burrow, however, continued to attract most attention. And there was a very good reason for this, of which I had had my suspicions from the outset, for in the right-hand burrow, the entrance to which was a mere crevice, apparently big enough only for a mouse, I subsequently discovered a puffin sitting very tightly on her egg. Further down the slope I found another sitter on the second egg of the season : a week or so later than usual.

This first egg laying did not, however, preclude further excitement, and three days later, on 11 May, I observed six puffins cocking bills and gaping and jumping back in alarm from a burrow on the north slope of Puffin Gully. Four of the six, indeed, were so alarmed that they eventually flew down to the sea. Occasionally I caught glimpses of the blurred movements of a puffin jumping backwards and forwards in the burrow, and one came out in a hurry, only to shoot in again past an enquiring cock. In the end two hens emerged in desperate combat and rolled down the slope. I found later that this was a single burrow with a puffin guffawing inside. After six weeks' residence on land the burrows were now beginning to exercise a stronger attraction than the sea, and when a mass flight of puffins streamed off the Slope at an alarm many of their fellows skeltered into their burries, instead of flighting as they would normally have done.

On 14 May as many as eighteen puffins might be seen in a single excited and ceaselessly active group, performing all the usual antics with typical fussiness. Three actually rapped bills together for a few seconds on the usual intruder butting in, until the cock of the pair, suddenly aware of what was going on, broke off to gape menacingly. Other incidents were not so easy to interpret : as when a cock approached a hen with a beakful of grasses in the most threatening 'gaping' attitude, and forced her to struggle backwards in fright, shaking all her grasses away. When these had all been scattered the cock checked his advance and both went and collected more grasses for their respective burrows! Other puffins with heavily soiled bills and shanks tumbled out of crannies and pattered up the boulders above my head. Although I had been finding their old eggshells of the previous year scratched out by the rabbits ever since my first coming in March, there were now one or two newly sucked shells in evidence among the boulders.

With a full house, as many as thirty razorbills and half a dozen puffins might be seen on a single boulder. High up above them prowled great black-backs, and the peregrine, paying one of her rare visits, stooped down on the thickly populated boulders. Once again I experienced the unique exhileration of being in the midst of a continuous flighting of hundreds of puffins and razorbills sailing buoyantly at a height of a few feet over the Slope into a northerly gale, as if drawn along by invisible wires. Against a strong wind the flighters had difficulty in turning into the circling mass of their fellows.

As the numbers of those sitting on eggs increased daily, at mid-May things quietened down, and those puffins standing about outside their burrows were somewhat subdued. Day by day the latter grew fewer, most preferring to ride in packs on the waters below the cliffs. Occasional sitters emerging from their burrows came swooping down the Slope at forty or fifty miles an hour to join them. For the last fortnight in May, indeed, the Slope and Puffin Gully were, to all outward appearance, almost as deserted as on those stormy days in April, when nearly all the puffins stayed out at sea.

Then, on the morning of 28 May, three weeks after the laying of the first egg, I was astonished to find a full house of puffins both on Puffin Slope and on the north-west sidings. Once again there was the flighting round and the massing with the razorbills on the boulders and all over the Slope : as many as one hundred and twenty puffins standing about Puffin Gully at one time in the familiar manner, without very much excitement. Most of them were cocks, but there were many hens and pairs, who occasionally rapped bills, especially at the mouths of their burrows : the cock turning his head nearly upside down in his comical, coy, stiff way before each bout of 'kissing'. Once at least a hen began the rapping. For the rest there was an occasional brief dancing and pattering around looking for a kiss, and one fight; a collecting of grasses by one or two here and there, and a marching in and out of burrows; and the odd *haa-aa*. Between four and six in the afternoon the great gathering evaporated in the usual way.

During the first fortnight in June affairs continued in this way, though the number of puffins standing about the Slope increased, as more and more pairs lost their eggs from various causes. These luckless birds hung about outside their burrows, repulsing intruders with that static but threatening, gaping antic, causing them to jump back a pace or two in a sharp, startled way; or began new preparations for a second laying. Day by day one noted little episodes and antics that must be woven into the complete pattern of this tale of puffins. On 29 May, for instance, there was a little bill cocking, and a male puffin, rapping bills with his mate, broke off to rap spasmodically and not at all ardently with an intruding female. The 'kissing' impulse was so strong in him that he continued to rap his bill in the air at intervals, even when not contacting with her bill. This was always a ludicrous sight.

Though relations were rather strained during this amoral 'kissing', his own mate, albeit very stiff and tense, took no offence at it. But the intruder, with that subtle awareness of danger so commonly seen among birds, was very fearful during her illicit 'kissing', and betrayed her apprehensions plainly by that startled 'ready to withdraw on the instant' attitude peculiar to puffins. In the end the conjugal 'kissing' was resumed at that most popular place, the entrance to the burrow, and was prolonged for as lengthy a period as I remember. As the intruder hen gathered courage to approach again, she was driven off by the cock, who renewed his rapping with his mate – to the continued interest of the other hen and two or three other puffins.

Throughout this fortnight the island was almost deserted by the puffins from four in the afternoon to ten or eleven the next morning except for an occasional bird coming out of burrows. But at noon, especially when there were big seas on (in contrast to their behaviour in April), there were enormous numbers on Puffin Slope – more, indeed, than had been obvious heretofore – with the old wonderful flighting into the wind. Sexual excitement, however, was waning. The cocks made a few half-hearted attempts at bill rapping which were received with even less enthusiasm by their mates, and what dancing there was, was not of an amorous nature, but an habitual part of the general pattering up the incline of slope or boulder. One or two sat sheltering under boulders and one circled over with a straw three times as long as himself. From the sea below came an occasional *haa-aa*. Climbing up behind a tall boulder below the Constable Rock and popping my head over the top, I had the pleasure of seeing nine puffins lined up on the edge of a boulder two feet from me, and others hovering almost stationary on the gale, level with my eyes, before plopping down gently alongside their fellows. This continual alighting of new puffins led to a certain amount of bill cocking from those already *in situ*, and this in turn to a strained uneasiness from their neighbours.

3. *The Fishers*

On 14 June, a few puffins were flying over Puffin Slope with shining tinfoil whiskers of little silver fish. The first young puffins had hatched. It was the tininess of these first fish, not one-third the size of those brought in by the guillemots, that particularly

Puffin carrying fish.

struck me. They overlapped the puffin's great bill so little that it was difficult to be certain that he was actually carrying a beakful when he whirred past at thirty or thirty-five miles an hour. The first fisher came up to Puffin Gully once, flew down to the sea again, and came up a second time straight into his burrow, hitting the heads of two razorbills almost blocking its entrance. After thirty seconds he reappeared at the mouth of his hole but did not fully emerge for another thirty seconds, when after a brief look round he flew down to the sea again to sip water and flap his wings.

Time and again I saw how shy were these fishers of alighting with their loads. They often circled over the Slope ten times or more before making a landing. The second fisher to alight in Puffin Gully followed this course, and when he finally alighted was very nervous about entering his burrow, continually starting back apprehensively after peering in. In the end a very young rabbit came out and made a little dab at him, whereupon he took flight, and the rabbit entered another burrow. When he came up shortly after, he ran into the burrow almost immediately on alighting, came out in just under a minute, looked around for a second or two and flew down to the sea. Most fishers stayed in their burrows for about a minute, and were sometimes accompanied by their mates.

While standing about waiting for the rabbit to come out of his burrow, the fisher's breast pulsated violently from his exertions, for he had eight or ten fish packed tightly in his bill, one squashed upon another. The hindmost was tucked away in the elastic folds of naked skin forming the rosette at the base of his bill, the foremost was gripped by its hooked tip: all nicely head and tail down the length of his mandibles. Although this ingenious method of packing was employed ninety times in one hundred, it was not invariable and an occasional fisher would come up with four or five sandeels, heads one side, tails the other. Pleasant to look at, the alternating head and tail arrangement of his fish is explained by the zig-zag course steered by the puffin when under water. Progressing thus, he will take a fish to the right of him and then one to the left, then right, then left, nipping each one with the hooked tip and working it down his bill very easily: for the elastic folds of skin at its base permit either mandible to be raised or lowered independently of the other. And although he may already have caught eight or nine fish, a very slight opening of his bill will enable its hooked tip to acquire a purchase on a tenth, the other nine being additionally held by the fat tongue, as illustrated by the delicate movement with which he picks up a grass or straw with his beak full of nesting stuff. Razorbills often came up with their fish packed alternately in the same way. Having exhausted those fish of the shoal immediately to beak, the fisher planes to the surface and hurries up to the Slope with his load still alive and kicking, frequently shaking his head when they tickle him with their tail smacking. By what extraordinary process is the naked skin of the buccal cavity pushed out into the orange rosette, necessary to an efficient fishing technique, several months before the young will hatch? For in the autumn it retracts into a thin line, at the same season that the outer sheath of the bill is shed.

In these early days of fishing many puffins were still carrying grasses and straws. The social gatherings still contained elements of tension and curiosity, and there were short bouts of bill cocking and mild 'kissings' – with the usual intruder attempting to butt in for a 'kiss' and being repulsed by the cock bill-tapper, still shaking his bill in the air. With this change in their daily routine the puffins no longer went out to sea at four in the afternoon. There was, instead, a full house on the boulders until dark. The lower parts of the Slope were especially favoured, for while many of the puffins who used the boulders for their social entertainment nested under them or in turfy burrows in their vicinity, a great many more collected on them from all parts of the Slope – when, that is, the razorbills permitted them to. As those on the lower boulders began to go out to sea, so their places were taken by those puffins dotted all over the Slope to the top of the island : the puffin dislikes solitude, preferring to be planted well down in the thick of his fellows whenever possible. There was, in particular, a turfy corner of a few score yards on the north-east top of Puffin Gully where one hundred and fifty or two hundred puffins delighted to gather. This was a corner seething with activity, for the most part without motive, and a continual popping in and out of burrows. A spacious cavern under an enormous boulder afforded them as much amusement as the floats of the lobsterpots on the sea below. There was a constant coming and going from it, and much scrapping, accompanied by the usual tumbling down the Slope and bouncing from boulder to boulder, bill grasped in bill. And there was much collecting of grasses, provoking a good deal of bad temper and that menacing opening of ferocious bills. They were noiser, relatively, at this season than at any previous time, their *haa-aa-aa* and *haa-haa . . . aa . . . aa* sounding from the burrows every few seconds.

The hatching of the chicks, setting free both parents and necessitating the bringing in of fish, resulted in a constant passage of puffins to and from the Slope, so that the mass circling over it was pretty well unchecked all day. Indeed by 22 June, when at six-thirty in the evening there was the fullest house of puffins I had yet seen, there were two hundred and fifty on the north-east corner of Puffin Gully, and to make an individual count of those that swarmed over every boulder from top to bottom of the Slope was impossible. On the other hand razorbills, still occupied with incubation, retired to their burrows or out to sea early in the evening, so that for the first time Puffin Slope to all outward appearances was peopled in the evenings by thousands of puffins only. Between ten o'clock and half-past, when all is murky, the nonsitting puffins vanish out to sea in their usual unobtrusive driblets and Puffin Slope is left to the gulls until four o'clock the next morning, when one or two puffins, weary of their night's sitting, pop out of their burrows down to the sea : the mass do not come in till seven o'clock.

The puffins on this island proved exasperating subjects for a naturalist whose creed of bird observation has always been based on the law of the least possible direct or indirect interference with natural and environmental conditions. From time to time, however, I examined many scores of burrows : to find in almost every case that egg or chick was hidden away round a bend or a rock far down the burrow, the entrance to which was often a very narrow aperture and most inaccessible. A typical haul from an hour or two of grubbing was likely to be one puffin sitting tight on her egg, one egg much stained and, as an exception, one chick three feet down a flat rock chamber, instead of an earthen burrow, gulping down a succession of fish which it picked up from the floor of the chamber, throwing them up with great aplomb to a chorus of deep contented grunts. The quantity and weight of fish consumed by the chicks of these sea birds is astounding, though the puffin chick is probably fed only twice in twenty-four hours.

The chick was a strange little object with its tufts of black down, dark-blue beady eyes, and broad greyish bill. On this occasion, in the early afternoon, it was alone ; but at eight o'clock the next morning it was frisking about behind the sitting male. The latter sat facing the entrance, and his enormous white face sank into his black neck ring. With his triangular eyes blinking (which I do not remember noting of a puffin in the outside world) and his great bill set in his baldish forehead, he was most owl-like. Although grunting once or twice, he never flinched from my gigantic mask blocking the entrance to his cavern : but when after five minutes I drew back to correct a crick in my neck and write a few notes, I found at my next intrusion that he and the chick had both vanished around a turn in the chamber, from which they did not again venture forth. And during the next one and a half hours no bird entered or left the burrow, though one circled past it a score and more of times, turning her head to look in and back at it.

With the hatching of the young razorbills on that day, the puffins' activity on the Slope was restricted, for the bigger bird was cock of the roost, and one would sometimes take a puffin by the scruff of his neck and hurl him off the boulder! The adult razorbills were now free to fish or sit about the boulders. This change resulted in a new order of the day, with razorbills occupying the coveted boulders in the morning and early afternoon, especially those on the lower parts of the Slope, to the almost complete exclusion of the puffins, who gradually took over from them in the late afternoon and evening. Occasional puffins, however, still dropped in with fish at all hours of the day.

The stock of whitebait was low this summer, and the puffins were now bringing up much bigger sandeels : four or five at a time neatly arranged head and tail. Gripped by the gills, the heavy bodies and tails hung down either side of their captors' beaks. All wet and shaggy about the head from the exertions of their fishing, the fishers were usually in a desperate hurry to deposit their loads, fairly scuttling into their burrows. Sometimes, however, the presence of a rabbit or razorbill in a double-chambered burrow caused delay, and I have known a fisher with seven or eight sandeels to remain on the terrace outside his burrow for more than an hour, standing for long periods and even squatting down, besides making eleven brief excursions down to the sea and up again without once relaxing his grip upon his enormous load of fish.

On the first day of July the puffins entered upon the last stage of their occupation of the island. At eight o'clock that morning, with a heavy sea running, there was a full house of both puffins and razorbills on Puffin Slope, and a wonderful flighting of a thousand birds slipping in sideways from the sea *en masse* after streaming over the boulders into the gale on their invisible wires : but not one fisher! What has regulated this abrupt cessation of fishing? Has the puffin's entire reproductive machinery run down? That the first individuals are beginning to moult and that overt signs of sexual and bellicose emotion are now reduced to a minimum, suggests that this is so. Most sat preening on the boulders or sleeping, one eye open, with bills tucked shyly back into wings and head feathers puffed.

Razorbills or no razorbills, the puffins now massed on the boulders and over the Slope from early morning to twilight, whenever heavy seas interfered with their pleasure on the water. Their last days on the Slope were not without tragedy. Ever since their coming at the end of March herring gulls and greater black-backs had prowled over the Slope, the puffins always apprehensive and wary of their presence on nearby boulders. One such herring gull, wheeling over the boulders on the evening of 3 July, dropped suddenly into the flighting puffins and knocked one down with a heavy thud of his swinging webs, breaking the puffin's neck very cleanly. Picking him up I marvelled at the great depth of soft feathering of this perfectly plumaged sea bird, especially at that of his head and cheeks, which normally seemed so smooth and unruffled that one could hardly conceive of their being anything but a hard polished veneer of waxed down. The puffin is probably the heaviest bird in proportion to his size I have handled and the most powerfully muscled. One cannot imagine a structural body more perfectly evolved and adapted to its several environments in its five dimensions under and on the sea, under and on the ground and in the air. Yet a vicious flip of a gull's webs and this perfect mechanism was destroyed in a second.

With the passing of another week the call of the sea became more and more insistent, and though a rare bird here and there was still bringing in fish, and many were still collecting grasses, comparatively few puffins came into the Slope before noon. With the razorbills monopolising the boulders, the turfy parts of the Slope were dotted with puffins standing at the entrances to their burrows, and occasional pairs or solitary birds going shyly in and out, to a chorus of *aa-aa . . . haa-aa*. There was a good deal of brief and mild but illicit 'kissing', and a cock squatting down, pecking at the ground in a strange way, rose and heartily rapped bills in quick succession with two hens passing him up the siding *en route* to their burrows. Another hen took the initiative in bill rapping with a cock who had no desire to 'kiss' and backed away from her step by step. The entrances to many of the burrows now had cobwebs across them and were overhung with curtains of grass. Others were flooded or dripped with water after the heavy rain; and never a sound or a sign of a young puffin from one of them except for the very occasional adult entering with fish. In spite of my twenty-four hour watches I had missed the nocturnal departure of the bulk of the chicks. Everything pointed to a bad season, with rats and flooded burrows as the main evils : for every egg and chick that I located and marked down for further observation vanished before its proper date for hatching or departure.

Some of the old birds were still carrying nesting grasses, and continued to do so up to 21 July, at which date others were still emerging from their burrows heavily stained on breasts and beaks with earth. Late impulses to build again seized those puffins that had lost earlier eggs to rats. By the middle of the month, when one puffin was still bringing in fish to a burrow high up in Kittiwake Gully, where there was a little colony of eight or nine pairs, there were times when there was hardly a puffin to be seen on Puffin Slope all day. From this time forward, half past seven or eight o'clock in the evening was their hour of assembly. At these hours there were more puffins on the Slope than I had seen at any time during the previous four months. As many as one hundred would collect on the flat top of a single enormous boulder, many of them very bleached of primaries, brown of back, and pale grey and bald of tonsure. After watching guillemots and razorbills intensively for some days, the brilliant vermilion paddles of those puffins still in full plumage hit the eye with an unusual vividness.

There was still some bill rapping continually interrupted by the unmated, and a repulsing of desirous females by satiated males, and even a cocking of bills by a little group of seven birds. But two hours of pattering over the boulders very erectly, with bills well tucked into chins, and continuous mass flighting, and they were ready to go out to sea again and fish for shrimps, and play and sleep for the next twenty-two hours. With the deepening dusk the empty Slope was once more left to the prowling gulls and the razorbill chicks piping sadly under their boulders.

By 26 July the puffins' occupation of the Island was practically confined to this two hour period in the late evening, when they also massed on the sea in unprecedented numbers. The waters below the Slope were studded with tens of hundreds of puffins in one colossal pack : little groups, cocking their tilted heads, spinning around one another with their white breasts high out of the water. There was a little dancing among those on the Slope, and two came bouncing with customary violence head over heels out of a boulder burrow, one leaving a beakful of tiny white feathers with his pursuer. Just before eight o'clock they began to flight *en masse* over the Slope, others joining them in successive mass flights off the boulders. Eighteen weeks before, they had come in from sea in the early morning after eight months' absence, to circle *en masse* over the Slope. Now before going out to sea for another eight months, during which time they would never voluntarily come to land, nor often close inshore, they once more circled over the Slope.

On the night of 30 July they flighted for the last time. The next evening there were a few on the sea below the Slope, and little groups might be seen whirring round the North Cape and fishing in the Tide Race with the shearwaters, but I waited in vain for them to make a landing. In their place the wild goats browsed over Puffin Slope on the dead stems of the thrift – a thing that they had never done before – and over all the boulders were only a young kittiwake standing on one and a young rabbit squatting on another.

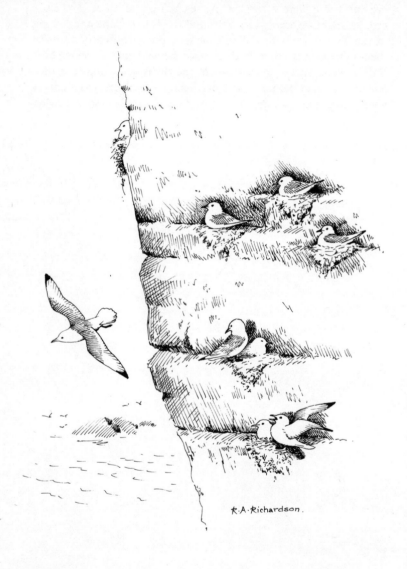

Kittiwakes nesting.

III

KITTIWAKES : TWENTY-SEVEN WEEKS IN A GULLY

1. *Beautiful Automatons*

Woven into the ceaseless crying of the gulls on a March day of tempest and rain squalls is a faint and momentarily elusive yelping *ew-ew-yaa/ew-ew-yaa,* wind-borne up the chimneys between the stacks to the top of the island. It is the little kittiwakes, hidden from above in the deep gullies fissuring the cliffs below the sidings. Their clamorous crying eddies strangely.

Though returning to island waters at Christmas, it is late in February or early in March before they compete with the newly-arrived razorbills for nesting sites on the cliffs. Unlike the razorbills and guillemots, once established on their ancestral nesting platforms, they will not completely abandon them even in the most tempestous weather, when icy gales blow their tails and wings up over their backs in a way that must cause them considerable physical discomfort. The deeper the gully or mere cleft penetrates the cliffs the better suited are the kittiwakes, whose peculiar characteristic it is to cling like leeches to their ledges, niches and cracks in the sheer face of the granite. To these nesting chasms they are uniquely attached. Only once during their six months' residence did a kittiwake come to the top of the Island – to the freshwater at Pondsbury; yet in Scotland and the North Isles freshwater bathing in the lochs is a notable feature of the kittiwakes' daily routine at the nesting cliffs. Seldom even did these Lundy kittiwakes follow the tide south of the Rock of Gannets in their fishing for whitebait and those diverse small fish lumped by Devon fishermen into a single genus, brit or britling — those incalculable millions of small fishes that daily provided food for some eighty thousand nesting sea birds, and for more than half as many again after the hatching of the chicks. The especial fishing grounds of the kittiwakes were in the Tide Race that surges west round the North Cape, swirling over and about the reefs and rocky islets of the Hen and Chickens, and setting out to sea at five or six knots in a hundred-yard grey belt as far as the eye can see. Out here thousands of white kittiwakes circled round with quick wing beats: hovering in an interminably weaving maze, securing a tiny silver whitebait at almost every plop into the water. Here, too, gathered young kittiwakes of previous years, puffins and immature razorbills and guillemots in a variety of bizarre white and black plumages; together with an occasional black-headed gull or a red-throated diver on passage; shags and cormorants; great and Manx shearwaters; fulmars; gannets travelling on their one-hundred-mile fishing ellipse from Grassholm; and mature and immature big gulls bent on plundering the kittiwakes of their spoils, swooping menacingly down on them with the squeaky cries so familiar to those who go out in fishing smacks.

Riven forty yards into the north-east sidings, which are bright with deep cushions of green thrift and its masses of pink flowers, is a gorge one hundred and fifty feet deep and eight feet across. On both its sheer faces nested three hundred and thirty pairs of kittiwakes, besides some two hundred and fifty pairs of razorbills, two hundred pairs of guillemots, and a few puffins in the honeycombed thrift. Only Puffin Gully, with three hundred and forty-five pairs, housed a bigger colony of kittiwakes. The little gulls lived in almost unbroken peace with their odd nighbours, save for an occsional mild bill darting at razorbills or guillemots who were too close to their nests, for a razorbill was not above annexing a nest for his own use. Naturally there was more jealousy when eggs and chicks arrived and a kittiwake would then sometimes fly at a guillemot with a full body-tilt.

That only rare shafts of sun lit up the twilight of Kittiwake Gully was no deterrent to the kittiwakes, many of whose nests were ledges deep in the dark depths of the chasm where water dripped continually. The absence of sun, indeed, would be beneficial to the nestlings. There were always kittiwakes planing over and into the gorge on their straight wings, primaries gently angled back to black tips, continually sailing up to the lodestone of the nest. Clinging tightly to narrow ledge and cornice, they usually faced into the cliff, their black wing-points, forked beyond square white tails, projecting over the edge, displaying their smooth dove-grey mantles, their snowy cowls coloured by soft dark-brown eyes ringed in red, and the primrose bills with which they preened their white breasts or thrust back into the partings of their grey wings. Many sit on ancestral accumulations of compressed grasses and guano: several of such monumental nests often heightening the entire length of a ledge in a great rolled slab. Those on the fringes of the old-established colony stand on the naked grey rock, uttering a querulous *pyewk*.

Their behaviour at the nest is reminiscent of fulmars. There is a continual delicate waving and darting of heads at rival occupants of a ledge, at new birds alighting on a ledge, at those sailing up to and by a ledge, and of male and female when they ecstatically pass their heads over and under each other's necks. This antic is especially exaggerated when one of a pair flies in to join the other on the nest drum: with the impulse to relieve one another on the nest present from the first days of their return to the gully, this may only result in one flying on to replace the other flying off. Associated with this almost incessant head movement is a vigorous clamour of *ew-ew-yaa/ew-ew-yaa* from widely gaping pale lemon bills. This reveals brilliant scarlet buccal cavities and extraordinary adobe tongues, paler than their throats, projecting in spikes the length of their bills from their junction two-thirds of the way down the lower mandible. Their clamorous head-waving coincides with a sharp and often explosive *kik-kik-kik*, and is invariably followed by a smacking of mandibles and a shaking of the head, as if they are gulping down some regurgitation or secretion. The gulping, as in the case of the fulmar, plays a dominant part in temporarily breaking up every activity on the ledge. Every bout of pecking even between adjacent nesters is soon interrupted by one or other of the combatants being obliged to break off for a bout of gulping back what is presumably a secretion stimulated by its excitement.

It is difficult to imagine any more excitable little birds. Kittiwake Gully is tumultuous with varying discords of that clamorous *wickgewr/wickgewr*, with often a higher-pitched *zewee* mixed up with it. This clamour heralds every arrival at the ledges, and is even uttered by a solitary bird alighting alone on a cornice. The excitement provoked by their own or by their mate's alighting is quite crazy, so that they often do not distinguish, momentarily, between rival and mate, pecking either savagely and indiscriminately: the bewildered female lying half prostrate on the ledge with drooping wings and spiked tail. At one moment nearly all the birds in the gully are dozing in an immobile state: at the next this tumult has spread in an instant from one to another of the five or six hundred kittiwakes present at the time. In small colonies of up to fifty or sixty pairs there are long intervals of calm and quiet, but in large colonies, where the stream of outgoing and incoming birds is almost continuous, the tumult seldom dies down completely. In the afternoon, however, they grow sleepy, and there may be periods of quiescence when only a high squeaking note comes up from far down the canyon. This is associated with a curious, intermittent pointing up and down of closed bills, with taut throats and half-shut eyes, the female continually breaking off to nibble at her mate's bill and throat, or both breaking off abruptly and only momentarily to shake open bills with the *kik-kik-kik* expletive. Both birds will often do this after nebbing, as if they dislike the taste of the other's secretion. This antic of the kittiwake, apparently isolated and meaningless in March and April, becomes in later months an important feature of sexual solicitation. Puffins, guillemots and the three big gulls employ an identical antic under similar conditions, and it is also present in less direct form in razorbills and the two cormorants.

It is during the intervals of comparative quiet that a marvellous thing happens. Suddenly, hundreds of kittiwakes zoom down from the ledges at a single impulse. Shoaling out of the gully in a dazzling white and grey pack like snowflakes in a blue heaven they wheel over the whirlpools of white surf and the deep green Atlantic swell.

Each bird zooms down the canyon with a prolonged humming *zew ... ew ... ew,* like the escape of air from a squeaker balloon – a new and beautifully attenuated kittiwake in flight, with extended neck and widely parted bill. From the black depths of the gully zooms out over the rocks at its mouth a continual succession of kittiwakes, soaring up with a dazzling brilliance of china white underwings and intensely black shafts. Their 'zewming' might be the faraway buzzing of bees on hot summer noons. From the hidden places down below ascends a continual cooing, as of rockdoves: a *cuk ... oo ... oo* (sometimes heard from a bird on the wing), providing a murmurous undertone to the dominant discordant cries. The occasional resurgent cooing of amorous guillemots is strangely amplified by the gorge into a thunderous caw. The wash of the tide over the reefs at the entrance to the gully also murmurs of summer on calm noons, and there are intervals when only the thunderous gulp of a seventh sea pounding far up the canyon disturbs the peace. As night falls only an occasional brief outburst of *ew-ew-yaa* surges and dies from the preening and resting birds.

Like most sea birds, kittiwakes come back to their ledges in pairs, and do not quarrel much over nesting territories, though there is a certain spasmodic jealousy between birds on adjacent nests – a tweaking of tails often ignored by the victim or a slight darting of bills. The instinct to own a nest or nesting site is, however, dominant and since kittiwakes, like many other sea birds, do not breed until their fourth year (in their third winter) they have with them a proportion of nonbreeding birds. A batch of these are seized each year with the desire to mate and secure nesting niches: they are responsible for the greater part of what trouble there is on the ledges. Even second and third year birds, particularly when big seas prevent them from fishing in the Tide Race, will perch alone on pale chocolate-coloured webs, forlorn and very quiet on unoccupied niches in the gully, apparently subdued and often uneasy at the babel of the nesting adults about them. Some of these young birds have yellow-green bills duller than those of the adults : others have black bases to their bills and grey-black hoods and black yokes or neck smudges, or only a little of that faint grey mottling about the head common to some of the nesting birds; but their eyes are black and bigger than those of the adults, which are dark brown, ringed with red.

But it is the unmated fourth-year bird that gets himself on to the nest or ledge of a mated pair, often for hours together, and bows his head right down against the face of the cliff. No amount of punishment by the owners will budge this passive resister from his pitch, and to the savage pecking about his head and beak he offers no retaliation, beyond occasionally shaking his head up a little. He illustrates a law applicable to ninety-nine per cent of colonial nesting birds and most others : that a territorial usurper will seldom show fight to the true owner of the territory and will always give ground in the end. Whereas two kittiwakes on adjacent nests will spar furiously, an intruder on its fellow's nest will never fight, will seldom await the owner's arrival at the nest, and will never make any forceful attempt to hold the nest. Where territorial combats do take place the combatants are presumably old birds, each of whom has an associative memory of a previous year's nest : these passive resisters are young birds who have not hitherto possessed a territory. Such an intruder is bewildering to the mated pair, who spend more time in darting and waving their heads at one another over his recumbent body than in determined onslaught on him, and after an hour or two of fruitless attack they are likely to settle down to sleep, until territorial emotions are again dominant, impelling them to renew their onslaught. For a period of perhaps several hours the third bird never lifts his head from the base of the cliff wall. And all this time the male and female have been pressing him hard on either side, or even sitting across his head!

If in the excitement of arrival at the nesting ledge there may be a confusion of identity between resident and intruder, a similar confusion may also exist with regard to an intruder actually on the nest, and a kittiwake has certain states in which he does not at first appear to recognise that his territorial rights have been violated. However, before the eggs are laid, the kittiwake's nesting site, even if it has ancestral foundations, is the fair equivalent of the oystercatcher's pre-nesting display territory, and many species of birds countenance the present of unmated young birds up to the time that nest building begins. The kittiwake does not go to this length, but late in April three birds may be seen amiably bill pointing on one nest for minutes at a time, until the harmony is broken by the middle bird jumping on top of the other two. This action sets in motion a train of disruptive incidents breaking up the unnatural harmony : the middle bird pecks at the intruder, who flies off and is followed shortly afterwards by the pecker's mate. Later the latter, the female, returns, and for some minutes the nest contains a normally behaved pair until the intruder also comes up and is again accepted for a brief space. But, impelled no doubt by a growing sensation of establishing a territory, he unwisely reaches across the middle bird and pecks at the female. Thereupon the male again pecks him away : only for him to return and be pecked away again for a third and final time.

As a third example of confusion of purpose, I found that nesting kittiwakes sometimes got on to the wrong nests. Two kittiwakes, for instance, were on a ledge just roomy enough for four, and one had his head buried in a corner of the ledge, in the manner described above, while the other attacked him savagely about the head : sometimes standing on his back, sometimes pushing against him with one foot on his back, apparently for lack of standing room owing to the intruder's awkward recumbent position along the length of the ledge : the peckings, of course, being continually interrupted by bouts of gulping. As usual the intruder offered only passive resistance, but eventually he unexpectedly and suddenly left the ledge, and after two circles out to sea, sailed up to a ledge directly opposite on the other side of the gully, and was there favourably received by a solitary bird as its mate! At about the same time the mate of the bird on the other ledge also returned.

2. *Seven Months' Cliff Life*

In March some sitting kittiwakes peck idly at wisps of old grasses on their toy drum nests and pretend to throw them to one side – in the manner of a herring gull, and referred to more fully in our study of the razorbill. But it was April before stray pieces of fresh or rotting thrift were to be observed on the ledges. Though it may have been coincidence, it seemed that those birds whose territories were bare rock began this mandibulating of nesting material before those sitting on nest drums of previous years. In these early days it was, of course, an impulse without direction : a mere collecting of material, flying around with it, dumping it down on a ledge, and forgetting it, for the wind to whirl it away. But one of these early impulses was of special interest since it elaborated an incident of kittiwake behaviour previously noted. I had under observation one such kittiwake continually flying in and out of the gully and circling over the sea at its entrance with a beakful of thrift before finally flying up to a nest drum and there depositing the stem of thrift: picking it up and putting it down a number of times in familiar manner. This performance, however, apparently took place on another bird's nest, for she was suddenly assaulted by the rightful owner, whereupon, picking up her stem she flew down the gully again: to return and alight, significantly, on a bare ledge immediately below the one she had first visited. Putting her stem down on this ledge, she shortly seized a large chunk of decayed black thrift already *in situ*, and mandibulated this vigorously, her mate standing by. Finally she flew out with another chunk of thrift and returned to put it down again.

At the end of the month a few kittiwakes began building in earnest, and in the first days of May a bird here and there was to be seen sitting on an almost perfect circular nest of dead grasses and the tips and roots of thrift : though it was mid-May before many nests contained much material. This nesting activity of the kittiwakes, like that of guillemots, razorbills and herring gulls, operated under the *block* system. In one big gully, for instance, there would be a number of nests under construction, in another of similar capacity only one or two, in a smaller colony none, while in a still smaller one there would be a continual stream of birds, sailing in with bunches of thrift, without any obvious dissimilarities of situation or other external factors to account for these variants. They carried this *blocking* to extremes, for when nest building became general in the second week of May, they conducted communal nesting expeditions, as many as a score together excitedly plucking beakfuls of thrift, with violent stabs, from a single cushion at some special site on the cliffs. Though shy of being observed in these activities, it became apparent that the members of a colony would repair from a gully far down the coast to some favoured patch of thrift, although there might be ample supplies in the immediate vicinity of their own nesting cliffs. In this manner they would bare to the roots a patch of several square feet by their mass plucking, and might be met half a mile out to sea carrying their beakfuls of stuff. So ill-directed was their purpose, however, that there was little material evidence on their ledges of their expeditions. The ancestral drums increased in size mainly from the fortunate accident that there was a limit to the amount of material a kittiwake could drop idly in one place, without eventually forming a heap. Naturally such a structure was very loosely compacted, and occasionally a whole mass of material would come tumbling down the face of the cliff.

Dead grasses, moss, or thrift, plucked from the siding or stolen

from other nests, were strewn haphazardly over the ledge and nest
– a vivid green on the bare earth or rock – by one bird alone or by
the male bringing it in to the female. This fresh material was
gradually dampened down by an incessant paddling up and down
of the bird's wet feet, until it was as deep a brown as coconut
fibre: a central depression being thus engineered in the ancestral
slab of beaten earth white with guano. This cat-like marking time
on the nest might go on without a break, not only for minutes but
for hours, and long after the fresh stuff had been trodden into the
old debris. This remarkable paddling might even be conducted
when a bird was sitting. She would also push away the loose stuff
into the rim of the nest by a vigorous back scratching, and at the
same time peck wisps of material in to her breast and flanks.
Many nests never grow more impressive than a mere litter of
grasses in the centre of the old drums. Others, before they are used
much, are circular ramps of newly-collected grasses built up by
that incessant drawing of outer stuff into the centre. In her efforts
to get more comfortable the sitter continually alters her position,
necessitating a fresh pulling in of the outer grasses and a renewed
scratching, tail dipping and paddling.

Only with the general onset of the nest building impulse in the
first week of May do the kittiwakes begin to mate, although many
of them have been on their nests and ledges for the best part of
nine weeks. Once against the *block* system operates : the birds in
one gully begin to mate several days before any in another. The
actual mating, performed on the nest, is remarkable. For a long
period, often five or ten minutes or more, the male stands on his
prostrate mate's back, delicately nebbing her head and bill, and
occasionally shaking his bill with the familiar *kik-kik-kik*. His
mounting may be preceded by two or three minutes of placing one
foot tentatively on her nape and, when he does mount her, by a
further two or three minutes of paddling about on her back, she
turning her head up to him : only in the end for him to jump off
again and 'gulp' before another attempt. Then, after the usual tail
wagging, with fanning wings, he bends his tail up horizontally
under hers, and she turns her breast and head with its red-gashed
bill right round and caresses him at each consummation. There
may be six or eight of these before the male finally stands on her

back again, gets off on to the nest beside her, or flies straight down to the sea.

The mating impulse does not reach its zenith until the third week in May, and is of short duration, for not every female kittiwake is desirous of mating, and those not desirous shake off the mildly importunate males very quickly, when both indulge in a bout of 'gulping' instead. On the other hand a female may solicit the male with that bill pointing and squeaking – which may also be heard during the actual mating – whose implications were obscure when the antics were enacted weeks and months before the season of mating. On such occasions it may be the male who is not quite ready for the mating, and he may jump on and off her back three or four times before proceeding to the mating. In some cases the female will bill point for as much as ten minutes, ecstatically pecking at the male's bill and squirming her body about in an invitatory manner, without inciting him to anything more satisfactory than a 'gulping'. Once the chicks have hatched, the old birds cease bill pointing, but those that have *lost* their eggs or chicks continue to point and squeak until the middle of July!

At the end of the third week in May, when half the kittiwakes had good foundations to their nests, emotions were running high, and there was much fighting, both among themselves and with razorbill neighbours. One male, indeed, with that familiar confusion of impulse and purpose, pecked his mate savagely when she alighted and disturbed his siesta on the nest. Intruders at the nest were seized by their napes and flung into the gully, and for the first time combatants continued to fight on the wing, after tumbling off the ledges, scrapping furiously in mid-gorge like toying pipits. Many persisted in their fighting after alighting on the water, often returning to their mates very battered about the head; and one such combatant had a bloody bill with a piece knocked out of his upper mandible. He was not seen again on subsequent days.

In the light of this unprecedented excitement I was not surprised to find one kittiwake sitting tight on two different coloured eggs, and another standing for a long period over one egg four days later on 26 May. Both had poorly constructed nests on small foundations. As in the case of terns, it would be difficult to find a cluch of kittiwake eggs identically patterned and coloured, though the ground colour tends to be maroon, stone or pale green, speckled and spotted with brown.

Other birds continued to build, collecting material in communal expeditions and bringing in enormous beakfuls of grass and thrift, strewing it with characteristic haphazardry about nest and ledge impartially. Those with eggs also continued to build, with the appropriate motions of bill, shanks, and tail, at considerable risk of rolling their eggs out of the nest. But where before these antics had appeared to be the direct outcome of the sitter's efforts to get herself into a comforable position, they now derived from attempts to position the eggs comfortably. This operation necessitated the frequent pointing of the egg with a pleasant twiddling motion of the bill. From the taking up of a territory to the hatching and feeding of a chick there is one continuous organic and physical routine, one impulse leading rhythmically to another, one stimulus provoking another. On the very day, for example, that the first eggs are laid, the female once again solicits the male with the now familiar squeaking and bill pointing, but on this occasion evokes a *new* response, for this time he *feeds* her. In precisely the same way will the chick solicit its parents for food.

Although the males take a share in the incubation, they pass much of their time fishing with nonsitters and immature kittiwakes in the Tide Race, or stand about on reefs and low cliffs near their nesting gullies, roosting on these extraterritorial cliffs at night. Throughout the night occasional sleepy outbursts come from their mates sitting on their nests: for in the first days of June all but the unpaired birds are sitting tight, usually alone, quiet and sleepy, with heads tucked back. One male stands pathetically on his dead mate, who lies spreadeagled over the nest. Numbers of the unmated still attempt to usurp the nests of their more fortunate fellows, and noisily turn one another off unoccupied ledges. As before, three kittiwakes will get upon one nest, and with familiar confusion of purpose, the resident male at first pecks his mate savagely instead of the intruder. Later he drives off the latter but then pecks his mate again for two minutes. As usual she is passive and unresisting, with lowered head and half-closed eyes, until at an extra painful peck over her eye she stands up, her torn neck dishevelled, and *pewks:* whereupon after much 'gulping', the male gives over his assault and she settles down to sleep and he to preen. Afterwards they indulge in the customary bouts of mutual yelping. Incessantly restless, the unmated solitary birds give wonderful exhibitions of aerial acrobatics in the gully, not only sailing down it on the updraft, with an unique trick of suddenly heeling over and reversing their direction of flight in a single scissor movement, but actually hanging motionless on the upcurrent (relative to the air speed), as if suspended from an invisible thread, and even eddying backwards: an antic accompanied by a babbling *oeur-oeur-oeur*. Often one will stand on a rock uttering this strange sound with half-open bill and tongue cloven to his palate.

After some thirty-one days' incubation nearly a score of kittiwake clutches of two hatched off in Kittiwake Gully on 24 June: the date also of the first razorbill chicks. Balls of white and iron-grey fluff with dark-brown bills, the chicks were already in possession of those remarkable excretory powers common to many sea birds and to some others, such as hawks and swallows. Laboriously backpaddling to the rim of the nest, with an unsteady flapping of wing stumps, like young cormorants, the tiny chicks, tilting their rears well, excreted outwards the prodigious distance of four or five feet!

For the most part the females sat upon or stood over their chicks alone, the males being absent for long periods: though that desolate male in Peregrine's Gully still stood on top of his mate, now rapidly decaying and hardly distinguishable from the guano on the nest. On the return of the males there is a great din: both birds standing on the edge of the nest by the chicks, cawing and 'gulping' as vigorously as ever, the female delicately nibbling the heads of both chicks and mate. Others fight on the water, tails shutting and spreading axe-wise, one atop of the other. When a herring gull swoops down on a hapless guillemot's egg and makes off with it to his usual anvil rock below Puffin Gully, there is a tremendous outcry from the kittiwakes like a swarming of bees or a rising of sandwich terns from their sandspit: a pleasant din coinciding with a spontaneous shoaling out of the gully of hundreds of male and unattached kittiwakes. This provokes, in turn, a mass cooing of guillemots, and on the return of the kittiwakes a mass *oeur-oeur* from the latter, both from those on the wing and those standing, protesting, on the ledges.

This Puffin Gully was worked daily, hour after hour, by two pairs of herring gulls nesting in its vicinity. One bullied an eggless kittiwake off her nest : she returned time and again to mob the tyrant furiously, with an angry *wac-wac-wac-wer-oeur*, and eventually drove him away. Those kittiwakes with chicks refused to be frightened from their young, unless actually knocked off the nest by a gull — a rare event — but sat tight, raising and arching their wings and bravely darting out their bills at the marauder. The latter, however, occasionally swooped in and took a chick before the kittiwake was alert to his intentions. The luckless parent followed the gull out, but returned almost immediately to her other chick. I only saw an adult kittiwake actually assaulted on three or four occasions : on one of which a herring gull seized a parent on the nest and tried to pull her off her chick. Darting with her bill at her assailant, the kittiwake drove him off but made the mistake of following him off the nest, whereupon another gull swooped in to take the chick. Mobbed by its fellows, it dropped the unfortunate chick in the sea for a great black-back to retrieve and swallow whole. The robbed kittiwake, returning to her nest, trod about feeling for something to sit on, and with the subsequent return of her mate, both 'gulped' noisily and preened on their empty nest. And so it went on.

The chicks point at their parent's bill and throat with their beaks, with an incessant loud and swift cheeping. This provokes her, after a short interval during which the nape of her neck considerably thickens and her head swings continually backwards and forwards over those of the chicks, to gulp up a grey-white pulp of whitebait without much effort : the swinging motion of her head being repeated before each regurgitation, and even after the chicks are full-fed and settling down to be brooded. The chicks take the mess from far down her gaping scarlet throat — their own buccal cavities and long spike tongues are pink — and the old bird swallows the residue of each regurgitation, for the chicks take only small morsels at a time. This gulping may be repeated by the parent a dozen times in five minutes, although the chicks are very mild in their solicitation and probably seldom actually touch her bill. One chick, unable to swallow a big morsel, drops it, the parent picking it up and reswallowing. Another chick pecks its fellow repeatedly after it has itself fed : whereupon the other immediately buries its bowed head tightly into the back of the nest in exact imitation of the passive adult female or, more often, the adult intruder when pecked by the resident male!

At the end of June, when the immature kittiwakes were moulting heavily and the oldest chicks were sprouting blue and white quills, the fortunate and unusual accident of a shoaling of shrimps just below the cliffs gave the old birds the chance to begin feeding the chicks, and incidentally themselves, on that food for which both they and herring gulls are most avid. The cliffs of the kittiwake gullies become stained the true granite pink, and from the Rock of Gannets northwards there was a lively scene, with hundreds of kittwakes and herring gulls feeding greedily on the jumping shrimps, taking headers into their red masses, and razorbills and guillemots diving under them.

After some ten days the chicks were nearly half as big as their parents, with black collars and wing markings and enormous pale grey webs. The parents of the biggest chicks began to desert them for considerable periods: a disastrous habit in such an environment, for those few pairs of herring gulls that actually nested among the kittiwakes and auks were now desperate with hunger for their nearly fullgrown young, and grew daily more bold in their piracy in Puffin Gully and over Puffin Slope and the cliffs of the north-west, marauding from dawn to dusk. One, getting right down among the kittiwake ledges, deliberately seized a chickless kittiwake by the tip of one wing, pulling her up the cliff until she managed to free herself. The ruffian made a second and unsuccessful attempt to seize her. Working farther down the face of the cliff, he got his tail tweaked by a sitting guillemot, whereupon he immediately faced about and barked. In the end the standing partner of another sitting guillemot twice fluttered up the cliff face to assault him, and finally drove him away. I never saw a lesser black-back, nor any herring gull or great black-back nesting *away* from colonies of auks or kittiwakes, take their eggs or young.

All this while and up to the last days of my residence on the island, kittiwakes, both with and without chicks, continued to carry nesting material : even immature birds, with dusky heads and big black eyes, bringing big chunks of stuff to empty ledges. On 9 July there was actually a wave of communal thrift plucking on the northwest slope: with a great and clamorous excitement, accelerated by the washing away of many nests and chicks by streams of water pouring down the sides of the gullies after heavy rains. More fortunate chicks sat under a continual drip of water.

The bigger chicks of a fortnight old and more are now mantled in smooth grey chain mail. Deserted by both parents for lengthy periods, they put in a great deal of time jumping petulantly up and down on their flat drums of grasses and guano, vigorously flapping their long black-barred wings to the accompaniment of a wheezing and creaking falsetto, a diminutive of their parents' gulping *krakatoa*. The length of their young wings is enormous, when they stretch and spread them luxuriously and beautifully over their tails. The sudden arrival of a parent at the nest often shocks them into complete immobility for several minutes. Later they bill point, like their soliciting mother, before being fed.

From now on to the departure of the main body of guillemots and razorbills, the combined uproar from the young and old of all three species, especially the kittiwakes, from dawn to dark and spasmodically during the night, is terrific : great waves of sound envoloping Kittiwake Gully, where some sixty per cent of the kittiwakes have one or two chicks. There is much tentative sparring, open billed but harmless, between adjacent kittiwakes with chicks, and even this late in the season three kittiwakes occasionally get together on a nest of chicks, with the usual

Kittiwakes at nest with a chick in juvenile plumage.

cawing and 'gulping' and head pointing, the intruder bowed forward in his passive way. One such returns twice again to a nest of chicks after being edged off, but is pecked away each time and finally settles on an empty nest above.

Occasional kittiwakes have an odd habit of hatching out one egg a week or more after the other, so that one may perceive the curious spectacle of two unequal-sized chicks on one nest : one a two- or three-day-old ball of fluff, the other a fourteen-day-old giant; or later .one partially and one fully fledged chick standing on the remains of a dead adult, pecking at another chick on an adjacent nest : both chicks, however, being fed by their other parent.

It was a full calendar month, towards the end of the third week in July, before the chicks, now of a size with their parents, took wing more or less accidentally from their eight-week cradle, after some days of incessant wing flapping from morn till night, to the accompaniment of their persistent squeaking 'gulping'. Their taking wing coincided with the last appearance of eggs anywhere on the island. They flew more ably than young terns or gulls, though those dancing over Kittiwake Gully with legs hanging and wide-spread wings experienced some difficulty, when turning, in countering a strong updraft that blew the wings and tails of other young birds still on their nests right up over their heads, almost dislodging them from their precarious quarters, They attempted to return to their nests or to effect lodgements in various parts of the gully many times before finally succeeding in half-tumbling landings : only perhaps to be pecked off again by the adults whose territories they were infringing.

These fully fledged young kittiwakes are very beautiful, for black and white is the most distinguished pattern in Nature – witness the grey plover in his breeding plumage – and they are black of eye, bill, lores and yoke, and barred in black on wings and tail, with pale brown shanks and webs. Yet with these young birds already on the wing (and they do not desert the gully for some days after gaining their powers of flight) some mature kittiwakes are still bringing in nesting material to mates without eggs or chicks. They go through all the familiar ritual of nidification, though nothing will come of such optimism. Immature birds still stand about 'gulping' squeakily, and even fighting with mature birds for nesting niches in the gully. Gulls still take the chicks, and a great black-back on the sea below allows one of its own young to feed on a kittiwake chick with it. But their stronger brethren are already traversing the seas between the island and the mainland. And though many frequent the gullies for the remainder of the month, they gradually vanish from island waters during September, the young birds apparently preceding the adults.

Razorbills with chick.

IV

RAZORBILLS: TWENTY-FOUR WEEKS ON CLIFF AND
SIDING

1. *Their Social Life*

Huddled in the lee of a great block of granite on Puffin Slope,
little drops of water from a light sea mist falling on my notebook, I
seemed once again to be listening to the soft wing music of
flighting duck. The air was musical with the sudden thuds of
turning wings, as a continual succession of razorbills whirred
away from my head, braking hard with instant spreading of
beautiful black fan tails, as pointedly serrated as those of drake
wigeon. Their cries were all about me: soft, vibrant, electric
whirrings, as of grasshoppers.

This was the morning of 2 April. Looking up the dun and olive
siding to the grey sphinxes embattling its crest, and the watchful
hand of the Constable Rock pointing to the misty blue sky, I could
see that the great scree of fallen blocks littering the grassy slope
was seething with hundreds of razorbills in ones and twos and
threes, a dozen on a boulder : while over them hurtled dense black
and white squadrons of their fellows in an unbroken black circle,
downwind over the sea, upwind over the Slope. Successive waves
of flighters dropped onto the boulders : some clumsily on their
fellows' heads, bouncing and falling off the boulders; others most
gracefully with waving wings, shuffling nimbly up the sheer rough
sides of the granite blocks – the short black claws of their webbed

toes, and perhaps, too, their stiff tails, enabling them to cling to the sheer face of a smooth wall of cliff. Once alighted, they stand or sit back on the full length of their black tarsi, spiked tails projecting : just as at sea they can always be picked up as much for the elevated pin tails and tilted heads of their dumpy forms as for the salient black and gleaming silver of their plumage. When the sun broke the veil of the thin mists these razorbills were exquisitely beautiful in the splendid contrast of china white fronts and glossy black mantles, with slender primaries crossed like scimitars over the hilts of their long spiked tails, and delicate white grooves on their gnarled black bills. Their tiny, peering eyes have a reddish-brown tint, but at a distance of more than a few feet the eye is completely lost in the intense blackness of the face – brown-tinted in certain lights. Almost parallel to the yellow gash of their usually slightly parted mandibles runs a white groove, from the corner of the eye to the base of the bill, which when wide open reveals a tiny tongue spike attached to the lower mandible. Although there are various uncoloured grooves in both upper and lower mandibles, the single white grooves in either mandible coincide when the bill is closed.

Pitching in on the boulders about me, often at a distance of only three or four feet, they peered at me shortsightedly, continually turning their uptilted heads and slightly parted bills. At this short range and for as far as I could see over the five thousand square yards of granite blocks littering the Slope, they settled down to the everyday routine of their new life. Two mated on a boulder at my feet, rather less vigorously than guillemots. Continually paddling with his webbed feet on the glossy back of the recumbent female, the male occasionally half unfurled his wings, as a balancing measure, or even rested his wing tips on the rock either side of her, like a guillemot. Spiking her tail high in a convenient posture and tilting back her head and opening her bill slightly, the female emitted a double ticking *'scrarl'*, deeper-pitched than the normal 'scrarl' with which he occasionally answered her. The mating is followed by sundry affectionate nibblings, reminding me of the cossetings of budgerigars, so affectionate are these razorbills. In April most of the matings appeared to be inconclusive, though some were certainly successful after much tailwagging, culminating in the final pressure.

From the chambers under the boulders comes the incessant bass caw as of an angry parrot : a prolonged and rasping *caarrr*, which is almost a roar at a distance of a few feet. This may be an expression of anger, of alarm, or of warning to mates hidden under boulders, though the electric whirring note is also employed for the latter purpose. There were mornings in April when Kittiwake Gully was full of the cawing and 'scrarling' of five hundred razorbills, as of some colony of bass-cawing rooks. At a sudden alarm a warning caw spread almost instantaneously from end to end of the Gully. The cawing seldom dies for a minute, for every suitable niche, chamber, or platform at the outer edges of the kittiwake colony swarms with razorbills. For once the kittiwakes, as if overwhelmed by this inrush of razorbills, are very quiet. Most of them, indeed, accidentally or not, are out fishing on the ebb tide in the swirling Race over the Hen and Chickens. The growling *caarrr* is also associated with the incessant head nibbling of mated pairs. Recumbent females on the boulders (the male will often sit, too) nibble affectionately and very delicately with the tips of their gnarled bills at their partners' plumage and especially at their conical heads, bushy with the pleasurable sensation. (Most males were bigger and bushier in the head than their mates). Very delicately, too, male and female interlock the hooked tips of their bills. This is in strong contrast to the savage beakholds of those occasional razorbills locked bill in bill, with half-open drooping wings, at the mouth of a cranny; or or of those tumbling interlocked down the siding, fighting furiously with flapping pinions, occasionally loosening their beakholds to stab savagely at one another : only to grapple bills again vigorously. When near the edge of the sheer cliff below the siding the weaker bird loosens his hold and flies down to the sea, but is followed by his adversary, who pitches on him in the sea and attempts to renew the combat. Then ensues a remarkable chase, both birds progressing with breasts raised out of the water and threshing wings for another five minutes after their ten-minute fight on the slope : the pursuer occasionally diving and swimming under water with bent wings, coming up from time to time to locate the position of his rival. But far from gaining by his submarine progress, he loses distance, and on his last submersion does not reappear within my ken, although his rival continues to thresh onwards for some minutes. In all, this was an extraordinary feat of sustained energy, but the object and origin of their curious wing-threshing progress half in and half out of the water eluded me. In a study of the guillemot we shall see that scores or hundreds of guillemots on the sea below the cliffs will instantaneously begin to thresh over the water in this laboured manner, and that solitary groups of razorbills or little parties in line may also be descried threshing over the sea thus. Sportive drakes of long-tailed ducks and scoter will manoeuvre similarly.

One razorbill will often seize a rival by the nape, and the two will lie spreadeagled one upon the other : every move of the victim resulting only in a tighter hold on his nape, until he succeeds in freeing himself and flies down to the sea. The razorbill is a bird whose diverse emotions and impulses appear to be even more liable to confusion than those of most birds, and as in the case of kittwake and guillemot, the dividing line between affection and aggression is thinly drawn. Thus an affectionate nibbling between a mated pair will not only be conducted in a manner violent enough to suggest illtemper between the two, but a purely affectionate nibbling will suddenly turn into actual savage fighting, in which one bird may be knocked off the ledge, only to return once more to an affectionate nibbling. (With each pair of razorbills nesting in their respective cranny, it was easy to establish the identities of a great number of mated pairs.) One might even watch two razorbills fighting most furiously in the sea for many minutes : going at it again and again, savage beak to beak and wings threshing the water. Then, after bouts of wing flapping, coming together again, not now to fight, but to nibble affectionately over a long period, 'ticking' pleasurably, one occasionally shooting through the water with threshing wings.

The razorbill is obviously a species whose impulses are strongly and easily stimulated, so that it is perhaps not very remarkable to find him slipping so facilely from one impulse to another. A razorbill fighting furiously with a rival, for instance, will switch in a moment to affectionately nibbling his mate. The razorbill and the guillemot impressed me most, I think, by their extraordinary and most unbirdlike responsiveness to physical sensations. There was no confusion on this point : some things were pleasurable to them, and some were distasteful, and they left one in no doubt as to which were which.

Before his mate the male razorbill occasionally bends his head right back over his mantle, in the manner of a cormorant, with a slight opening of that gamboge buccal cavity that is in such artistic contrast to his black and silver plumage. He follows this antic by strongly pecking his indifferent partner's averted head, eventually provoking her to further endearments, which take the form of mutual preening. This preening of one another's feathers is a dominant feature of the cliff life of razorbills, and especially of guillemots. Ninety-nine times out of a hundred a scrap between two guillemots is brought to a standstill by one of the combatants breaking off for a feverish preening : in which he is usually at once imitated by his rival.

The laying back of the head is rather a rare razorbill antic. Most frequently the male (and also the female) elevates his head and bill vertically, his slightly parted mandibles vibrating swiftly with the rattle of castanets, while his mate nibbles his taut throat, and he shivers in an ecstasy of pleasurable sensation : for this antic is usually associated with extreme physical pleasure or excitement.

These pleasures are subject to certain complications : for as in the case of nearly all wild birds I have watched, both in flight and on the water, especially in the months before incubation, a third party can be seen attaching itself to the affectionate pair. This is a young unmated male or female, and any deaths in the ranks of the mated birds will be made good by one of these. These third party razorbills habitually try to land on the ledges of nesting pairs, when of course resentment is felt and they are pecked away. But the implications of the third party's presence are not always immediately recognised. A female, for instance, coming in to her nesting ledge at mid-May, nibbles briefly and diffidently with a male, whereupon another male jumps down from the ledge above, but makes only a slight peck at the first male. The three then stand amiably on one ledge for a minute before the latter, betraying a growing awareness of being on forbidden territory, flies off to another ledge, when the second male immediately mates with the female for a prolonged period.

Ones and twos and sometimes scores of razorbills are continually taking off with a most delicate grace from their boulders on Puffin Slope. With heads and tails depressed, penguinwise, and paddles attenuated like a seal's hind flippers, they go down to the sea with only a swift sinuation of pinions, contrasting strongly with their

Razorbills flying down to sea over nesting boulders

customary quick-beating, whirring flight. After the initial
flutterings they beat away down into the gale over the sea with the
slow, powerful flipping wing beats of a mousing short-eared owl,
their wings lifting high over their backs like those of a
joy-flighting oystercatcher: the delightful nonchalant flight of a
nightjar or a great shearwater, but without their sharpness of
wing. Whoever first promulgated the theory that the razorbill was
a bird of weak flight unlikely to migrate a great distance can never
have visited a breeding colony of razorbills – or of puffins or
guillemots, for that matter. Unexpectedly long of pinion, the
razorbill's flight suggests a latent power equal to that of a
short-winged plover or tern. Conceive a black cross with white
outer edges to its stem and short white slots centred in the lower
edges of the cross, and you have symbolised the razorbill in his
exquisite flight. At rest, when his wings are closed, the white
cross-slots become half-moon circlets of white on his black mantle.
Some flighters break the circle of their fellows and go right out to
sea, but instead of alighting on the wide splayed paddles associated
with the whirring flight, which succeeds the flippant hawking
once the bird is on an even keel, they straighten out and glissade

into the sea on their bills, bringing their heads up sharply after contact. The sea at the base of the cliffs is spangled with packs of only a few pairs or of several hundred razorbills. Brilliant white and jet-black floats, they swim high in the sea, black paddles hanging almost vertically in the clear water : spinning and flapping, like teal in winter display packs, continually 'kissing' and head nibbling. And there are constant explosions in the water from razorbills submerging with instantaneous dives. Looking down from the cliffs of the North Cape, one could watch them swimming steeply down with half-furled wings, their sharp primaries sloping almost vertically back, and planing up to the surface, after their lightning dives, with bent wings : a beautiful resilient motion. Continually breaking water in unexpected places, they are forced to dive again with splutter of opening wings by kittiwakes plopping on them with daintily threatening webs. During their intervals at the surface they bow their tilted heads to sip water incessantly, often rising to flap their wings, treading water swiftly on their paddles, while their bass 'scrarling' carries hundreds of yards over a calm sea.

Though frequenting island waters at Christmas razorbills are first seen on the cliffs late in February, or early in March, about the time that the kittiwakes take up residence on their ancestral nests : but not until the coming of the puffins at the end of March do they make land in big numbers, vying with the puffins and shearwaters for the turfy burrows and especially the boulder caverns on Puffin Slope. Their catholicism in the choice of nesting places also brings them into conflict with guillemots. In April there are several thousand razorbills all round the northern cliffs. Later, small groups and odd pairs colonise both coasts of the island down to Quarter Wall in the east, and right round the west coast to Mermaid's Hole in the south, for the big colonies of all four species of auks and kittiwakes were tenanted days or weeks earlier than the smaller colonies in the extreme south. Although the biggest colony of razorbills, some two thousand pairs, perhaps, patronised the boulders of Puffin Slope, where their social activities could be most closely studied, the ledges and cornices of the steep gullies and colossal pyramidal stacks formed their most effective background. Such stacks as St James' Stone fairly twinkled with their black and white beetle forms. On the other hand a single pair of razorbills might be perched precariously on the only narrow ledge on a sheer slab of cliff hundreds of feet square, for a feature of their colonisation was that while in some places they nested in massed colonies of several hundred pairs – though I only knew two instances of razorbills incubating contiguous eggs – in other places solitary pairs and fours and fives were scattered over an enormous area of cliffs, sidings and the crags above the sidings. It was a familiar sight to see little knots of white bellies gleaming from the ledges of lichened crags that beetled out from the sidings three and four hundred feet above the sea, and there were not many such sites on the island to which the razorbills did not penetrate, although there appeared to be ample room for an increase in the density of the twenty-one thousand nesting on the island. One has, however, to bear in mind the astronomical numbers of small fish needed to fill the plump bellies of some eighty thousand nesting sea birds. That most of the fishing after incubation had begun was conducted in island waters suggests that the supply of fish was well up to requirements, for at the Farne Islands, where the total sea bird nesting population is probably greater, a proportion, at any rate, of the auks passage several miles to and from their fishing grounds.

At the end of April the bulk of the nesting razorbills came in for good from offshore waters, though they still tended to leave the cliffs and sidings earlier in the evening than the guillemots and puffins. And even in May they might all have gone out to sea by four in the afternoon.

2. *The Unfamiliar Egg*

It was mid-May before the razorbills began to go in and out of their rock chambers and crannies in the cliffs very frequently, emerging with sparkling breasts soiled by these initial pre-incubationary activities. Puffin Slope swarmed with them, and as many as thirty might be crowded on a single slab of granite. Matings were still incessant, four or five pairs doing so at a time, although others were even now taking up territories. Hitherto they had only sat quietly within their burrows for brief periods. The major portion of their few hours on shore on calm mornings had been passed in social activity on top of the boulders or in a passive standing about in the vicinity of their burrows, interrupted by continual flighting down to the sea and circling over the Slope.

But in the days that followed the female razorbills sat for an increasingly longer diurnal period in their crannies, and one or two appropriated old kittiwake drums. At this critical season the males, like the male guillemots under the same circumstances, rise to the height of their emotions : unmated birds continually jump on to the backs of any females in the vicinity, paired or otherwise, with a desperate fanning of wings. The latter, however, keep their tails down and always refuse them, as they are beginning to refuse their own mates also, though there are still a great many proper matings. One female even pecks a male, possibly her own, off another female's back.

There was good reason for this waywardness. On 21 May the first eggs were laid, great numbers of birds, unlike guillemots, laying at once. The next day there were many hundreds of eggs dotted about the cliff ledges all round the island and under the boulders on Puffin Slope : again, there was a tendency for blocks of birds to lay at the same time. Their eggs are white, sometimes brown, with a varying degree of brown pencilling and blotching, often concentrated in a dense zone of colour at the rounder end. Though very long, they have in lesser degree the heavy, but pointed pear shape of guillemot eggs.

On the morning of 22 May there were some ten razorbills sitting in Kittiwake Gully, some on the naked rock, others on scoops in the earth between the rocks, one in a rocky cavern. Most of the eggs were wedged into declivities in the rock and were often left unattended for considerable periods, though before actually laying the razorbill appears to sit for several hours. Even when present, their owners were often shy of sitting on them, and in one case a male made three attempts to incubate and flew down to the sea three times in twenty minutes while his mate stood by the egg. At the end of that period both flew down to the sea and back again, when the female made one brief attempt to incubate and five minutes later a better attempt – to the great interest of her mate peering down at her from a rock above. But after actually settling down on the egg for a second, she rose again, got off, and pecked some dust under her.

Her egg, as was very often the case, was awkwardly placed against a ledge of rock, so that after another attempt to sit on it she got off again, this time to swallow some grit. Two further attempts at incubation followed in which every movement of body and bill to adjust the egg was accompanied by a great, and what sounded like highly pleasurable, caw than her usual 'scrarl'. It was noticeable that many razorbills had much trouble in settling down to incubate their eggs, taking perhaps twenty minutes to get them properly covered : though this was often owing to the awkward places in which they were laid. Some had an amusing trick of putting one web on top of their egg before shuffling it under their wing. Here, as in the case of the guillemot, individual temperament, or age, or inherent makeup, played its part. Some razorbills sat tightly from the beginning, with heads drawn back into their shoulders, hour after hour, day in day out. Others constantly neglected their eggs, and one with an egg in a rock cavern at the top of Kittiwake Gully passed most of the hours of daylight sitting outside the burrow or playing with her mate, who yawned continually with that flexible forking of mandibles common to the cormorant, or 'vibrated' with vertical bill – not that this indifference affected the chances of the egg, for a chick was successfully hatched off.

On coming in to take over from her sitting mate, the female tickles his vibrant upstretched throat with a great cawing, and he, having been gently pushed away from the egg, continually picks up and swallows little bits of dirt and stuff and places them beneath him – as any male tern does when leaving his eggs.

The razorbill has a curious though very necessary habit, considering the enormous size of her egg, of incubating it under one falling wing, and you will see one continually adjusting her wing for this purpose, pushing it down between the face of the cliff and the egg. Her wings shiver before she takes up position, and her outside wing shivers while she is getting the other settled over the egg and for a short time after she has finally settled down. The wings of those birds which have difficulty in settling on to their eggs shiver continually, even when they are standing well clear of them.

Two hours later perhaps, the male takes over from his mate after she has tickled his vibrant throat. She, too, throws stuff back to either side and under her when leaving the egg, and there is the usual great cawing while the male settles his wing down, and especially when she leaves him and flies down to the sea. Male and female change about frequently on the egg, and the interval may be less even than two hours : the females usually returning to stand by their sitting mates after an absence of only five or ten minutes during the daytime, often going off and coming up again a number of times during the males' period of sitting. The latter, however, tend to remain out at sea for the full duration of their leave of absence. But they are good sitters, and a male who has been sitting for some hours – all the morning since dawn perhaps – continues to sit, after welcoming his mate's return with the usual caw. Although sitting for a further twenty minutes after her return, he rises on three separate occasions and fiddles with the egg, shifting it about, and preens before settling down again with a caw. When in the end he gets off to allow the female to get on, he performs the usual ritual of billing in dust and stuff, going to some trouble to secure this from crannies a foot or more away from the egg.

One gathers certain impressions from these early-laying razorbills : that they are in the immediate process of getting into a new routine; that the eggs are unfamiliar objects of unknown behaviours ; and that, from the affectionate nature of their cawing at each billing of the egg, they respond to it as a living object.

In such quick succession do all the razorbills lay their first eggs that within three days of the initial laying Puffin Slope and its gully are almost as outwardly deserted as on those early stormy days when nearly all the birds stayed out at sea. In such sites as Kittiwake Gully, where all the incubating razorbills are obvious on their rocky platforms and ledges, their numbers appear unchanged, for their mates come in to stand by their sides. But on the Slope, where they are hidden away in their boulder crannies and chambers, the only obvious sign of the wealth of subterranean life is an occasional owner of a burrow running with open, snarling bill at a prowling herring gull and putting him to flight : he himself vanishing into the burrow with the coincidental surge of territorial jealousy provoked by the gull's approach. With all the puffins sitting in burrows too, there now ensues a period of inactivity until such time as the hatching of the chicks releases a new wave of activity.

After a week of egg laying, that is at the end of May, hundreds of pairs of razorbills have lost their eggs to gull, man, or rat, and they have more leisure for standing about, with once again the massing on the boulders. The males continue to display great mandibulatory affection for their mates, whether sitting or not,

Razorbill standing on a rock with outstretched wings.

and an occasional mating enlivens proceedings. They yawn incessantly, with or without a waving of the wings, raise their heads vertically with opening beaks and lay them back and almost on their mandibles, vibrating with the clicking of castanets. Many females stand outside their eggless burrows, and on a male coming in from the sea, the pair will shuffle together into the cavern and there, with bowed heads, make a great pretence of fiddling about with an imaginary egg. The female of one pair after nibbling with her mate, their heads down in a cranny, repeatedly dips her head and nibbles the rock and her webs in the manner of a guillemot, though she has no egg. And once (indeed on the only occasion during the five months) a pair stand firmly upright on their toes.

By four or five o'clock the Slope is once more deserted for sea and burrow, for the razorbills are always the first to go down to the sea in the afterpart of the day, planing over my head with a vicious hum. But they atone for this by returning the first in the morning, odd birds beginning to pitch on the boulders between half-past three and four o'clock, when it is pretty light, single birds continually whirring around the North Cape at that hour. From now on the special hours of razorbills and puffins are most accentuated : the morning and afternoon belonging to the razorbills, the early evening and twilight to the puffins. As June lengthens out and the attraction of the sea begins to dominate that of the burrow, the razorbills go out earlier and earlier in the afternoon, and the puffins come in later and later in the evening : so that only a few units or scores of either overlap on the boulders.

3. *Fishing for the Chicks*

On 23 June a herring gull took a razorbill's egg from St James's Cove, the contents of which he afterwards disgorged before his chick as an embryo razorbill. The next morning the big chick of a great black-back on the north west sidings, upset by my sudden appearance, disgorged an embryo razorbill and shell. A heap of eggshells nearby proved him to be the offspring of the monster who so harried the unfortunate guillemots of the North West Stack. This was Razorbill morning on Puffin Slope, and after staring somewhat dreamily at Kittiwake Gully for a while, I became aware that the first razorbill chick had hatched off after some thirty-five days in the shell : its mother excitedly shivering her wings, its father very curious of it, and both indulging in a bout of vertical 'vibration'. She made a little tent of her shuffled wings around the dark-grey chick in the manner of a guillemot, but the chick was obstreperous and insisted on billing with the male, who, by continually weaving about his mate, was able to thrust his bowed head under her breast to the chick. Within its limited space the chick was very active from the beginning, and kept the female continually on the shuffle, endeavouring to 'tent' it up safely in a corner of the cliff at the back of the ledge. Even so it persisted in pushing its bill through the parting of her drooping wing and mantle, so that she had to cosset it back gently with her turned bill and tighten up her wing to close the aperture. Although he took five or six brief flights to sea in an hour, the male brought up no fish. Both parents were very jealous of the proximity of other razorbills, pecking them away from their especial slab of the creviced ledge; for in the delightful way of these auks, those razorbills without eggs or chicks were intensely curious about this new phenomenon, peering down at it from a number of higher vantage points, the parents pointing up their heads at them with parted mandibles – that menacing opening of the bill recognised as a threat by puffins and razorbills, though so far as the razorbill is concerned it also denotes affection, alarm and sexual emotion : just as his caw, always bass but pleasantly mellow, has various modulations and inflexions expressive of different emotions.

Later in the day a powerful squeaking *tsee-ee-ee* drew my attention to five or six more chicks in crannies and ledges of the sheer walls and cliffs about the Devil's Chimney. One was still sitting in its shell, with only its stout black bill and curious white-grey head dry : the female jumping excitedly up and down from a ledge above its cranny, with that comical 'clothes-peg' opening and shutting of her 'scrarling' bill. The next day the chick had dried off into an iron-grey on the back.

It was the prettiest sight to see the parents change over on their chick : a departing female continually returning, with a contented caw, for a vigorous neb with the male and a pointing and cosseting of the chick, on whom the former settled himself with vibrant wings very efficiently, the chick poking its bill through his wing. It was fifteen minutes before she could tear herself away and fly down to the sea, leaving the usual idlers – of which the parents grew less jealous as the days passed – still comically peering down from above at the chick, leaning right forward over the edge of the ledge with heads tilting enquiringly first on one side and then on the other. Overcome with curiosity, one such idler could not resist the impulse to go right up to a cranny in which a chick was being fed and peer in, though threatened by the parted bill of the sitting female. Another fought with an idler guillemot, the guillemot stabbing with his bill and beating viciously with half-furled rigid wings, the razorbill with menacing bill but closed wings. Neither bird being on a nesting site, the passage-at-arms ended in a draw, though the guillemot soon flew down to the sea.

Four days after hatching, when on 27 June there were a great many chicks off in Kittiwake Gully, the oldest chick, who preened his white breast assiduously, was perceptibly blackening on the back. His parents were now rather sharp tempered and there was even a little stabbing of open wings at one another between bouts of nebbing. Above them a razorbill noted for her incessant pleasurable cawing over her egg, was today cawing in precisely the same way over her newly hatched chick. It was interesting to find

that those razorbills marked down as desultory incubators were
also those who most frequently stood away from their chicks or
even quite deserted them : the converse also being true. In any
case, as the chicks grew, so the parents would stand clear of them
more and more frequently, nebbing and displaying noisily, the
chicks nipping their tails. One old bird sitting clear of her
offspring drew nesting stuff towards her before brooding.

The old birds did not begin fishing until mid-morning, between
ten and eleven o'clock being the rush period – this was true also of
guillemots. On 1 July, for instance, the first load of fish was not
brought up until half past eight. The delivery of fish to the chick
was a delightful operation to watch. The first fisher brought up
five gleaming whitebait, but it was four minutes before the chick
woke up to his arrival, opening its bill hopefully, revealing its pale
yellow buccal cavity and flesh-coloured tongue. At the outset it
was unable to negotiate a small promontory of rock, and in the
course of getting to the male, a spasmodic impulse to preen (so
early!) closed its open bill. In the end, however, it reached its
parent on a ledge a little above and took the fish directly from the
bill of the latter, who leant forward in a curious hunched-up,
immobile attitude, with his head well down and slightly on one
side. The chick occasionally missed its aim, and took the fish by
the longer drooping tail portion hanging down from the old bird's
bill : but miss or take, the latter continued to stand patiently until
his load had been drawn, the chick swallowing the fish without
difficulty. In the meantime the previously brooding female stood
by at a little distance without interfering, and the idlers peered
down curiously into the crevice at the chick picking up fishes he
had dropped, equally impartial whether he swallowed them head
or tail first. After standing about for five or six minutes the fisher
flew down to the sea, returning without fish an hour and a half
later.

The number of whitebait or sandeels brought up varied
remarkably from one fisher to another and from one time to
another : any number of fish from one to nine being possible,
though five or six was most usual. No less variable was the manner
of their delivery. One fisher standing about uneasily with five
whitebait flew down to the sea again before returning to feed three
to his chick, swallowing the other two himself. Another with three
shining tails all on one side of his beak, stood about for several

minutes before delivering. A third brought up five sandeels, with two three-inch ones at the base of his bill, which the chick took from him and gulped down with very little trouble. Two, however, were dropped across the webs of the fisher, who picked up one very delicately and held it out to the chick again. The latter picked up the other itself, first by the tail and then by the head, still alive and kicking. The fisher then brooded the chick, the female standing by. A fourth fisher with three whitebait displayed an obvious dislike of having to jump down into the deep crevice housing his chick : his shilly-shallyings, before finally plopping down, were of great interest to neighbouring idlers. A fifth, arriving with six big sandeels, was mistaken by a female brooding in a rock recess for her own mate, for she rose from her chick, who got up with a yawn. Nothing transpired, however : though another bird scrambled up on to a higher ledge and peered down at the female, who subsided again on the chick. After four minutes the fisher dropped down beside his true mate and stood beside her for another ten minutes, during which period the true mate of the other female arrived with five big sandeels, got into the recess behind her and, poking his head round her breast, fed his chick without any delay. The first fisher then finally delivered five of his load of six to the chick, who thereupon retreated under its mother again but later emerged to take the remaining fish from the patient male. Some razorbills returning to their nesting territories seemed to mistake those momentarily, and on Puffin Slope a fishing razorbill sometimes alighted on the wrong boulder – to be pecked away after standing about for a while, fly down to the sea again and come up once more, this time to the proper entrance to his burrow, boring his bushy, conical head well down into his breast to avoid the eager bills of the idler razorbills and guillemots who sometimes accosted the fishers halfheartedly. I often used to marvel that a razorbill coming in from the sea and whirring up a couple of hundred feet or more into a gully teeming with some thousands of other razorbills, guillemots, and kittiwakes, or to the jumble of boulders on Puffin Slope tenanted by some four thousand of his own kind, five thousand puffins, and several score of shearwaters, could make a beeline through hundreds or thousands of his flighting fellows and alight on his exact ledge less than a foot square, or within a few inches of the mouth of his burrow!

Four fish at one series of gulpings seemed often to be the limit of the chick's immediate capacity, and usually, though not invariably, the fisher – nearly always the male – took over the brooding sooner or later after feeding, as in the case of the guillemot. Here, for instance, on 4 July, is a male with seven sandeels of varying size packed in anyhow in his gnarled bill. After taking three of these, the chick settles down to rest again : whereupon the female takes one from her mate and eventually presses it upon the chick. She then attempts to take another, but the male grimly holds on to his remaining three, turning his head away from her and trying to feed the chick himself. In the end she manages to pull a second eel from his bill, but after trying unsuccessfully to feed it to the chick, swallows it herself, and also a third that she takes from him, while he picks up and swallows the seventh and last that has dropped on the rock. She then resumes her brooding. A quarter of an hour later the male parent of the oldest chick, now eleven days out of the shell, brings up five or six fish which the chick swallows ravenously, dropping several in his desperate eagerness to secure them, after his twelve- or, probably, fifteen-hour fast, for the old birds still go out to sea early in the evening. The fisher as usual settles down to brood it, the female flying down to the sea after five minutes' standing by. Between three and four o'clock fishers are coming up, one every five minutes, but by half past six Puffin Slope is almost deserted of attendant males. The last fisher comes up at a quarter past seven, but flies down to the sea again without delivering his load. On the Slope the brooding females are hidden in their boulder caverns, but at eight o'clock many females in Kittiwake Gully are standing clear of their chicks, which preen industriously and fan their wings, the old birds continually 'scrarling' to them – not that the chicks take much notice of this, although they will point bills with their parents.

It is a most interesting instance of inherently divergent behaviour that while on open nesting sites on exposed cliffs one parent or the other was always in attendance on the chick, those nesting in the rock chambers and turfy burrows of Puffin Slope were wont to leave the chick quite alone for long periods. In such a way as this might two different races of razorbills evolve : for already on the island there were cliff-nesting razorbills and burrow-nesting razorbills of whom I soon learnt to recognise such typical divergences of habit as this. The period of absence increased with the growth of the chicks, so that on the tenth or eleventh day the feeble pipings of deserted chicks were to be heard all over Puffin Slope, though not elsewhere. By this time the chick was assuming the typical white breast of the adult and blackening heavily on head, nape, necklace and mantle, though still retaining the eggtooth mark on his bill. Yet while retaining this embryonic hallmark, it was already displaying a faint white inlay on its head groove. It was also assuming adult mannerism, parting its bill menacingly at the idler razorbills peering down from above, their curiosity unabated.

About the twelfth or thirteenth day, at the end of the first week of July, a new and unwonted hastiness was noticeable amongst the fishing razorbills. For the first time a chick in Kittiwake Gully was brought two lots of fish, some seven in all, in thirty minutes, one by each parent : whereas hitherto the normal interval had been three hours, with probably only two deliveries in the twenty-four. The last of the seven fish was dropped and later picked up by the fisher, and the chick was just about to take it from him when the other parent neatly filched it from the male and fed it to the chick herself, after which she 'vibrated' and nebbed with the chick and settled down to brood it. Very shortly afterwards another chick was fed twice in twenty minutes, and for the first and only time in five months an unmated razorbill brought up one fish and immediately swallowed it. Then a parent arrived with eight enormous sandeels for the big chick in Kittiwake Gully, now thirteen days old. He stood on the ridge above the little rock enclosure, but the chick, stretching up to his dangling load, failed to reach them : so, after two or three minutes' indecision, the fisher dropped six all at once into the gully while the female took the seventh and later the eighth, feeding both to the chick.

Seven chicks out of nine in this small cleft of Kittiwake Gully have now been fed in the hour between eleven o'clock and noon, two of them twice, and there has been a continuous stream of fishers to all parts of the gully. The size of some of the fish brought up appears ludicrously inappropriate, and one birds whirs up with two enormously broad britling three inches in length, one of which proves as much as the chick can manage : the fisher retains the other for some minutes, to the interest of a nearby guillemot standing beside his brooding mate, before flying seaward with it. Many of the sandeels are four or five inches in length. This day, 6 July, was the last on which any great number of fishers came up with fish, and all over Puffin Slope sounded the piteous *psee-ee-ee* of chicks lonely in their burrows.

By the 9 July the biggest chicks, some sixteen days old, had full white throats and lower cheeks and wavy white headlines and were quite black on the back, with a few wisps of grey-white down adhering to their heads. They were, however, very shaggy in contrast with the glossy smoothness of the adults. One or two had faint white inlays to the grooves in their bills, although the adult retains only the headline in its autumn plumage. The inlays are actually minute white feathers or bristles, and the headline comes right down on to the bottom edge of the upper mandible. So fat were the chicks that they seemed hardly able to waddle about their rocky retreats.

The next day the comparatively few fishers that did come up were often in a desperate hurry to deliver their loads, pushing their mates out of the way and bustling in to their chicks. One fisher brought up a single five-inch sandeel, and another a tiny whitebait and an enormously broad and headless three-inch britling, which his newly hatched chick swallowed after sixty seconds' violent struggling, with flapping stumps of pinions. The fishing activities of some razorbills were becoming a little confused, and a male brooding his chick at first pecked away his mate, arriving with fish, and after feeding hustled away some razorbills standing by.

What did this speeding up of the delivery of fish indicate?

On the morning of 11 July I was astonished to find that the biggest chick in Kittiwake Gully had vanished during its eighteenth night after hatching, although both parents were still standing on its ledge. On Puffin Slope hardly a chick was to be located, and by the next morning a whole shoal of chicks had gone from Puffin Gully and Kittiwake Gully, including some ridiculously small ones only partially black. As yet, however, the lower slopes of the latter gully swarmed with chicks of all sizes and colours. Some of the very small grey chicks were very confident, others shy with open bills : but all the big black chicks were wildly nervous, seeking to bury themselves, head first, in narrow crevices, with violently flapping wings, or pecking savagely at my fingers, revealing the pale yellow of their buccal cavities and the tiny back-sloping teeth with which they manipulated their fish so easily. Their eyes, like those of the old birds, were a filmy brown with black pupils.

I found it incredible that such tiny creatures, less than one-third the size of the adults, could have gone down to live on the sea. In any case, how could they have got down? For those which I watched specially in the cross-gully out of Kittiwake Gully could fall only on a narrow, vertical ladder of rock sixty feet below, and throughout their short lives on the cliffs a few square inches had hitherto marked the limits of their activity. Nor were any to be seen on the sea below. Besides, either one or both parents were standing by every ledge and cavern deserted by its chick, and though rather silent and subdued, were still ejecting intruders (also very quiet now) from too close a proximity. From time to time they would fly down to the sea, returning, however, without fish. On the other hand it did not seem probable to me that the gulls had cleared the lot, for up to this time I had never seen a gull pay any attention to Kittiwake Gully.

4. *Epic Journeys*

At twilight on 14 July I was out on Puffin Slope watching a great flighting of puffins, but not one razorbill among them : nor were those razorbills without chicks present on their ledges at this late hour. But from under an enormous boulder, whose flat top was the social playground of one hundred puffins, came the incessant piteous piping *psee-ee/psee-ee* of a lone razorbill chick. I went down to locate him and found him standing up, black head well back, looking up to the great world outside. Quite clearly he wanted his parents very much – there were one or two other chicks also crying on the Slope – so I crouched down against another boulder to await events, not knowing what I was going to witness.

About nine o'clock both parents suddenly alighted on the boulder without, however, going down below to the chick who was still piping. A quarter of an hour later only the female was left standing silent on top of the boulder, peering about shortsightedly and occasionally looking down at the hidden retreat of the piping chick. Sometimes moving a few inches down the boulder, she returned time and again and even squatted briefly. Once she dropped on to the thrift on a level with the cavern under the boulder without, however, going in to the chick. In the end, when it was getting very dusk and she was the only bird left on the Slope, all the multitudinous puffins having gone out to sea for the night, and only six or seven gulls wheeling menacingly low overhead, I began to fear that nothing would come of it. But immediately after this the old bird began to 'scrarl' intermittently, and I knew that I was in the right place. Quiet when the gulls passed over, she 'scrarled' and 'vibrated' with vertical beak at intervals to the piping chick, in between three or four brief flights down to the sea, often peering down at the cavern but never making to enter it. The chick continued to pipe plaintively, a most pathetic, appealing cry – respondent to that tantalising 'scrarling' outside his cavern.

And then began a marvellous episode. It began with the realisation that the chick's piping was coming from farther down the siding under the boulder. And with this the parent flew down to the sea and did not return : so in the gathering dark I scrambled down over the cushions of thrift and granite blocks closer to the boulder and found the chick, looking rather like a little auk, standing upright under the bottom seaside edge of the boulder, his satin belly as dazzling white as a dipper's in the gloom. Looking out at the sea, one hundred and twenty feet below, he continued to pipe incessantly, his mother 'scrarling' harshly and intermittently on the water, hidden from both of us in the darkness, her call rising above the wash of the surging tide and the cries of the gulls, as she spun and bobbed on the swell.

There intervened another long period of anxious waiting, cramped against a rock. Then about half-past ten the chick began hopping and tumbling down very nimbly and swiftly from terrace to terrace of the thrift, and from boulder to boulder, with little flips of his tiny pinions, choosing the least precipitous path with great skill. But after making such good progress for a few yards he scuttled under another big boulder and stayed there for a long while, piping hard to his 'scrarling' mother. What were her emotions down there on the water? She was torn between the sea and the chick, responding first to one and then to the other. She may possibly have instinctively associated the cries of the prowling gulls with danger to her chick, but she certainly could not assess, as I could, the enormous risks of this epic journey.

Not until it was almost completely dark did the chick venture again from his lair and set forth, after much shilly-shallying,on his heroic descent. But this time, piping all the way, he went on down the siding at great speed, hopping and tumbling : so swiftly, indeed that he got down to the sheer tide-wet slabs at the sea's edge a few feet in front of me, stumbling and sliding in the darkness. At his appearance just above the water his mother intensified her 'scrarling'. Thus encouraged the chick tumbled into the sea and, still piping, swam out to meet her, dived, and came up to neb bills with her. Then spinning around one another a little, mother and child swam away to sea, occasionally diving together, and I lost them in the darkness.

Climbing up the cliffs slippery with seaweed, at eleven o'clock, I heard the piteous piping of other chicks voyaging forth on this perilous and astounding journey, and the 'scrarling' of their parents waiting on the water.

As I stumbled home the two and a half miles across the moors to the Old Lighthouse, reflecting on the events of the evening, with the strange sobbing cries of the shearwaters gasping about me, I thought that this had been an experience transcending all as a naturalist: for this tiny chick had only broken its shell some seventeen or eighteen nights before at most, perhaps only thirteen or fourteen, and had never moved more than a few inches from its birthplace during this period.

So this was how the chicks got down to the sea : but what of those hatched off on the narrow ledges of cliffs two or three hundred feet sheer above the sea, or those at the bottom of chimneys in the crags of the north-west slope nearly four hundred feet above the sea? I had read that chicks hatched in such places were taken down on the wings or backs of their parents. But such an action would necessitate a complete departure from razorbill normality, and I had seen nothing preparing me for such a method of departure. On the other hand, I found it difficult to believe that these tiny chicks, many of them still wearing a partial down, could fly with their little stumps of wings, or that they could fall hundreds of feet without injury. The events of the evening had not resolved any of these questions but had only shown the chick to be vastly more active than one could have expected.

On the morning after this momentous discovery, I found that

all those crannies from which the chicks had departed, including that of the oldest deserter in Kittiwake Gully, now five days gone, *still* had one or both parents standing by for varying periods : though most went out to sea again long before dark. They were jealous of their territories, and one fought with a guillemot who attempted to brood her chick in the declivity formerly occupied by the razorbill's chick : much to the noisy alarm of the guillemot's chick. This continued presence of chickless birds at their territories provoked three awkward questions : What happened to the chicks, once they were led away from the island, when both parents were present at the ledge? For they were never to be seen anywhere in island waters. By what means did their parents find them again after such an absence? And what were the relations between the two? For although fetching the chick down to the dominant habitat, the sea, the old bird is still possessed by a lingering attachment to the nesting spot. In this connection I was interested to observe that the chick was not necessarily encouraged to expedite its departure by starvation : for of three big chicks noted the previous day as likely to leave during the night, one, which I had not seen fed, had duly gone, but so also had one which had taken seven fish, while the third was *in situ* and received six fish.

Many old birds were bringing up fish, and while one female fed the chick, her mate 'vibrated' and nibbled her head and also her fish, the last of which he took from her and delivered to the chick, besides picking up another and swallowing it himself. Another male, not being able to reach down his last fish, tucked into the base of his bill, to a chick in a crevice, deliberately (to all outward seeming) turned his head towards his mate so that she could take the fish and feed it to the chick – which she did.

Little black and white sacks of fish, these chicks now, but very active : continually preening and exploring all over the limited space of their rocky platforms, often hopping up and down with a most vigorous fanning of their little wings and reaching up on their toes (only once observed of an adult) as if seeking to scale their prison walls. How came it that this activity was only now apparent after a considerable number of chicks had gone down to the sea? Were not those chicks who had gone off first equally in need of such strengthening exercise? The parent of one such energetic chick, becoming rather excited over its activities, dropped down from the ledge above and eventually got it tucked under his wing with its black head poked through his mantle. Shortly after this, however, the chick took seven small britling from the female and immediately excreted on to the back of a bird sitting below, hitting the head of the chick protruding through her mantle (feeding and evacuation were often consecutive among the chicks). The male then gave up his charge, and his mate took over.

Those chicks with no parents standing by sometimes slept with bills tucked back into wings, and one lay on the rock with one leg and web stretched back flatly, with its wing spread over it. All the chicks were still fed twice, about every three hours, some at dusk even, with the exception of one black chick which was not fed at all. The adults still fought a great deal, and at least one mating took place every day among those unsuccessful with eggs or chicks, as had been the case all through the summer.

By the night of the 17 July a great many chicks had gone out to sea, only about fifty remaining in Kittiwake Gully, and at half-past six very few parents of those away to sea were on the ledges. Shortly after nine o'clock one mystery was solved when an old bird came down from the top of the gully some two hundred feet up, accompanied by a big chick which made a perfect flight down, its diminutive wing stumps whirring as swiftly as a bee's, its little paddles spread wide in the appropriate manner. A 'scrarl' of excitement from other razorbills lining the route extolled its triumph. Had the chick begun its descent on its mother's back, and taken off from her half way down, so buoyant had been the latter stages of its flight? However that might be, the little fellow made a perfect alighting on the water, with even that slight submergence peculiar to the old birds. And away went mother and chick to sea, not diving.

Then from the cross-gully another chick dived voluntarily off its ledge, followed by *both* parents, and also made a perfect flight down to the water at the bottom of Kittiwake Gully : and away out to sea, paddling so swiftly that it fell over itself in the water, swinging from side to side like a dinghy in the hands of an inexpert oarsman.

But other chicks were not so amenable : for after more than an hour's coaxing by its 'scrarling' parents one chick has still not been persuaded to quit its ledge by a quarter past ten, when it is nearly dark. 'Vibrated' to by its attendant parents, the chick comes out of its crevice after about ten minutes, but immediately goes back again. Another ten minutes and it reappears : only to make for its crevice once more; momentarily checked by the effects of the old birds' 'vibration', it is nevertheless back in its retreat within five minutes. Then follow in quick succession three more outs and two more ins, and a great dancing up and down a-tiptoe, usually facing the cliff wall, and a fanning of tiny wings. Three more ins and outs, and it ventures a long way out over a crevice in its platform of rock, but returns to its lair after several minutes, and comes out and goes in again. By this time the female is growing very impatient, for throughout this long period she has been constantly 'vibrating' with her bill either vertical or laid right back on her mantle – which was rather a rare antic earlier in the season. She now changes her tactics and continually scuttles fussily and hastily up to the crevice, imploring the chick to come out. But all to no purpose. The chick will not leave its lair this night.

There are other equally obstinate or indifferent chicks, who are not to be drawn forth before the impulse, whatever its precise nature, moves them. One very black chick, previously brooded, does a wing-fanning dance around its rock – but nothing comes of it, and the parent broods it again. One or two other parents, standing at the edges of their platforms well clear of their chicks, 'vibrate' hopefully, but eventually settle down to brood again. The size of the chick does not appear to be the deciding factor in the date of its departure, for some very big chicks remain while other smaller chicks, often with quite a covering of down, go off. Nor does the parent have the final say in the matter. If the chick lacks the inclination to go off, no amount of encouragement by the old bird will force it to. However, three more chicks went down before it was quite dark : one not flying so strongly, hitting the water with a great plop, but swimming out to sea quite happily, falling over itself in its excitement.

On 19 July all the razorbills whose chicks had gone off were putting in an appearance in ones and twos from time to time, although the earliest chicks had left at least ten nights before. Others were hanging about on the sea below. Moreover, certain chicks whom I recalled as having been 'vibrated' to on the night of 17 July were *in situ* and were being fed. And, more astonishing, that very obstinate chick in the crevice was included among these. Closely brooded by the male, the chick later recieved seven whitebait from the female, which it took standing perfectly upright on its toes.

At twenty minutes past eight that evening this chick was at its old game again. By this date its head and mantle were absolutely coal black, except for a little white patching on the front of its necklace, though the white of its head and bill lines were not very distinct : whereas a chick in the niche above, though no blacker, had very distinct lines. Both parents were in, and the chick pottered about on its toes, flapping round its platform, the male in close attendance. The female then took a couple of brief flights down to the sea and up again, the male 'vibrated', and both nibbled with the chick. After more flights and 'vibrating', the female's absences gradually became of longer duration, though she looked in once at the entrance to the chick's retreat to which it, as usual, continually returned. Half an hour of this and she flew down for the last time, whereupon the male, after another 'vibrating', squatted down and was very affectionate to the busily preening chick, continually nibbling it and finally brooding.

A quarter of an hour later he got up and, after five minutes, 'vibrated', while the chick peered over the edge of the platform several times. He then went on to another platform, but ten minutes later, when it was a little dusk, joined the chick and peered with it down into the gully. And very shortly, after an instant's hesitation, the chick, followed by the male, took the plunge, on this third night, in a perfect flight down. Submerging quite gently on alighting, it headed for the mouth of the gully in pursuit of its parent, shooting forward in little propulsions on the surging of the tide and swinging to and fro in the swirl of its parent's backwash, the little white squares of its flanks bright above its tiny black webs feverishly paddling out behind.

Meanwhile the chick on the ledge above had been exploring extensively around the walls of its rock platform, but after displaying great energy was brooded at five minutes past nine. Half an hour later the old bird got off, whereupon the chick ventured for the first time on to the outermost slab and continually peered over the edge, the female peering with it. And off it went almost immediately. At the same time another chick, after peering down in the usual way from a ledge right at the top

of the cliffs, made a fine flight down and beyond the entrance to
the gully.

At a quarter to ten a chick at the bottom of the cliffs by the
entrance piped loudly to its parent and two other razorbills
swimming in the water a few feet below. Its *tsee-ee-ee*, not unlike
the winter cry of the grey plover, signified that it had been left
alone on the ledge : those chicks with parents utter a soft, almost
inaudible piping. It had evidently scrambled down from the cliffs
above, and it dropped off almost immediately, the old bird diving
under it at its alighting on the water.

Twenty-five minutes later another chick went off from about
the same point, whistling hard while swimming out to sea with its
parent, who also dived on meeting it. By twenty past ten, when the
light was very dim, the last of the chicks had gone off for that
night, and the last of the old birds had brought up fish. I left, to
the groaning of a solitary remaining puffin.

All the old pairs of razorbills were present on 20 and 21
July, ten and eleven days after the departure of the earliest chicks,
and the last egg known to me vanished though both parents came
up to the nest site hopefully. There were now only about a score of
chicks left in Kittiwake Gully, and at ten minutes past nine on the
evening of the 21 July a parent and a chick went away to sea, she
turning round to neb him, he occasionally bumping into her and
turning his proudly tilted little head from side to side as he swam.
Five minutes later there was the less usual spectacle of both
parents going off with a chick. One bumped into the chick in the
flight down, but it alighted safely on the water. Far up on the
highest crags, nearly four hundred feet above the sea, a herring
gull was waiting beside a razorbill who had been 'scrarling' to her
peering chick for a long time. The razorbill had more patience,
and in the end the gull moved off to his roosting cliff. When it was
nearly dark, and two more chicks had gone off, I climbed up
beside the chick on its lofty eyrie, but its ardour for adventure had
been dampened for one night.

By 23 July the remaining chicks were clearly fighting a
losing battle with the sea, on which shoals of old birds spun and
nebbed. The four or five fishers coming up with whitebait to their
black chicks were all in a desperate hurry to deliver their loads.
One brought up an enormous young mackerel to its tiny grey
chick, which the latter nevertheless disposed of, after disgorging it

the first time and picking it up lengthwise from the rock, instead of crosswise as it had taken it from its parent's bill.

At twilight the next night I saw two chicks come down from Kittiwake Gully with perfect landings. The parent of one alighted beyond the mouth of the gully, so that for many minutes the chick swam up and down the gully, continually calling its *pswee-wee/pswee-wee*, until in the end it swam through the surf at the entrance and joined its parent outside.

Although the parents of the first chick to leave were present at four o'clock the next day (fifteen days after its departure!) there were very few razorbills generally, and on the evening of 26 July Kittiwake Gully was virtually deserted – though the kittiwakes were as clamorous as ever – and only some eight razorbills with chicks remained. At a quarter past nine, however, a chick suddenly appeared from nowhere in the water at the bottom of the gully and swam directly out to the open sea, crying its continual *psee-ee-ee/psee-ee-ee*, with wide open bill. For some minutes it plied around outside the entrance to the gully, often looking up at the cliffs : but no parent came to meet it. Its fate was inevitable, for it was still quite light, with a fine sunset reddening the North Cape. I waited sadly. Down came the gull, as deadly quick as ever. And though the chick dived, and though three guillemots, waiting on their own chicks flighting down, made an onslaught on the gull, the latter hooked him by one shank and carried him dangling to a nearby reef. There the gull beat and tore the life out of him, though he struggled valiantly and with astonishing tenacity.

Shortly after this tragedy an old bird and her chick went off from down below, the chick turning very neatly in flight to avoid a rock at the bottom of the gully, alighting on the water without a sound.

July saw practically the close of the tale. By 30 July there were only six chicks left in Kittiwake Gully, and though some old birds were still standing by deserted territories, the parents of the earliest deserters came no more. The terns waiting on the sea below the cliffs on 28 July had also gone. On the last evening in July there were only three parents left in Kittiwake Gully, one of whom 'scrarled' impatiently to a tiny grey chick, but soon brooded it again. There was still one old bird with a chick on 4 August, but after that I knew of only one on all the island : a tiny grey chick with a white head in Puffin Gully. The call of the sea would prove too strong and his parents would leave him to his fate at the bills of the gulls.

Guillemot with chick.

V

GUILLEMOTS: THIRTY-SIX WEEKS ON STACK AND CLIFF

1. *Life on a Ledge*

On this calm dull day there surged hundreds of feet up the cliffs to the top of the island an explosive *currr,* rising and falling like the murmur of sea shells or a resurgent cooing of multitudinous rockdoves. For four miles and more from the Rock of Gannets on the north-east, round the North Cape and all the way down the west coast to Seals' Hole in the south, the explosive murmur rose and fell on the air eddies above the thunder of the breakers. Peering over the sidings, I could make out far below tens of hundreds of tiny guillemots massed like beetles on the sloping faces of great pyramids and the rounded summits of pinnacles, or packed in ranks on the broad ledges and deep niches of colossal stacks. There were few sharp crags or pointed cones on the Isle of Puffins, but innumerable rounded, or rectangular, segmented stacks and sphinxes of granite, weathered green, grey and orange by lichens.

This massing of guillemots was always marvellous to watch. Its essential details varied little from one part of the coast to another. On the rugged Atlantic coast there is a steep embattled amphitheatre of green thrift cushions and granite outcrop, rounded off short at its middle over sheer hundred-foot cliffs. The southern arm of this horseshoe cove, stretching far out into the

Atlantic, is the cathedral pile of St James's Stone : three great pyramids of rough stone segmented into a thousand square-hewn cornices and broad ledges dear to nesting sea birds. The first and second pyramids are linked by a narrow coll of thrift riven by two fifty-foot fissures, up which the white tide seethes : the rounded pinnacle of each pyramid is surmounted by a great black-back. From these rugged pyramids surged the incessant roar of guillemots and the 'scrarling' of black and white razorbills twinkling from every niche and frieze to the pyramid's top. On the granite bluffs of the short northern arm of the horseshoe herring gulls barked and wailed. Into either corner of the convex lip of the amphitheatre's slope are driven chasms of brown cliff, where guillemots and razorbills and querulous kittiwakes cling to the sloping slabs of cliff face.

In these early days, late in March, the guillemots were very shy, and continued so up to the time of incubation, pouring off their ledges at the first sight of a man a quarter of a mile distant. In an unbroken stream twelve abreast they whirred down from the cliffs with paddles spread wide, palms down, and stretched flatly either side of the white flank slots above their smooth brown tails, skimming over the waves with the arrowy flight of kingfishers half a mile out to sea. For minutes the five or six streams pouring off all the cliffs and stacks encircling the cove would be unchecked. The rays of chocolate-coloured backs and silver bellies converged on a vast assembly of their fellows swimming over acres of sea, among whom they alighted glissading on to the water and plunging underneath. Some of those already on the sea were white-cheeked immature birds, a few of whom frequented island waters throughout the spring and summer.

Temporarily free from their attendance at their ledges, they make a great to-do of bathing : turning right over on their backs, paddles in air, with brilliant gleams of white bellies, vigorously throwing up glittering sprays of water. They swim very low in the water, their smooth fawn shoulders almost awash, and are thus distinct from high-floating razorbills and twinkling dots of puffins at any distance. Looking one or two hundred feet down the sheer cliff into the limpid green sea, where every pebble and boulder was clear, one could see the glaucous shapes of many guillemots swimming under water with slow-beating half-furled primaries and clasped paddles stretched behind, opening when they turned.

When their milky-grey shadows swam steeply down, one could follow the wavy white flashes from their flanks and secondaries, until they went out, like comets, in opaquer depths. Their apparent slowness belied their prowess as fishers.

Like teal, and indeed most duck, these guillemots released much excess energy in their natural element and disported themselves merrily : leap-flying from their dives three or four feet clean out of the water, and skidding over the surface with two or three bounces off their plump white bellies on alighting from their 'fly'. Like teal, again, the playful antics of one bird immediately affected a score and then perhaps a hundred more of his fellows in the vicinity, so that in an instant whole fleets of guillemots previously bathing and sipping water peacefully were diving and swimming under water in shoals – a curious spectacle – or wing-threshing in droves over the calm sea, leaving in their wakes a multitude of churned rays, as if a herd of giant water skaters had been skating over the ocean.

It was interesting to a naturalist to see that the pattern of their play was almost precisely similar to the teal's : in their submerging with sudden dives and shooting up from under the water at their fellows, tweaking their tails, the assaulted guillemot leaping a couple of feet clear of the water. And there was the usual diving and sipping of water common to all sea birds when nervous or excited. Often they planed up to the surface in their smooth way immediately under puffins, tweaking their tails similarly, so that they, too, were constrained to shoot away in their comical, alarmed manner. Puffins betrayed a certain wary uneasiness in the presence of guillemots or razorbills, with whom they did not seem to be altogether popular, and in these mixed packs on the sea below the cliffs there was always a tendency for their big companions to shoot vindictively at them, as duck at duck.

Single guillemots continually returned to their ledges, circling up to the cliffs like puffins, squarely whirring : to alight with long and tapering wings arched as gracefully as those of small waders. But after an evacuation it would be hours, or the next day, before the ledges had their full complement of birds again.

Of one hundred and fifty thronging a yellow-stained platform, twelve feet long by three feet broad, or packed six deep along a broad ledge, half perhaps face in to the cliff wall, as they will tend to do in months to come, when they have eggs or chicks. Some stand, others are recumbent, asleep, with heads tucked as close as possible into the cliff face, white membranes nictating over their big red-brown mild eyes, which become gleaming golden orbs when they tilt their heads at me in the morning sun – although actually the irises are brown about black pupils.

The other half face outwards. A row of silver bellies and a forest of slender brown heads bowing gracefully at my sudden appearance round the cliff : a host of lissom snakeheads darting fearfully, with a soft staccato cooing audible only within a few feet. Typical penguins they seem, so full-fed on britling that their fat white bellies are as spherical as eggs.

Guillemots afford opportunities for study under natural conditions which must be unique, or almost so. For some eight months the most intimate details of their everyday life and behaviour lie open to the eye of the observer. Nothing is hidden, as in the case of most other birds, mammals, reptiles, fish and insects. The egg is laid upon the naked rock. Except when jaded from having to maintain a constant critical output of notes instead of just pleasurably watching the details of this remarkable scene, I was always deeply conscious of my good fortune in selecting this extraordinary bird.

When it came to piecing together consecutively into coherent book form my kaleidoscopic welter of notes, I thought sometimes that it would be a task beyond my powers : this story of a ledge and of many ledges of guillemots : a ledge of, perhaps, only three or four pairs, or of fifty or one hundred pairs.

On broad ledges where space and numbers permit, and to a lesser extent on narrow ledges and densely crowded platforms, there is a great deal of stepping delicately about the ledge with bowed heads and a penguin hop, or a high arching of pinions at every step with leisurely grace, and as among all water birds a frequent raising and flapping of short wings. There is much affectionate billing between mated birds and head nibbling on the part of the male : an attention not always welcomed, and more often than not impatiently evaded by the female, who is of a more placid disposition. She is more intent on posturing herself over an imaginary egg and keeping her precise place on that square foot of rock on which she will eventually lay her real egg, or sleeping, often with her head tucked right back under her wing. It is the incessant irritating attentions from males that are mainly responsible for the interminable roar of cawing on the ledges, when protesting female and excited male utter their wide-billed explosive *arrg-arrg-arrg*, often prolonged and dying away like the distant rumble of thunder. In the hidden depths of a great chasm in the cliffs the bass, uneasy *arrr* of more than a thousand guillemots is sonorously amplified by the precipitous granite walls and booms up to me in an overwhelming organ roll of sound. This is the characteristic deafening resurgent cry. Explosive variations on this, not unlike the distant crying of geese, are all expressive of great excitement on the part of either bird, when they stab sharply at one another with stiletto bills and darting heads, the male continually shooting over and under his mate's head with intent to nibble her face and throat. These continual intermarital bouts of half-angry stabbing, leading to a certain jostling of neighbours, engender still more energetic and savage stabbings between adjacent males, with yellow flashing buccal cavities and further resurgences of resentful cawing : a crescending guttural *gwoo-er* . . . *gwooerr-gwooerr-gwooerr*, which, in more peaceful moments, dies to a contented *worr . . . gg* uttered through closed bills : one of the most humorous sounds that ever came out of a bird.

The dominant object of most guillemots alighting on a broad ledge is to hustle themselves through the ranks of their fellows as close as possible into the face of the cliff, which will be the most popular site for incubation. If the alighter is conscious of having a territory somewhere in the vicinity of the cliff wall she is usually successful in barging her way through : but if she is an unmated bird with an undeveloped sense of territory she allows herself to be pecked right along the ledge, and eventually flies down to the sea again. On the restricted space of their square foot of rock, territorial emotions among guillemots are strong, especially on those broad platforms where, packed eight deep and twenty-five in a row, there is a great deal of competition for the favoured sites close up against the back wall. Distinctive bridled guillemots suggest that some at any rate of these are held to the very foot, not only from their first coming at Christmas, but for year after year. Infringement on these few square inches of territory is strongly resented, and the aspiring intruder is hustled from one forbidden territory to another, and finally driven off the ledge. Some of the unpaired young males hang on to the edge of the platform with violently fanning wings in a desperate attempt to maintain a foothold. Real or mock stabbing combats between adjacent pairs are incessant, except for those rare intervals when an absence of alighters on the platform has permitted the excitement of individual birds to subside into a quiescent period of preening, lazy nibbling and sleep. One of a pair at such a time lays her head upon her back dreamily with closed eyes in an ecstasy of enjoyment, while her mate nibbles her throat with infinitely tender and delicate tweezerings of his fine mandible points. These silent sleepy interludes contrast strongly with much more frequent periods of excited caresses and impatient evasions. The darting petulance of rival males may develop into a furious fight of slashing bills and drooping and half-furled beating wings, to the smothered accompaniment of guttural *arrr*s. Often spreadeagled one upon the other, the combatants end abruptly, panting and dishevelled, when both have the sudden impulse to preen : or when one is finally ejected from too close a proximity. Where the ledges are narrow these furious struggles are conducted with desperately fanning wings by those birds unable to secure footholds on the rim of the ledge, one or both eventually falling backwards down the cliff, knocking off one or two angry kittiwakes from lower cornices.

There is always a certain cautious animosity in being between adjacent kittiwakes and guillemots and razorbills : an animosity for the most part of closed bills and tentative dartings. A kittiwake, however, is not afraid to seize by the tail a guillemot or razorbill violating her territory, the two falling together into the canyon. She, for her part, immediately relinquishes a guillemot ledge, on which she has passed an idle minute preening, on the owner's return. There are two avian laws relating to the possession of territory. The first is that no matter how great the disparity in size and strength − the guillemot and the great black-back, the pied wagtail and the sparrow hawk (how frequent this association!) − the big trespasser invariably gives way halfheartedly before the direct assault of the little bird with territory, once the latter has settled in it and grown accustomed to it. The second is that when its young are threatened the small bird is fearless in their defence. 'Invariable' is a dangerous term to apply to the habits of birds, but I cannot recall any exceptions to either of these laws.

If the holding of a territory is a dominant feature of the

guillemots' cliff life, it is probably not, however, the primary cause of their return to their ledges in the first place. From the early days of their return they mate incessantly, or rather they go through a succession of antics that do not differ in the observer's eye from those employed at a later and more appropriate season. By the middle of April indeed they are still mating at ten o'clock on rare calm nights. I have not studied any other species so strongly affected by this impulse. In twenty minutes you may see and hear two or three score matings among the thousand birds under observation. Yet every field naturalist knows how comparatively rare an event it is to observe the mating of most species of wild birds. One of the strangest things about birds is that while most of their behaviour runs parallel in essentials one chances now and again on instances of an extreme divergence of behaviour. Thus while guillemots have been performing their mating antics day after day since Christmas, kittiwakes, who returned to Island waters at the same season, taking up residence on their ancestral nest drums late in February, do not begin to mate until May. Why should one or two species – for the razorbill is a good second to the guillemot – be organised so differently to the many hundreds of their fellows?

Even when not actually mating, the guillemot always looks to be about to mate, for in the congested conditions of the ledges, the male, who usually stands behind his mate, is likely to be paddling about on her very tail. This may well be an additional stimulus to the continual urge to mate and, indeed, the male often hugs his mate suggestively, and actually mates with her in an upright position. In a normal mating she is recumbent, with the male standing on her back and balancing himself with spread wingtips resting on the rock on either side of her. He occasionally nibbles her nape gently with the sharp points of his open mandibles, though not holding her with them, while she continually throws up her head at him with wide-opening bill, sounding a loud protesting *gurt-er/gurt-er,* that rises raucously above the general chorus of cawing, hundreds of feet to the top of the cliffs. Walking over the island, one is left in no doubt as to the precise activities of the guillemots hidden down below. If eager for the mating she will utter this cry when only nibbled by her mate, or before he begins to mount her, but she is usually the first to put an end to the performance, which may be prolonged for many minutes, by tipping him off: after which there may be a little head bobbing and turning from side to side. Neighbouring and, as often as not, contiguous guillemots pay no attention to these marital affairs : whereas one would expect them to be stimulated to some degree of excitement.

In April occasional single guillemots or pairs mandibulate stray grasses or straws from old kittiwake nests : though the species fashions no nest in the present stage of its evolution. One bird with a small piece of lichen in her bill puts it between her legs, picks it up again, walks around, allows her mate to nibble at it, and finally *throws* it between her webs. There are always some guillemots pointing their sharp bills at, and sometimes into, crevices in their rocky platforms, as if responding to some latent impulse to seek nesting material. More significant still, one bird close up against the cliff wall has a whitebait in her bill which she holds in the special guillemot grip almost flush with her mandibles, its tail waving a little to one side of their points. The big fish pushes out creases of naked skin as yellow spots at either side of the base of her bill. (I only once saw a fish held differently by a bird with immature pale feet. This unattached individual held his single small whitebait crosswise at almost the tips of his mandibles. Dropping it after about fifteen minutes, he picked it up lengthways properly, with most of the tail end hanging out : but after another five minutes twiddled it crosswise again, eventually swallowing it.)

Making no attempt to swallow her fish, she continually bows her head and points her bill under her belly between her webs – to feed a chick two or three months unborn, and certainly not consciously anticipated! The rhythmic cycle of organic change within her is already accustoming her to the appropriate external responses vital to the future welfare of the chick and procreation of the species, Nature's only concern : just as every guillemot from the early days of its initial return to the nesting ledge is continually bowing its head to its webs – to bill into position an egg that will not be laid for four or five months to come! A pair often do it together, delicately tweezering the rock between each other's webs, twiddling each other's bills at the same time, and making a great to-do about bowing themselves close up against the face of the cliff. Their incessant bowing of heads at any excitement or uneasiness is not hard to explain when we see that a similar bowing of the head to bill the egg or feed the chick – its primary and proper use – has become so much a habit in the guillemot's preincubationary period on the ledges that any additional stimulus, from anger to fear, is also likely to lead to bowing.

The extraordinary thing is that the male, while nibbling the fish affectionately, makes no attempt to take forcible possession of what he must recognise as an edible object : the two of them twiddle it between their webs very animatedly. Later, however, the female willingly surrenders it to him, whereupon he also attempts to feed an imaginary chick. She then recovers it, and in the end takes flight with it from the ledge and far out to sea. Yet neighbouring guillemots are in no doubt as to its edible qualities, and one, after making several rather tentative darts at a fish in a fellow's bill – actual possession usually being nine points of the avian law – eventually overbalances in his eagerness and tumbles backwards into a cranny, the owner as usual flying seaward in the end still holding her prize. Less often the owner may swallow her fish after standing about with it for five minutes or half an hour, or it may be pulled in half by a tug-of-war between two birds. The new owner of a half also stands about for a short while before swallowing her portion. All those birds bringing fish to the ledge at this season whose sex I was able to check were females – for the holding of a fish is no bar to a mating or attempts at mating – though this does not rule out the possibility that a great many more, unchecked, were males.

Early in May the majority of the guillemots have come into their breeding cliffs for good and are fishing in island waters. There is a continual whirring of auks around the North Cape. As yet, however, the guillemots are still colonising new sites on the cliffs, and maximum density is not attained until the last week in May immediately previous to the laying of the first eggs. By this date the back and south faces of a big colony such as the Long Roost are plastered with as many as three thousand guillemots, and the ceaseless surge of explosive cawing is deafening across the hundred yards of square cove, where hundreds of razorbills lay their eggs under a great moraine of tumbled boulders.

About the middle of May the intensive mating between pairs slackens somewhat, but is replaced by a new feature of communal life on a guillemot ledge. Those young males who have not succeeded in gaining mates continually attempt to mate with any female in the vicinity, creating a maximum of disturbance and combat on every ledge and platform : two, perhaps, rushing at a female newly alighted on their platform, and making the most desperate attempts to jump on her back. These improper advances necessitate a continual savage defence by paired males, and after a severe pecking of such a Don Juan by the male, he and his mate indulge in a bout of head bowing to an imaginary egg. Just as any unpaired female, without an established territory, alighting on a ledge is chivied right along its length by a succession of savagely pecking residents, so no resident female alighting on her ledge is sacrosanct from the attentions of these young males. The latter are astonishingly persistent, and struggle for seconds at a time with the usual violent fanning of wings to maintain a foothold not only on the already packed ledge itself, but on the back of the protesting female, often winnowing their way up to her very shoulders! The unfortunate female, assaulted by a succession of males, is often forced to fly down to the sea again. Before their assaults, two or three of these may be seen throwing up their bills vertically, with gaping tangerine buccal cavities. Now up till this time this has been a rare antic – indeed I have no note of previously observing it – but from now on it becomes increasingly frequent. Its significance lies in the fact that a similar antic is a prominent feature in the sexual behaviour of puffins, razorbills, kittiwakes and all the other gulls, shags and cormorants.

The young males are not the only ones whose emotions are now at their most intense. While there are intervals of quiet on the flat-topped stack of the Devil's Chimney where a huddle of fifty or one hundred guillemots sleep recumbent, or stand one upon the tail of the other, there is for most of the day a ceaseless and astounding surge of cawing. This springs mainly from the now generally unwelcome advances forced upon their mates by the old males. Desperate to mate, a paired male is not above importuning the female partner of an adjacent pair : though the somewhat tentative nature of these advances suggests that this is another instance of confusion of impulse and purpose. Such licence, however, adds to the general disturbance provoked by the excitement of the young males.

2. *Temperamental Sitters*

After performing the mating ceremony intermittently for more than four months, the male guillemots were still unsatisfied, but at long last the females rejected their advances, for the good reason that on 22 May the first eggs were laid. Once again the *block* system operated, so that while on one rocky platform of St James's Stone there were seven eggs, I could locate only two other sites with eggs, three in all, on the remainder of the island. Very pleasant it was to look down from the steep cushions of thrift in St James's Cove at the blue eggs half hidden beneath the brown and white guillemots sitting back on their tarsi and leaning forward a little over the eggs. One with her egg in a rocky declivity was recumbent upon it, not covering it very well. Another, uncertain of the nature of this new phenomenon, pattered uneasily to and fro between her egg and the edge of the platform, continually half stopping and moving in little jerks towards her egg, before settling down on it with shuffling 'tented' wings, sliding one web and shank along either side of it. Yet another of the seven, rising from her egg, stood upright on her toes – a thing I had not previously seen a guillemot do – and flapped her wings.

Nor on the next day could I find any eggs in the northern half of the island, though there were a score or more of guillemots sitting on the Devil's Chimney. In these early days they were easily provoked into deserting their eggs for hours at a time, and there were already broken shells lying about. Whenever she settles down on her egg – and being a nervous and excitable creature she is continually doing this – the guillemot pushes out and drops her wings a little from the shoulders, forming a tent or wigwam about the egg, while she rolls it between her feet with her bill. Some keep their wings partially 'tented' while sitting on their eggs, others close them in the normal fashion. It will be understood that owing to the enormous size of her egg, the guillemot leans foward over it rather than sits on it. On a broad platform or deep recess in the face of the cliff such as that on St James's Stone, the sitters are lined up three or four deep, all leaning one on top of the tail of another as close in to the back wall of the recess as possible. On the flat table-top of the Devil's Chimney there was a tendency for the sitting birds to get into leaning huddles, heads in to the centre. On such a crowded but weather-exposed stack this tight sitting of the females in rows and heaps all touching, generated a heat advantageous both to egg and sitter, who might sometimes be at the edge of, or actually in, a pool of filthy water.

Although on the evening of 23 May the score or two of birds on the Chimney were mostly incubators and their mates (one standing a-tiptoe again), and not many of the latter after half-past five, the incessant plaguing of females by bachelor males desperate to mate continued. One actually tried to mate with a bird sitting on a white egg and, when she refused him, pecked her savagely about the head, almost knocking her off the egg. Even their own males occasionally tried to mate, with explosive *arrr*s, but without success, the females being impatient even of head nibbling. Indeed I saw no successful matings at this date. One male brought up a fish and stood by his mate with it, but very quickly swallowed it. He stayed with her for a long time, affectionately nibbling her head, peering at the egg, and pattering around her and all over the fairly deserted table top. His shuffling about on the whole length of his tarsi is a perfectly natural and graceful movement though it may not sound so, and he has an amusing habit of lifting his webs off the rock and swinging round on his 'elbows'.

By 26 May there were a few eggs in various places about the northern half of the Island, though as yet by no means all the guillemots came in to the ledges regularly every day. For two hours I watched two birds with eggs in Kittiwake Gully. Incubation had brought with it new impulses, for after twice twiddling a straw with her long bill, one bird later twiddled some green stuff and pecked back grit between her webs. These primitive nidificatory impulses were interesting, for the guillemot now lays her egg on the naked rock. Yet some guillemots have the inherent impulse to mandibulate potential nesting material and peck such stuff in to their bodies, which every true nest-building bird does, as described in the account of the razorbill. Although these impulses were stronger in some guillemots than others, most might be observed 'pecking in' at one time or another, and some might be observed actually mandibulating straws and grasses two or three times a week.

The second egg was incubated for only five minutes of the two hours, sometimes being quite deserted, though for most of the time the pair stood beside it. This partial or complete disregard of eggs in the early stages of incubation was characteristic of the guillemot, and one found eggs lying about unattended all round the island. But as their period of incubation lengthened so some guillemots began to sit very closely, and one or other of most pairs were in at all hours of the twenty-four. There was no getting away from the fact that among their thousands the guillemots displayed a considerable range of individual temperament. A few, indeed, sat tightly from the beginning and for hours at a time without visits from their mates; and one bridled female was present daily throughout my five months' watching in Kittiwake Gully. Some were frequently in attendance, but were so nervous that the slightest untoward incident upset their incubatory routine, so that they either left their ledges altogether or shuffled nervously to and from their eggs for several minutes. Others deserted at the slightest provocation, sometimes shuffling their eggs off the ledges in their confusion, to leave them unattended for hours – gifts for the gulls. Those that sat tightest belonged to small colonies or odd groups scattered among big colonies of kittiwakes or razorbills. But once again the *block* or group-contagious system was dominant. No territorial disadvantages could explain away the fact that in certain places such as the North-West Stack or Puffin Gully, whole blocks of guillemots, four hundred together, streamed off precipitately at the least alarm, up to the very end of their residence on the island : an evacuation initiated and hastened by the restless young males, for after such a streaming off, the few remaining *in situ* comprised the stauncher sitting birds with mates standing by. Yet in similar situations, such as the Devil's Chimney or Kittiwake Gully, such a phenomenon was never or rarely to be seen : eighty or ninety recumbent sitting birds leaning in rows, one overlapping the other, right up against the back wall of the platform for hour after hour. That the guillemots of the North-West Stack and Puffin Gully were especially persecuted by gulls cannot be accounted the basic cause of this communal nervousness, for in such places as the Devil's Cut, from which they were continually streaming off, I never saw a gull, and in other gull-infested colonies they sat tight.

The increase in eggs was very slow, and the reason was not far to seek, for all and every day the herring gulls and great black-backs robbed them of the eggs they deserted so easily : especially the herring gulls, for, as ever, the black-backs subsisted mainly on what they filched from the former. So fiendishly persistent was their piracy that I wondered many a time how any chicks could possibly be hatched off. At the end of May the ceaseless sailing of the gulls over the colonies of guillemots was a feature of island life. On some stacks, as soon as a guillemot laid her egg and deserted it again in her careless way it was pounced upon by a herring gull, who was robbed in turn by a black-back. And there were actually no eggs on the North-West Stack at this time, although it housed one hundred potential nesting pairs. By the middle of June a maximum density of twenty-eight eggs had been attained by dint of second and third layings, but this total gradually diminished, and I never saw more than eight chicks hatch out. Puffin Gully suffered even more heavily. Out of the one hundred nesting pairs not one brought off a chick, whereas along a single ledge north of Kittiwake Gully thirty pairs of guillemots took away to sea some twenty-five chicks.

When all the gulls nesting on the sidings and cliffs among the guillemots had become aware of this source of food at their very nests they became exceedingly bold, pitching on the ledges where guillemots were standing or sitting, and snaffling eggs from those momentarily inattentive : but though very anxious to do so, the robbers would not face the darting bills of those guillemots actively defending their eggs. If, however, the stack was denuded of most of its colonists by their streaming off, those gulls sailing overhead or watching from the cliffs or from their nests on the sidings were at work immediately, and the chances of any deserted egg surviving until the return of its owner were small. One guillemot who had been standing nervously a little clear of her egg, uncertain whether to take flight with the streaming horde of her fellows or return to her egg, rushed at one such robber with an agonised squawk, too late.

The reactions of individual guillemots to this persecution were dependent upon three factors : primarily the time they had been sitting, but also the behaviour of those about them, and their individual temperaments. Younger birds and males were not likely to have so strong an inclination to sit as the older females — though one bridled male I watched was a very much closer sitter than his mate. Thus a guillemot already mentioned made a great to-do about the loss of her egg, but another stood on a pinnacle beside a gull eating hers, dividing her time between peering down at him without overt excitement, preening, and flapping her wings. A third, standing clear of her egg, allowed a black-back to walk off with it without making any fuss over its loss, and some minutes later went down into the next declivity and happily mandibulated and 'leant' on nothing for the remainder of my stay. Others, as we have seen, stuck tight to their eggs, however menacing their assailants, and sixty seconds after the assault were all sleeping and preening peacefully.

Nearly every accessible colony of guillemots included one or more of the bridled variants, whose red-brown eye is encircled during the breeding season by a white ring of tiny white bristles, while a white groove, similarly inlaid, curves back from the eye and down over the cheek. The effect produced is exactly that of a white monocle and cord. Among 3,000 guillemots in eight colonies watched by me daily there were thirty bridled birds, and a further ten among 2,000 in colonies less well known to me. Since there were probably additional unrecorded bridles among the latter, their overall numbers amounted to about one per cent of the total population.

Incubation got into its stride in the first days of June, and in late evening as many as two hundred and fifty guillemots might be seen sitting on the flat summit of the Devil's Chimney, the majority half recumbent, others leaning forward over their eggs in the proper manner. A number of males stood by and shuffled about, for ever on the move in their restless way, nibbling their sitting mates affectionately about their eye furrows and taut throats : an attention sometimes welcome, sometimes evaded. There were matings and attempts at matings among those without eggs. Some lasted for more than a minute at a time though the impulse was often imperfectly put into practice, the female throwing off the male directly he was on her back, or getting herself up against a rock in such a position that he could do nothing. Nearly all the matings were associated with the standing a-tiptoe antic. From now on up to the time of final departure in August there were always occasional matings taking place : indeed towards the end of July there was quite a wave of them, mainly at the instigation of chickless females holding fish.

Nonsitting birds did not stay in very late, and by nine in the evening those incubating were almost all deserted by their mates, who formed a sportive necklace of chains and links on the water below the cliffs in a column of two or three thousand, a quarter of a mile out to sea. Hundreds more preened on the reefs, fluttering up on to them from the surging tide, and even here the males attempted to mate, for those females who had lost their eggs also disported themselves on the sea and sunning rocks. It was very pleasant to see these low rocks at the base of the cliffs swarming with penguin-like guillemots (but seldom a razorbill) sunning themselves after bathing with their customary energy or disporting on the sloping base of the Rock of Gannets, one hundred and fifty plunging into the sea together to swim *en masse* under water. The cork floats marking lobster pots amused small groups of guillemots, razorbills and puffins, swimming around in shoals and continually jumping on and plopping off the corks; curious puffins paddled in to the landing steps at Kittiwake Gully to see what we were about.

Those guillemots incubating on the cliffs above were content to sit very quietly and peacefully side by side, panting in the evening sun and occasionally gulping with a curious reaching up and forward of opening bills and flashing deep-orange throats, somewhat after the manner of a displaying shag. They sat patiently thus, hour after hour, eyes half closed. By the middle of the month many, after sitting all day immobile, were stained yellow with filth from head to tail from the spattering ejections of those above and from the gummy guano plastering the rock on which they sat.

It is the saving of their species that when incubating, the sitting guillemots feel no impulses of territorial aggression. You could observe among these guillemots a sight you would have to go far to see in the world of nesting birds : one sitting guillemot gently and industriously nibbling the throat and head (especially about the eye and groove) of an adjacent sitter, who turns her head back and shuts her eyes blissfully.

The protesting *gurter* of the females was less and less to be heard as the days went by. But they displayed every sign of irritation at the excited billings and continual mating attempts of the males cawing their affectionate *wug-wug-woor-wug-wug-wug* : those restless males with their scrapping and preening and explosive cawing and their marching about on tiptoe, especially on the topmost platform of the Devil's Chimney where there were few incubators but always an unmated or eggless female or two standing about with a fish, or pointing it down to an imaginary chick – the obvious target of every unattached male. But this only showed the strange power of an immediate environment: no sooner did the males take over incubation than they became equally immobile. And that they did sit was confirmed by that useful oddity, the bridled guillemot. On the whole, the changeover during incubation appeared to take place in the late afternoon or evening, and after noon the number of nonsitting birds standing by their mates gradually dwindled, until in the evening few but sitting birds remained.

The latter were not particular as to their methods of incubating, and the egg might be broadways beneath them, or lengthways thick end under, or thin end under, which was the usual and proper method, when it was partially or completely contained in a brooding pouch of feathers dropped around it. But of that pleasant fable that guillemots incubate with their eggs on their webs in order to increase the incubatory temperature I could not discover more than three instances out of many hundreds of birds I watched closely; for the good reason that, when sitting, the webs of their toes were usually shut tightly together and their tarsi naturally extended down either side of the egg even when it was broadways on, in the normal outward-pointing fashion of their standing and walking. Indeed they often moved about the ledges in this way, rolling the egg along with their bellies. White, most curiously patterned with veins of plum or black or brown, turquoise, peacock green and an infinite variety of bright greens or blues, lightly or heavily blotched in dark-brown and black, all guillemot eggs were distinct from those of razorbills by reason of their heavier and more accentuated pear-shaped form. But nowhere on the island were there any red eggs, until I began to wonder whether I had dreamt that on the Farne Islands I had handled guillemot eggs of an exquisite pastel pink blotched with brown.

In the last days of June most of the guillemots with eggs were sitting very tightly, though the gulls were still taking them from the more nervous individuals on the most persecuted stacks at five-minute intervals. Alighting birds ran over the huddled backs of their fellows and ended up happily preening on one another's backs. Some of these were unmated males who came in to stand and shuffle about, loose-winged and flat-footed, in their usual helpless, street corner manner of being left out in the cold. There was much fighting among these young birds and with the old males, in the postures of fencers : the combatants lunged with continual ripostes of darting bills from heads pointing over shoulders. They fought till a stronger impulse to preen took one of them abruptly, whereupon the other, instead of profiting by this distraction of his adversary, invariably broke off and also preened in an inconsequent manner as if that had been his intention all along.

Others of these alighting birds were eggless females with fish, whose coming occasioned a vigorous bowing of heads among those sitting. One such arrival, jumping down on to a lower platform, was mildly assaulted by one of the unmated males standing about with others of his kind : whereupon she flew down to sea again. Even those birds with sitting mates brought up fish. But on the whole this was a comparatively quiet season among the guillemots and I had more leisure to watch what was going on down below on the sea.

In the spring britling and whitebait had been the guillemots' staple food, but in latter weeks sandeels had been prime favourites. In pursuit of the sandeels had come mackerel, and after the mackerel a school of hundreds of porpoises. Off the Rock of Gannets the school divided, the two halves going north and south of Puffin Slope and Gannet Bay respectively : gambolling smoothly and rhythmically in and out of the water in shoals of humped backs; shooting through the sea's filament, churning it into surf with their prodigious speed; leaping feet out of the water, to crash back in high cascades of spray, causing consternation among the swimming auks, so that hundreds of guillemots, razorbills and puffins took spattering flight together over the sea and rose into a broken mass flight : the gulls sailing out from their nesting slopes to join in the fun. The especial beauty of the scene lay in the rhythmic surfacing by the porpoises in pairs and shoals, as the two schools joined again and shoaled away south-east.

3. *Nervous Chicks*

The student of animal behaviour is guided and given notice of what to expect by the merest trifles at odds with normality. Guillemots had been bringing fish up to their ledges since midwinter, but these they had always held in their bills. On 24 June, however, there was for the first time in six months a fish lying on one of the platforms of the Devil's Chimney. What did this foreshadow?

An explanation was forthcoming at half past eleven the next morning when a chick was chipping its egg on the Chimney, and on the following day the first offspring of five hundred pairs of guillemots could just be made out under its parent's wing : very sooty of back and sooty-white of breast.

On 27 June I began to watch this new phase in the amazing cliff life of the guillemots when, after a great deal of getting together on the part of the parents and a prolonged and deep head bowing of the fisher, the chick was fed. After some thirty-four to forty days or more of incubation, most of these early guillemots had at last got into the habit of sitting tight, and they sat very tight on their newly-hatched chicks : so tightly that often only a slight pushing out of the shoulder of one wing betrayed the fact that a bird was brooding a chick and not incubating an egg. Some tucked their heads back into disengaged wings or turned them back with bills laid across wings, and crowded together even more closely than heretofore, taking no offence at other birds' chicks poking at their breasts : though under the emotional excitement of alarm a sitting bird would peck away another's chick. A strange cowl of long grey spikes hung like a mane low over the chick's nape, contrasting oddly with the soft dark-grey fur of its back, and the iron-grey of its breast. When it stood up and fanned its tiny wings – for the chicks were occasionally very active after the first two or three days – it displayed a white belly.

Though both parents sat for several hours at a stretch, changeovers were often to be seen, both birds cosseting the chick, preparatory to such a move, obviously very intrigued by it : and both elbowing out their shoulders and tenting their wings about it, with their sharp primaries sickled back to their tails.

The changeover usually took place on the arrival of one parent with a fish, to the accompaniment of the familiar loud *arr* of greeting. The chick might take the fish almost immediately, but more usually there was a considerable preliminary period of interminable bowing on the part of the parents, associated with the customary cooing. An excessive manoeuvring, helpful and unhelpful, by both parents was more or less traditional before a small chick was finally allowed to take an enormous sandeel, longer than itself. This it might jerk three-quarters of the way down its throat, before it paused for a breather and completed the engulfing at a second attempt. However loudly it squeaked and opened wide its bill in an upward reaching gulp, the fish was not passed to it until a satisfactory tent was made, shielding the transaction from the vulgar gaze. This making of a tent had once served the purposes of protecting the fish from the greedy bills of neighbouring guillemots and of preventing the chick from staggering off the edge of the platform in its eagerness to secure it. But this antic, like most other avian antics, has somewhat outgrown its original usefulness : for not once on many hundred such occasions did contiguous guillemots attempt a raid upon the fish during its delivery to the chick; nor did the chick itself display great anxiety to obtain it : often indeed it seemed hardly to appreciate that its parent had a fish for it, and soon abandoned its attempts to secure it, burrowing into its other parent's wing again, if the fisher was awkward and dilatory over his delivery.

In one such instance it was ten minutes before the brooding bird eventually moved away from the mouth of a little cavern containing the chick, and allowed the fisher to take her place. Whereupon the latter pushed himself right up into the mouth of the cavern, tenting his wings about it. After looking round a number of times and titillating the fish, he finally bowed his head to the chick, hardly dry from its shell, and the fish vanished. The original brooder then flew down to the sea for five minutes, returning to stand by the brooding male for the remainder of my stay. The parents often formed so tight a tent around the chick, the tented wings of one overlapping those of the other, and bowed their heads so low that it was impossible to see the chick take the fish. And the sitter was often so loath to leave the chick that the fisher, who evidently associated the feeding of the chick with a spell of duty, had to walk around in front of her and cut his way in between her and the chick, forcing her away. Even then she would remain standing by, perhaps tickling his taut throat : the two continuing to preen each other industriously for twenty minutes at a time, their eyes closed, their heads bushy with pleasure.

The guillemot is of a nervous and excitable disposition, contrasting strongly in this respect with the equable and confident razorbill or puffin. It was, therefore, particularly interesting to find that this nervousness was inherent in the species : for if a parent guillemot rose from her chick at a sudden alarm, treading all over it in her usual blundering fearful way, the latter would scream an agonised but musical *quew-yer-wew/quew-yer-wew* nearly as loudly as the somewhat similar cry of an adult kittiwake, and stagger to and fro over its ledge, apparently distracted, with that same helpless, indeterminate shuffling backwards and forwards of the adult. And it would continue to scream until the parent covered it once more, when the screaming would die down to the usual seeping *weeoo* only to rise again should the parent move but an inch or so from it. In its early days a chick appeared quite desperate if deserted by its parent, seeking wildly to burrow under her belly or wing, which was always its main objective, even if the old bird was standing on a knife edge of jutting rock : its favourite position being with its bill, and often its head, poked up between her wing and back in the same attitude as a razorbill chick. An old bird might sometimes be observed spending minutes at a time tucking or attempting to tuck her chick firmly under her with her bill, just as she had done with her egg, and even tucking back a few bits of stuff after the chick! One such 'tucker' trying to push her chick under her, interested another bird who came up to assist her, actually billing the chick! And though it was pecked away for its pains, the operation continued to intrigue it and three other birds who peered closely. The operation, however, was quite unsuccessful, for as soon as the chick was pressed under one wing it immediately scrambled out again.

The nervousness of the guillemot chick contrasts with the placidness of the razorbill chick; just as some adult guillemots betrayed a much greater nervousness and excitability than others, so different chicks displayed wide divergences in temperament. Most of them tended to become less nervous as they grew bigger, but one chick in Kittiwake Gully showed an excessive nervousness up to the very time of departure from its ledge on the twenty-second day after its emergence from the shell.

Ingress and egress on the densely packed flat top of a stack such as the Devil's Chimney became more difficult than ever, as more and more birds sat tight on their chicks – the brooding guillemot looks the most benevolent, soft tempered and mild of birds – and those guillemots alighting and departing must do so over the heads and backs of their fellows. The noisy *arrr* of newly arrived birds nebbing with their sitting mates was incessant, and there was the usual affectionate byplay between fishers and brooders. For the hatching of the chicks meant an increase in the numbers of birds arriving with fish at all hours of the day, and an increase, not only of those with chicks, but also of those with mates sitting on eggs and those unmated. The latter prowled all over the stack top mandibulating their fish, provoking hopeful head bowings from wearly brooders. One solitary fisher dipped her fish several times in a puddle of filthy water. Eggless males still continued to jump eggless females, and eggless pairs might be seen ardently twiddling battered snippets of fish between their webs : sometimes one alone, sometimes both together. All these, and most of those not immediately sitting or brooding, went out to sea in the evening, and in the morning little packs of them, a score or two at a time, went whirring round the North Cape, bound for their various cliffs.

By ti July chicks were widespread and numerous. Ten or twelve days out of the shell and growing fast, they were now a

Guillemot standing on ledge with chick.

very dark grey-brown, much darker than their parents, and were assuming the winter-white cheeks of the immature and old birds. These big chicks, in contrast to their generally lethargic smaller brethren, passed much of their time standing clear of their parents, and were much more active. This standing clear sometimes produced amusing results, for one parent persistently tented her wings around an imaginary chick, closing up on three of her fellows brooding in front of her, while yet turning back her head to neb with her real chick standing clear, and eventually trying to bill it under her wing without success.

By this date many chicks had very wet territories, after the torrential rains and full gales from the west of the previous fortnight, and the brooding birds continually wagged their tails out of the pools of filth. But the chicks, no less than the adults, are of a physical toughness and hardihood that is incredible, and one did not find chick guillemots dead from the weather, as one does, say, chick terns, despite the far more exposed nature of their habitats.

At ten in the morning fishers were coming up to the Devil's Chimney every minute or two minutes and fighting their way into the scrum of brooding birds. The fisher usually managed to get to his chick pretty directly, with his head held high in the air and his beak with its precious fish out of reach of his fellows. In this same high headed way a guillemot used often to alight among his fellows without a fish at midwinter.

This constant coming and going of fishers and mates of sitting birds naturally led to dissensions on crowded stacks, and there was more savage fighting than at any previous time, the chicks being knocked about a good deal. Two scrappers often gripped bills fiercely, but briefly, for this was not their normal method of fighting. There was always a most comical air of self-righteous indignation about those guillemots assaulted by their fellows on arriving at their ledges and an air of self-congratulation and rubbing of hands when such in intruder was pecked off his ledge. The guillemot displayed such an extraordinarily wide range of emotions and so vigorous and businesslike were all his actions that one could metaphorically see him turning down his sleeves, when he turned round from the defence of his territory to attend to domestic matters with his mate. After fighting, a bird would often stand a-tiptoe. This standing a-tiptoe was not to be observed of adult guillemots prior to incubation, but the bigger chicks more often than not stood quite erect on their slate-coloured webs and walked with ease, fanning their wings.

Those unmated or chickless birds standing about with fish were themselves of passing interest to idler guillemots and razorbills on the same platform, and it was amusing to see a stocky razorbill trying to reach up to the fish of a tall, slender-necked guillemot. Two guillemots, one with a chick and one unmated, would sometimes have a tug-of-war with the latter's fish, the former feeding her half to her chick, two others later seizing the remaining half from the original bird and feeding their quarters to their chicks! Or a chickless female, who has been going to and fro and standing about with a fish for half an hour or more, will begin to tent with her mate close to another guillemot's chick. The latter, however – and I think this remarkable – evinces little interest in the fish. Its parent, however, after first ignoring their activities, does at length peck the intruder male twice rather diffidently, and then turns her back on him and tents herself, though the chick remains outside. Should, however, a big chick stray into the brooding spots of other old birds with chicks, it is savagely pecked away : despite the fact that those brooding sit contentedly touching one another. But in the confusion of alarm or excitement a brooding guillemot would occasionally allow a deserted or desperately frightened chick to burrow under her other wing. This, however, was not a normal practice, and I do not agree that guillemots habitually brood each other's chicks. I saw only two such instances, and two or three of chickless birds brooding temporarily unattended chicks. These luckless guillemots who had lost their chicks to gulls were naturally always anxious to cosset the chicks of their neighbours, but seldom got the opportunity and were in any case, immediately evicted on the return of the chick's parents.

On crowded stacks I observed that the delivery of the fish to the chick tended to be more immediate than on sparsely populated ledges : the chick taking it tail first and swallowing it whole. The arrival of a parent with fish was invariably responsible for an enormous outburst of vocal jubilation on the part of the sitter and of other birds standing by. And in July Kittiwake Gully was even noisier than at any previous time : a great wave of sound from all three species continually surging and reverberating over the

Gully. All day long from the Devil's Chimney the plaintive, agonised *wrreeoo/wreeoo* of many chicks floated up a hundred feet to my eyrie on the opposite cliffs, though nearly all were hidden under the seething mass of old birds. Chickless birds, standing about with fish, tented imaginary chicks with their mates, passing the fish from one bill or one tent to the other, making great attempts to feed these non existent chicks with enormous and often much flattened sandeels : titillating them in their bills, slapping them in pools of water, and laying them with infinite care under their bellies, all to the usual cheery accompaniment of the roguish, protesting *arrr* and an excited bowing of heads and nebbing of bills. Once set in motion, the reproductive machinery must continue to turn over for its normal duration. The loss of egg or chick cannot break the appropriate sequence of impulses and antics.

They continued to 'imagine', and unmated guillemots continued to bring up fish, until the final departure of the guillemots from the Island! Like the unmated or chickless razorbills, they were most interested in the feeding of the chicks of their luckier neighbours, peering attentively down from a slab of rock above, with sharp down-pointing bills, or walking around them at a safe distance. Of no less interest, both to those with and without chicks, but especially to the latter, were the activities of the bigger slate-grey chicks, a fortnight old, who clambered all over the limited precincts of their rocky enclosures and had now begun to bob up and down in a mild way like their parents. They grew more and more like hedgehogs, with their straight, sharp heads and bills, and prickly cowls of grey spines. Now about one third the bulk of their parents, and half as tall, they had acquired full silver-white bellies, throats and cheeks, with the winter-black lines curving across the latter. Their bellies were white, much whiter than those of the old birds. Their black eyes had deep orbital grooves, and the whitish blibe of the eggtooth was borne up to the time of their departure.

4. *The Marvel of the Departure*

On 9 July some guillemots deserted second or third clutches, and some feeding chicks were, like the razorbills, in a desperate hurry to deliver their loads of fish. The sea was calling again. For the first time, two days later, a brooding guillemot took a fish very abruptly from her newly-arrived mate and delivered it to the chick herself. The fishers had now begun to bring up enormous dark-blue-backed mackerel : enormous, that is, relative to the size of even big guillemot chicks who, however, swallowed them as the merest trifles. Henceforward, young mackerel formed the chicks' staple diet. The latter were normally fed at three hour intervals, like the razorbill chicks, certainly twice and probably three times during the day. There were, however, many exceptions to a diet of mackerel, and of two guillemots coming up with fish together, one brought a whitebait, the other a mackerel. One delivered his fish immediately : the other, after he had stood about for a long time, performed an endless tenting and bowing of heads with his mate over the chick. One pair changed over, the other did not.

On 17 July I was first aware that some of the chicks known to me had disappeared, and at nine that evening I was astonished, again, to see a guillemot and chick swimming out to sea from Kittiwake Gully, both continually diving, the parent in the van. Only that morning I had wondered why there were no sizeable chicks to be seen anywhere on the island, although the earliest of them had been hatched off some twenty-five days before. Not having then observed the razorbill chicks flying down the cliff, I could not bring myself to believe that the guillemot chicks on such stupendous stacks as the Devil's Chimney could descend safely to the sea in such a way. Here, however, was a chick swimming out to sea with its parent in the familiar razorbill way, and the disappearance of its fellows was at any rate partially explained. Those early chicks on St James's Stone must have left their platforms the best part of a week earlier.

Out on the sea just beyond the Gully there have been from the beginning three or four guillemots waiting on, continually sipping water, occasionally calling their explosive greeting cry and less often the mating cry. All the twilight the Gully has been clamorous with the incessant cries of excited big guillemot chicks – a loud and penetrative, but musical and liquid, swift *quee-wee/quee-wee/quee-wee* – and the softer basser *wee-oo/wee-oo* of smaller chicks and continual 'vibrating' of razorbill parents waiting on the ledges. As the light fades so the adult guillemots become feverish with nervous excitement and incoherent in their anxiety. Later a great fanning of wings and resurgence of cawing, and a piping of chicks, below my perch on the side of the gully tell me that one chick venturing from its egg place has trespassed upon its neighbours' territories, and that the old birds are fighting. Another chick suddenly comes down from its ledge and hits the water with a terrific plop. None the worse for this, it immediately swims the wrong way back up the gully. Its parent, who had flown down with it and beyond it to the entrance of the gully, squawking with excitement swims back up the gully to it as fast as she can, wildly screaming her harsh *arrr/arrr,* in answer to the chick's incessant piccolo *quee-wee/quee-wee.* That piteous cry will ring in my brain for all time, and with it a hundred vivid, poignant, associative memories.

Then for half an hour and more I watched an old guillemot gradually drawing her chick out from its platform on to a narrow neck of rock jutting out into the gully, both continually calling : the old bird using almost every cry in her vocabulary. Frequently squatting down, the chick makes its way inch by inch along the neck, drawn by the parent shuffling backwards and tenting her wings encouragingly. Finally the chick is at the outermost point of the ridge, looking down into the gorge. In the end the old bird impatiently points her bill down under the chick's tail and hoicks it off into space. That, at least, is what it looked like, and so might well have been reported, but since the guillemot spends a great part of her cliff life in pointing down her bill to her nesting ledge, I could not accept this as an act of deliberate intent : particularly as I never saw such a hoicking-off again. Unceremoniously shot into space, the chick went sailing down with desperately whirring wings, to hit the water with a greap plop : the old bird following it in a fever of anxious crying, and away they went to sea, the chick hard on her tail, swinging about like the chick razorbills, who were generally better flyers than these bigger guillemots. With five razorbills and three guillemot chicks off from the Gully, there were at one time four old birds and their chicks to be seen heading out to sea.

Two days later the old bird who had pushed her chick off was still present, and several others, and also razorbills, were waiting on the sea below the Gully. The very nervous guillemot chick mentioned previously had gone from the cross-gully on this, the twenty-second day after its hatching. At eight in the evening many guillemots were already waiting on the sea, but another fifty minutes passed before the little guillemots awoke from their diurnal lethargy and began to dance about their ledges, fanning their little wings, their plaintive *quee-wee/quee-wee/quee-wee* heard for the first time since the previous night. An especially energetic chick that had attracted my attention on 17 July dashed about unsteadily on its toes with violently fanning wings, to the explosive applause of its parent : a quarter of an hour later it was brooded once more. A second chick on a narrow ledge also began to squeak and run around – but it was another five nights before it eventually went off. At a quarter to ten a chick whirred down from the cliffs behind me, piping hard, and was attended on the water by three adults, at one of whom its parent dug savagely. A big chick opposite looked like going down, but never did. At this hour there was a tremendous uproar from the old birds waiting for their chicks on the water at the bottom of the gully, and from those still bringing fish up to the ledges, or frantically excited at the activities of their chicks, answering their incessant *quee-wee/quee-wee* with their guttural *arrr*. When I left half an hour later the big chick was still peering over the edge of its ledge from time to time, and the energetic chick below was still hopping around in the intervals of being brooded. The big chick went off the next night, although one parent was present all day on 21 July.

At a quarter to nine on the night of 21 July a parent and chick are already on their way out to sea, where a dozen old birds are waiting, continually calling their explosive *arrr*. These waiting birds habitually take up with every chick and parent going out to sea, swimming closely about the little one and examining it, apparently expecting it to be their own, and accompanying it fifty or a hundred yards out to sea before turning back. From different parts of the Gully chicks call to one another persistently – which was something new in my experience of birds. One low down gazes up the Gully for a great while, firmly planted on the length of his tarsi, keenly interested in what is going on, and continually answers his fellows with his penetrating, diminishing *quee-wee/quee-wee/quee-wee*. A long drawn out and feverish *arrr*ing down below becomes frantic when two old guillemots finally get their chicks safely into the water. The two chicks get mixed up with the old birds in the swirling of a big sea surging up the gully, and their parents fight furiously over them, protesting noisily. A third old bird, calling at the entrance, swims up to join them, but, after accompanying them a long way out to sea, returns – as these hangers-on always do.

One chick makes continual assaults upon a foot-high ledge behind his platform, getting three quarters of the way up with fanning wings. Later, after continually peering over the edge with this chick, and repeatedly almost slipping off in her eagerness, its parent can no longer curb her excitement and takes a header down to another parent and chick swimming below. Together with an interested hanger-on she plays a crazy diving and calling game with the parent and chick. In her absence an old bird with a chick of her own on a ledge below, hops up to the abandoned chick. When the latter's parent returns a quarter of an hour later she pecks this bird savagely down on to her proper ledge, and also the latter's chick, which had followed its parent up. During the next quarter of an hour two more chicks go away to sea, and when I left at dark many were still calling. Going home on a calm night across Middle Park, there came faintly to me through the darkness the piteous crying of the chicks half a mile away in Jenny's Cove : *quee-wee/quee-wee/quee-wee.*

The departure of a proportion of the chicks made little difference to life on the platforms and ledges. One or two old birds were still sitting on eggs; some still mated; unmated guillemots still brought up very raw looking fish, seized fish from one another, or stood about mandibulating them, not swallowing them even at this late date! Fishing and the feeding of the chicks went on until dark – and did so up to the final days of evacuation – though ten or eleven in the morning remained the favourite hour. At that time enormous mackerel were brought up at the rate of one a minute, fishers relieved their sitting mates with the familiar noisy demonstrations, and bursts of *arrs* greeted every new arrival with fish. One chickless female mandibulating a fish nevertheless contrived a proper mating, with fish-muffled *gurta.* The din in Kittiwake Gully was as deafening as ever, with sudden waves of cawing from kittiwakes, a sound like vibrant castanets from razorbills, and that delicious, close-billed *woo-orrr* from hidden guillemots far down below rumbling and grumbling away.

Against all likelihood I had now seen for myself the chicks of both guillemots and razorbills getting safely down to the sea from their lofty eyries under their own power, without any aid from the old birds, and able to swim and dive perfectly in heavy seas. But I still found myself unable to solve the problematical descent of those chicks whose dropping flight must dash them on to the boulders of the sidings under the topmost crags or on the jagged reefs at the bases of the great stacks. And so on the evening of 22 July, when it cleared a little after fog and rain and cloud had enveloped the island for three consecutive days, I went out to the Devil's Chimney at a quarter past nine and found a parent and chick already swimming out to sea. A great many guillemot chicks appeared to have gone off the Chimney and there was hardly a razorbill to be seen on the sheer slabs of the high cliffs walling in the Chimney on two sides, though I heard one lone chick piping later in the evening. On the flat summit of the Chimney there was incessant scrapping : for the very good reason that chicks were gradually being edged, jostled and tented forward to the outer edge of the table top from the dense mass of birds at the middle. This naturally led to a continual infringement of territory, to the tune of the customary noisy *arrr* of the old birds and an incessant squeaking from the young. Once at the edge of the Chimney the chicks would peer about and down at the sea in typical fashion, constantly piping to other pipers on the cliffs a hundred yards and more away. Their tenancy of these outside positions was precarious and hazardous, for those adults continually alighting on the Chimney and taking off from it knocked them sprawling and, worse still, upset them on to lower platforms, where they were savagely pecked by the owners of those territories. One such chick indeed was not only pecked, but picked up by the scruff of the neck and flung about. Another chick who had been piping most bravely at the extreme edge of the top platform, its parents continually bowing their bills down to it encouragingly, was knocked by an alighting bird on to the platform below, and after one or two vain attempts to scale a three foot wall, and being pecked into immobility by a nearby brooding adult, stood huddled up in the corner waiting – for what? One of its parents, who had flown down to the sea at its vanishing (associating its disappearance with its descent to the sea?), flew up again to stand on a ledge over the chick; but beyond peering down occasionally, made no attempt to get down to it (and thereby trespass on other birds' territories), and stood preening.

In one of the incessant scrimmages an outer-edge chick was knocked flying off the top of the Chimney : to fall one hundred and fifty feet upside down, paddles splayed wide, crashing horribly on a jagged bulge of rock scores of feet down the stack, and rebounding into the fury of boiling surf thundering over the reefs at its base. Through my binoculars I tried to see if I could pick up its floating corpse ... but it was no corpse I saw, but the little chick diving under each curling surf crest and actually making headway through the breakers smashing on the reef. In a couple of minutes it was joined by its faithful parent, appearing as usual from nowhere, who led it out of the swirling whirlpool into the great swell of combers rolling and pounding from the Atlantic. Two other waiting guillemots took up with the chick, and for some time the four plied around and about the base of the stack, before the chick and its parent headed out to sea, diving through each curving roller like an eider and her ducklings.

This chick's survival was so incredible that I took it to be a happy exception, for I could not believe that the average chick falling a hundred feet on to a jagged rock would not smash its skull or break its legs, or not be drowned by the battering of that foaming cauldron. But later another, piping chick, which had gradually been manoeuvred to the edge of the top platform, was squashed by an alighting adult. As scared as ever, it ran up a ledge along the edge of the Chimney, chivied by a succession of territoried old birds, and finally stood peering down at the sea, repeatedly pecked by two nearby adults. But it paid little heed to the pecking, apparently concentrating on the sea below, and very shortly it took off, making a very fine flight many hundreds of feet out and down on to the farthermost reef : both parents suddenly appearing to lead it out to sea from the boiling surf, though they had not accompanied it in its hazardous ordeal along the ledge. With the fading light there was an absolute pandemonium of crying from the old birds and chicks all round the stacks and sheer cliff walls of Jenny's Cove, rising high above the pounding of the breakers.

Scrambling up the steep siding of bracken and boulders in the gathering darkness, I went home along the winding sheep path. A gold half-moon hung in the stormy western sky. Legions of rabbits scattered into the bracken. All round the island cliffs hundreds of guillemots were making their heroic descents in the darkness. But what of those chicks that fell into the horrible jumble of scree and boulders at the base of the Chimney, or of those razorbills hatched off deep down under the enormous granite blocks piled high on the square beach of the Long Roost? Of these it could only be said that while at one time the boulders were noisy with their pipings, later, after the appropriate interval, there was silence, so that they too must have made their successful getaway : I had seen that the chicks of both species could climb very fairly up the sheer rock, hopping and scrambling up with vigorously fanning wings, with the greatest determination and tenacity.

By the fourth week of July a majority of the old birds were growing most impatient of their terrestrial ties, and might be heard calling to their chicks from the water as early as four in the afternoon, and some all day, without persuading the chicks to descend at such gull-dangerous hours. A great many of the old birds had already gone for good from the south-west of the island – to which they had come latest – and by 23 July nearly all the chicks had gone from St James's Stone, though their parents were standing about *en masse,* just as they did before incubation began, with a great deal of savage fighting. The Stone was plastered with idle razorbills and guillemots, the sea and air spattered with them.

On the luckless North-West Stack a dozen old birds were sitting with two or three chicks, upon one of which a black-back swooped down, but was driven off by the single parent standing by it. A herring gull, however, carried off the chick while the parent was busy with the black-back. The robber carried the chick to its own young, but dropped it *en route* : it may have found safety in a crevice. (Many of the guillemots showed astonishing courage in resisting herring gulls and putting them to flight, even moving down from their ledges to assault them and running back to their chicks before the gulls could swoop in again.) Later, the black-back took a chick from another cliff and swallowed it whole. Another was eating a kittiwake chick on the water. Sickened by the butchery on the north west cliffs and the waste of life it entailed – for gulls do not lack for other food – I was glad to escape to the peace and quiet of Kittiwake Gully free from gulls.

Three evenings later only a score of the four hundred guillemots in the Gully remained, very few of those without chicks being present. One known chick had gone before my arrival, but at twenty past nine a second comes down, and a third, making a perfect flight down with its parent from the top of the Gully. A fourth, whose parent had just dropped down, is looking very excitedly over the edge, and quickly fly-drops down, hitting a reef fifty feet below with a terrible smack but swimming off happily to join its parent some distance outside the Gully. A fifth comes down at long last to join its parent, who has been swimming up and down at the bottom of the Gully for a great time, while from far back up the Gully comes the loud mynah-like piping of a sixth chick continually swimming up and down, not knowing which way to swim, other chicks answering it from the ledges above, and still farther back a seventh piping chick. After another ten minutes number six is met by both its parents, and in the end number seven also finds its way out safely to its parent beyond the Gully's entrance.

As I climbed the three hundred steps up the cliffs in the bright moonlight at half past ten, when the north-west was still flushed, the babel of calling and piping from the Long Roost and all along the north west cliffs was terrific.

There were only about one hundred guillemots and twenty chicks on all Devil's Chimney at five the next evening, instead of one thousand. Many of the old birds were waiting on the water and calling : one chick already with them, continually piping. (They have two or three different pitches of piping, these young birds.) One old bird after another, swimming up to see if the chick was theirs, pecked it savagely on finding that it was not : no doubt with some associative reaction that the chick was in a territory belonging to them. Others cosseted it and one with a fish swam around it for a long time, but it appeared to have no parents. It was not uncommon at this season to see a chick on the water with a drove of as many as eleven old birds swimming after it. It was probable that the call of the sea after three months' continual, and seven months' spasmodic, attendance at the cliffs, was growing too strong for certain parents and that they were now deserting those chicks that could not easily be persuaded to leave their ledges. For they now began streaming off the Chimney and the wall of cliffs backing Jenny's Cove at my coming, just as they did before incubation began, and in the Devil's Cut, from which they had never ceased to stream, there was not one remaining. From morning till dark a herring gull was in attendance at the Chimney, making unsuccessful attempts to get into the chicks past their parents. The next evening, however, and on the 31 July I was astonished to find a full house along the populous wall of cliffs of Jenny's Cove and on the Chimney, though I could only make out only nine chicks. This was the final appearance of the bulk of the guillemots.

Even at this final ascent to the cliffs there was no slackening in the tempo of activity of these amazing birds. Most of them, now released from attendance on chicks, are free to shuffle everywhere over their platforms : a flat-shanked shuffle made graceful by the high carriage of the guillemot's sharp head and bill on his long slender neck. Interest in the doings of their fellows is continuous, involving a constant peering down with slightly tilted heads at those on platforms below. An enormous amount of noisy fighting a-tiptoe goes on, and there are still many matings; chicks are fed and chickless birds with fish still play at feeding imaginary chicks; and there is the strange sight, not previously observed, of the old birds dancing over the platforms with fanning wings, exactly as the chicks do! The coincidence of this act occurring only now for the first time in the past five months, after a month or more of the chicks doing the same thing, is too significant to be discounted. Kittiwakes, particularly the females, automatically assume many of the postures and antics of the chicks *before* the latter have actually hatched. Here is a guillemot *without* a chick assuming these juvenile postures apparently from unconscious imitation of the many chicks about it : just as, whether coincidence or not, there was that other strange revelation of an adult bird first standing a-tiptoe (as the chick would do) at the time of the laying of the first egg.

There were still a score or so of chicks in Kittiwake Gully on the last evening in July. Some of them, though very big, were still disinclined to venture forth, and one hid in a little cave and did not come out on to his ledge until twilight. The evenings were quietening down, few of the old birds calling from the water, though quite a number of chicks were going off from the north-west cliffs.

Three days later there were only five old birds and one chick on the Devil's Chimney, though many of the ledges in Jenny's Cove were still very full. But the next evening, 4 August, these, too, were nearly empty, for there was a great clearance generally about the island during the night of 3 August. Only seven old birds with chicks remained in Kittiwake Gully, though at nine o'clock the latter were still going off from the north-west cliffs, picking up the usual escort of waiting birds on the water. This was the only occasion on which I saw a dead chick floating on the surge down one of the gullies. One chick made a perfect flight down followed by its parent, but the execrable gulls, as persistent as ever in their swooping, frightened the other chicks under the wings of their parents, who were still stoutly resisting the onslaught of the gulls, chasing them from the ledges; and no more chicks went off before dark.

By the morning of 7 August there were very few guillemots left anywhere on the island, and only two adults and three chicks in Kittiwake Gully. There were no auks of any kind on the seas around the island. One had to sail a mile out to sea before encountering the first parent guillemot and her large white-cheeked chick and several small packs of adult and young razorbills; and from two to five miles before meeting with solitary dusky-cheeked young puffins, while the majority of single guillemot parents, accompanying piping chicks of varying sizes, were ten to eighteen miles off the island. One found it difficult to understand why the chicks should go straight from their nesting ledges to so great a distance out to sea, though if they had stayed in island waters they would probably have suffered a heavy mortality from the gulls.

In three weeks almost the entire population of chicks, perhaps six thousand guillemot and five thousand razorbill, had been evacuated. And though the chicks I actually saw venture down to the sea for the first time were only a very small percentage of these, there was never any hint that they received assistance from the parent birds. It is possible that in other parts of the British Isles guillemots and razorbills might take their young down on their backs and wings, but having seen those on Lundy plunge down on to both water and rocks, usually leading the parent in flight, it seems to me most improbable that such a radical departure from the normal should occur. How, then, has such a statement been allowed to creep into reputable works? Would it be possible for an honest and capable observer to make such a mistake? It will be remembered that a certain confusion did arise in my mind concerning the precise method employed by the first razorbill chick I saw fly down from Kittiwake Gully. A similar confusion might arise in the minds of other naturalists, were they only to watch one or two flights, for until one has actually witnessed it, it does not seem credible that the tiny wings of these chicks can support them. It was still less credible that the chicks could fall hundreds of feet on to rock or into boiling surf, and escape injury or drowning.

VI

SHETLAND HO!

Six years had passed since that spring and summer when my wife and I had lived for five months in the old lighthouse cottage on the very top of Lundy, and I had watched daily and often nightly at the nesting cliffs and sidings. It was inevitable therefore that, after this long interval, we should be thinking of another summer with sea birds; and again I wanted to watch a bird that nested in large communities. There was one ideal subject, the gannet, better known in Scotland as the solan. There were ten large gannetries in the British Isles; but various problems associated with access and suitability for study reduced these to one – that on Noss, off the east coast of Shetland. Moreover Noss – a small island, approximately $1\frac{3}{4}$ miles by $\frac{3}{4}$ of a mile, and inhabited only during the summer months by the tenant farmer – was also the breeding ground of the great skua or bonxie and the arctic skua, in addition to large numbers of kittiwakes and auks.

And so, on the evening of 3 September – the hottest day in the Highlands that summer – I took ship from Aberdeen on an exploratory expedition, and early the next morning caught my first glimpse of the northern isles when the mists sundered, revealing the craggy Viking frame of the Fair Isle, that wonderful port of call for migratory birds, twenty-eight miles south of Shetland. Two hours later the *St Magnus* began to pitch and roll in the tumultuous roost of tides off Sumburgh Head, the gigantic toe of Shetland. Then, for another couple of hours we steamed steadily up the long leg of Mainland before there loomed out of the sea, almost directly ahead, the hazy outlines of two steep-sided, cone-shaped headlands – our first intimation that we were opening up the Sound of Bressay. The west cone was the Ward Hill on Bressay : the east cone Noss Head. Lying roughly parallel to Mainland for six miles from north to south, but almost meeting it at its north end, the hilly island of Bressay was responsible for the magnificent harbour of Shetland's port and capital, Lerwick.

From the rocky shores of a narrow sound on the east side of Bressay, Noss – the Nose or Rocky Point – mounted seawards from its green voe-bitten brim, half a mile long, in a gentle hill of green pastures that swept upwards to a spacious flat of moorland and the ultimate steep and hayrick crown of Noss Head, which terminated in the tremendous overhang of its great sea cliff, the Noup. White gannets plunged into the crystal waters of the Sound and down into the chalk-green and milk-blue deeps above the white sand. Droves of periscopic-necked shags and cormorants fished in the dark purple shadows of the reefs. Strings of shrilly piping tysties (black guillemots) and families of eider ducks swam out from little clefts, or geos, in the jagged inclined rocks edging the sound.

Halfway to the top of the island the Cradle Holm – an enormous table block of cliff more than 160 feet high and severed from the island by an L-shaped chasm – lay a little below the south corner of the large inverted bay, also L-shaped, of Rumble Wick. From the southern corner of the Wick a small promontory projected twelve or fifteen feet from the cliff top, and from it I found that I could look down and across to the adjacent cliff face, on which several hundred pairs of gannets were still in residence, the nearest only ten or twenty yards distant. From this vantage point I could also see most of the thousands of gannets occupying the ledges along the 400-yard back wall of the Wick and, at a great distance, not far short of half a mile, those on the south face of the Noup, which rose like a pyramid 592 feet sheer from the sea. After only a short stay at Rumble Wick, I continued on my tour of inspection, climbing up the almost vertical steep of the Head to the summit of the Noup and across its straight crest, which was less than 100 yards in length and sliced off so cleanly on the seaward side that no part of the cliff was visible beneath: just a 200-yard drop to the sea.

Here, then, was an island of 850 acres, of which 150 acres were pasture and the remainder predominantly boggy peat moor with a stunted growth of heather and a luxuriant growth of tussock grass. On the steep of the Head were extensive fields of *juncus* and, right round the island, a coastal strip of green grazing with, in some places, an extraordinarily dense mat of the silky-haired ribwort plantain and, on the Cradle Holm, a jungle of sorrel. The island was no longer permanently inhabited, sheep were not an influential factor, there was no fowling or egg collecting. Therefore Noss was the purest type of bird sanctuary and virgin territory for a naturalist. Considering the inaccessibility of most gannetries these conditions could hardly be bettered, and I arranged to arrive in Shetland at the end of March or early in April the following spring – a date that would coincide with the return of the earliest bonxies to Noss and would be well in advance of that of the arctic skuas; I hoped to stay until the first young gannets left the cliffs late in August or early in September. I should not be able to cover the full breeding season of the gannets, for they began visiting the nesting cliffs late in January or early in February and did not finally quit them until some time in October: but comparatively few of them would have laid eggs before the end of March. My plan would be to make my main study the gannet, with secondary studies of the bonxie and the arctic skua.

With these plans and hopes in mind we locked the doors of our house in the Grampians at 6 a.m. on April 2 and set out for Inverness on a morning straight from summer: but when our plane landed at Sumburgh Head six hours later, after a brief halt in Orkney, we found ourselves in the cold grey north and had said goodbye to summer. After an absence of seven months I stood once again on the Bressay shore and gazed at the promised land across that narrow sound of limpid amethyst and peacock-blue waters banded with dark purple. There was little evidence that Noss stood on the threshold of a new breeding season, though there was a just perceptible whiteness of kittiwakes and fulmars sweeping to and from the distant cliffs, and from time to time gannnets rounded the Ness and disappeared, bound for Rumble Wick and the Noup. The Sound itself would have made an interesting seasonal study, for through it was a constant traffic of birds, grey seals and cartwheeling porpoises. Its brow edges were littered with the shells of limpets and razorfish despoiled by common gulls, herring gulls and swaabies – as the great black-backed gulls were known in Shetland. Pairs of fulmars sat about the turfy domes of old corn drying kilns, on the square chimneystacks and copings of abandoned houses, and on the grassy banks, over which they swept noiselessly, hovering inquisitively a few feet above my head. Others gyrated in little flocks on the waters of the Sound, where drake kaaloos (long-tailed duck), blowing their musical hunting horns – *caw-caa-calloo, caw-caa-calloo* – dived with a sudden opening of wings like the opening of a flower's pointed sepals. A solitary tystie was also diving at long intervals with a barely perceptible splutter of wings, emerging perhaps with a small crab after a submergence of up to forty seconds. It dismembered the crab by shaking it vigorously and pecking at it on the water, diving to recapture it after each delegging, swallowing the legs but not the body. From time to time twenty or thirty gannets would converge on the northern approaches to the Sound, when they perceived one of their kind to hover and plunge, and join in the fishing.

Two days after this preview of Noss in the spring there was an alarum from a flock of oystercatchers, mounting high over the Sound from the Noss side, and a pair of rock pigeons dashed along the brow edge with a flash of dark green. A minute or two later, two large brown birds, with silvery Ys glinting on their wings, came out of Noss through a milling crowd of gannets and gulls. A little later a third bonxie came out on the same line of flight. In the late afternoon a gale began to blow out of the north with squalls of rain and hail, and the grey-blue waters of the Sound were lashed into a smother of whitecaps and blown spray. The gale – the strongest since the Old Year – blew without a minute's cessation until the morning of 10 April. Snowy surf broke in foaming crests on the brown reefs at the north end of the Sound and disintegrated in curdling smothers of milky whey. The deep pool of white sand in mid-Sound blazed like a green jewel in its purple bed of barrier reefs, but grey skirting curtains of successive squalls blotted out intermittently the dark-blue northern sea, and it was obvious that no boat could cross the Sound. This was all the more frustrating because I could see two bonxies flighting close together over the interior of Noss, and subsequently a third, and there could be no doubt that they were taking up their nesting territories on the island.

More gales, torrential squalls of rain and mocking intervals of sun-blue seas and clear brown islands, until I had almost given up hope of ever getting into Noss; but during the night of the 21 April another gale abated and the next morning I set foot at long last on the promised land, three weeks after arriving in Shetland. For many weeks no human being had landed on the island, and everywhere I saw great dark fowl standing watchful in ones and twos on heather ridges, or sitting confidently on green mounds in the surrounding heather or bent, glowering like bulldogs, preening, or sleeping with heads turned back. All the way up to Rumble Wick — where I found two-thirds of the gannets in the control gannetry already sitting on nests — I was subjected to a barrage of barking protest from hundreds of herring gulls nesting on the cliffs, and when I reached the Cradle Holm, to the deep cries of several scores of swaabies and the first summer-homing lesser black-backs on the steep grassy sidings opposite the Holm. Though arctic skuas, puffins and arctic terns had yet to return to the island, and though thousands of cliff birds had yet to take up permanent residence, hundreds of guillemots and kittiwakes were occupying ledges on the face of the Holm; rock pigeons dashed out of the geos, in which tysties were sitting up on cliff platforms. and deep down in the chasms shags perched erect on well-built nest drums.

On 25 April, after another gale, I finally settled down to my first leisured study of the gannets. At last, after an interval of seven years, I was free to enjoy once again that kaleidoscopic spectacle that had few parallels in the world of Nature — the breeding cliffs of vast numbers of colonial-nesting sea fowl. The scene was one of great animation and ceaseless tumult. From the long west wall of the Wick, and more faintly from its east wall the Noup, there rose to my eyrie, crescending and diminishing but never totally subsiding, a raucous medley of diverse and musical cries, from thousands of individuals of several different species of sea birds, blended into one harmonious din, one pattern of sound, from which only now and again could one detach separate components — the squeaky braying *wick-gewer, wick-gewer* of kittiwakes, the prolonged and humourous *woo-orr-rr-gg* and other familiar protests of guillemots, the intermittent cawing of fulmars and, dominant, the harsh grating rise and fall of the gannets' interminable *gurrah, gurrah, gurrah.* And ever in the background was the hollow booming of the sea, surging to and fro in the high-arched caverns and geo-cracks in the wall of cliff : an intermittent moaning which at first I attributed to seals.

With the exception of the great west slab of the Noup, where only fulmars and a few herring gulls nested among the blue-green, whorled clumps of roseroot and masses of soaking scurvygrass, there were tens of thousands of sea birds, most conspicuously gannets, nesting all round the inverted L of the Wick from its south corner to the extreme east end of the Noup itself. The mauve and red sandstone face of the Noup was shaded a dull green and yellow with thrift and lichen; tarred with black overflows of rain water spilling over the cliff from the drains cut across the green Head above; and whitewashed over its middle two thirds with a cream distemper of guano and liquid excrement, voided by endless rows of gannets and kittiwakes and thousands of guillemots huddled together on long ledges and broad cornice platforms. From time to time a solitary bonxie, or a pair, sailed out over the Wick, and flapped along the cliff wall, emitting a buzzing *keg-keg.* At their passing snowy clouds of kittiwakes would 'shoal' off the cliffs, eddy round, and swoop up to their ledges again. In the chasm of the Wick weaved hundreds of gannets, fulmars and kittiwakes, while the dark oily-blue waters below, which were spangled with white hieroglyphics traced by chains of guillemots, continually erupted in glaucous-green fountains thrown up by the shallow dives of gannets plunging obliquely, as a preliminary to bathing.

Evening drew on and by 8 p.m. there were very few birds on the wing. From the dizzy heights of the Noup the sea grew dark and cold, and I was glad to go down through the bonxie grounds in the gading light three quarters of an hour later to the friendly cooing of eiders in the sound and the piping of the oystercatchers around Gungstie – that lichened, blue-slated homestead on the long green Ness above the sound – and enter what was to be my true home in Shetland for most of five months to come.

VII

A STUDY OF A BREEDING COLONY OF GREAT SKUAS

1. *Life on the Bonxie Grounds*

When I settled down to study the behaviour of the bonxies I observed, from the vantage point of the Maiden's Paps – that central bulwark of bluffs ranging right across the breadth of the island above the moorland – that each pair or solitary bonxie stood commonly on its own special mound, with perhaps one member of a pair sitting in the heather a few yards off the mound. There was something of the appearance of the golden eagle about these heavy standing, conical-headed bonxies. There was that same ruddiness about the head, with its shaggy lanceolate, yellowish mane streaked with brown and white: for there was much white speckling on the heads of some and hoary etching down the necks of most of them, and a greater or lesser degree of whitish and yellowish raying and barring on their mantles; while one or two had thick white rings round their eyes. At a distance and in flight this pale streaking might not be apparent and the bonxie appeared a traditionally dark-plumaged fowl: but in actual fact no two birds were similarly plumaged and there was a wide range of colouring from reddish-brown to biscuit, the paler birds being especially light coloured on breast and shoulders and appearing tawny-white in bright sunlight. Only one or two were devoid of any white markings.

121

R·A·Richardson.

Great Skua swerving to attack.

Green oases in the surrounding bog and heather, it was apparent that their mounds had been used year after year, for the trampling feet of their heavy owners, together with guano in the form of excreta, castings and fishbones, had eradicated the heather and coarse herbage, treading out and fertilising smooth green mounds of grass and moss a few feet or yards in diameter, mainly circular in outline. The determinate factor in their origins had been that, being in the first place slight eminences, they had provided commanding viewpoints and were thus the obvious standing place in a nesting territory. Where a true hill, such as the Maiden's Paps, was available, with a view over all the moor and up the Head, thereon some of those pairs with territories in the hidden corrie above the Paps were to be seen standing more often than on the little mounds within their territories. Physically, the mounds were mainly rest and digestive places, and most bore both long castings and the bleached cast wings and feathers of kittiwakes, while one or two bore little flakes of purple stone, picked up around the crumbling dykes. Psychologically, the mounds were the hubs of nesting territories.

In the beginning I could not pass closer than within twenty-five yards of a pair of bonxies on their mound without disturbing them : but after two or three weeks a pair would remain sitting with no sign of uneasiness, until I had approached to within ten yards of them — seven yards being the minimum range at which one might walk past a mound without its tenant or tenants taking flight.

When flight was ultimately and reluctantly decided upon it was preceded by a heavy hop or two across the mound, or perhaps a waddling run off it, before their heavy torpedo-shaped bodies were launched into the air with quick beats of immensely broad wings. The pair would then circle around me with a feeble buzzing *kek* or *kyuk*. Owl-like, curiously moth-like, were the comparisons that occurred to me as they beat around on unbending pinions; but when they banked, and the eye was arrested by the brilliant white half-moons slanting across their primaries, it was the buzzard that came to mind. When one pair finally took wing it was likely that others in the vicinity would follow their example, until perhaps a score or more were in the air. In these days, prior to nesting, the bulk of them would then gradually slip away to sea in overlapping circles. Two of a trio, perhaps, would buffet each other in midair, with a squeaky gullish screeching, falling to earth with grappling talons; or one of three would 'float' a little way with wings arched over its back, mane 'hackled' and beak wide open, uttering a quintuple *keeyuk*, to which its two companions would reply with monosyllabic *kek*.

From the Bressay side of the Sound, a day or two after their return to Noss, I had observed two bonxies 'floating' close together over the Hill of Setter. With wings lifted high over their backs they had rocked with the effortless buoyancy of a tumbler pigeon and the grace of a golden plover joy-flighting. In this manner, with wings raised three-quarters to the vertical and tips bent outwards, pairs, trios and sometimes solitary birds floated across the island, with that whistling *keeyuk*, which might be preceded by a harsh *gyang-gyang-gyang*, a deeply nasal, almost goose-like honking. This winged display was a feature of the bonxie's aerial life, both over the hinterland of Noss and also over the cliffs and wicks. So also were the prolonged twisting pursuit flights to and fro across the breadth of the island of couples at a considerable height. Then, swift urgent wings hurtled over my head with a roar as of surf breaking on the cliffs, and there would be a tremendous rush of air from others volplaning with swept-back wings from a great height. Less often three or four would soar together over the Noup, straight-winged as ravens, when weather conditions were favourable. A bonxie and a raven in flight together were much of a size, though the former's wings were, unexpectedly, much the narrower.

These frequent aerial passages over the breeding grounds stimulated those pairs and single birds resting on their mounds to emulation. Rising to their feet they would arch white-blazoned wings so high as almost, perhaps quite, to touch at their backward-curving tips (as some small wading bird might do), displaying thus the white patterning on the undersides of the primaries; and throwing up their heads, utter with wide-open beaks (thereby revealing a lavender-white interior) that repetitive *keeyuk*. Having thus reacted – and three or four solitary bonxies might be displaying at one time on adjacent mounds, possibly not even rising to their feet to do so – a strained bowing of heads and hackling of manes would follow, before they closed their wings and sat down once more in their places.

These were not the only conditions in which this display was employed. An intruder, alighting by a solitary bird on a mound, would be repelled and driven away by a full display with wing and voice. Similarly, three birds would stand together with raised wings, and make short flight thus – when the wingbeat rate was accelerated beyond the normal. At the conclusion of such a flight, one would settle first by one of its companions and then by the other, and two of the three might ultimately fight. This would result in some desultory flying around of those birds on nearby mounds. Most of the bonxies undoubtedly returned in pairs to their breeding grounds, but there must necessarily have been some unmated ones among them, and there were few species of birds of which individuals did not lapse into temporary amorousness from time to time. As the season advanced, however, each mound or mounds became sacrosanct to one pair only.

One would also run with raised wings a few yards off the heather to its mate on the mound and, on a solitary bird being joined by its mate returning from sea, the two would arch their wings and call briefly before settling down together on their mound. This was the normal greeting between a mated pair. But here is a bird running around its mate standing on the mound : the latter, however, flies away at this demonstration and the demonstrator sits down in its place. My attention is then drawn to another mound bird, which first drives off a second alighting and then, after standing in strained silence with hackles raised for some seconds, again assaults it : whereupon the two, now being off the mound, fight unconvincingly with striking talons. Then both fly round and alighting on a different mound fight again, then fly round again and alight in the heather; and now the second bird, probably a female, walks round the male for two or three minutes in an attitude indicative of a desire to mate. With head pointed to the ground and stretched out in the manner of a gull, she makes tentative little runs at the male who, however, pecks at her; and in the end the two settle down a few yards apart in the heather. The hour for the consummation of the mating was not yet due. Perhaps it was overdue, for five minutes after I had retreated from the mound of a pair that had laid their first egg that morning, the female alighted on it, followed two or three minutes later by the male. The latter, after walking round her with head reared up, talking hard, jumped with raised wings to her back, but alighted behind her, whereupon both arched wings and called.

When the female was willing then the male would advance towards her, waving half-spread wings, and balancing on her back the two might mate immediately. After consummation there would be a brief wing raising display. The consummation however, was not always as swift as this and might be preceded by much rearing of heads (predominantly by the male) to the accompaniment of a repeated *kek-kek*; nor was it always successful, for a male might jump on and off the female's back five times without consummation. Here, for instance, is one of the pairs that stand commonly on the Maiden's Paps, with a true territorial mound in the corrie above. The two run forward, rearing up side by side, with the male uttering a variant of the *kyuk*. Then the female solicits him with the customary head pointing and he jumps on and off her back five times before consummation. After this they walk down the side of the hill and drink at a pool before making over to their true mound by another pool. There they run together with heads bowed and stretched out and the female solicits again. Two days after this the latter laid her first egg.

As soon as I appreciated the significance of the territorial mounds I realised that this habit of a pair making one eminence in their territory a traditional stand, to which they repaired daily – and no doubt tended to do so yearly – would provide unusually favourable opportunities for numbering each and every pair and following up their subsequent breeding history; though this presumed the nest would be made somewhere near the mound. The actual pegging out of the mounds was not, however, such a simple operation in practice as in theory, and there were days of continuous rain (when note taking was almost impossible) on which I put in more than seven hours at a stretch at pegging. One pair, for example, might use two or three alternative mounds permanently; or temporarily during the absence of a neighbouring pair; or, after incubation had begun, temporarily during the absence of a nearby bird while its mate was sitting on eggs some distance from its mound. Again, a pair rising from one mound would pitch on another as much as a hundred yards distant : while another pair would sit in the heather with two or three vacant mounds in the vicinity and yet, when ultimately disturbed, alight on some distant mound. Right up to the post-fledging season I was continually checking and rechecking my peg numbers.

Only once was a bonxie ever seen to take any notice of a peg, swooping down on it after I had stuck it in at the edge of the mound; and I took much pleasure in observing a bird here and there sitting close up against its peg. So confident were they, indeed, that a pair would even alight on the mound on which I had left the white peg sack, while I was carrying a few pegs to other mounds. On the other hand a peculiar mystery was associated with these pegs from the time that I first began putting them in until the very last days of the season, when only a score or two of bonxies were still on the island. Throughout this period the pegs were continually being pulled up and left lying on the mounds or sometimes removed a yard or two off them. I was still finding them out on 7 September. When this tampering first began I took to stamping them in with my boot, leaving only an inch or two protruding. They were then so firmly set that it seemed impossible that even so powerful a bird as a bonxie could pull them up. Nevertheless the practice continued, and though I never observed a bonxie attempting the task, it was incredible that the sheep, which only visited the bonxie grounds sporadically at night, could or would perform such an operation, and no other agency could be imagined – though that a bird should have such a grip in its beak, or such a power of leverage, was hardly credible.

2. *Attack in Defence*

It was as early in the season as 10 April that one of five bonxies at the Sand Vatn on Bressay had mobbed my collie slightly : but for the first week on Noss I passed through the bonxie grounds without a suspicion of molestation, and it was not until the morning of 29 April that a bird on the Setter 'flats' high above the Cradle Holm stooped at me from behind. The next evening this same bird zoomed down on me nine times, dropping its feet slightly, though I was sixty yards distant from what I had presumed to be its mound. It would either approach me head on, just above the ground, and zoom up with the buoyant lift of a fighter plane a split second before crashing into my face, or swoop down on me from the sheer slope of the Head in the background. On the third morning it attacked me when I was one hundred and fifty yards distant, and on the sixth day its mate also mobbed me, though one of the two gave up after three or four attacks. This pair (number 19), laid their first egg on or about 30 April – the earliest on the island.

If the bonxies' taking up of territorial mounds was the initial factor enabling a naturalist to study the individuals of a colony, their subsequent attacks when their mounds were approached provided an index, thereafter, of the precise state of each pair's breeding calendar : for it was customary for the bonxie to begin mobbing a day or two before the first egg was laid. Exceptionally, one might mob intermittently as much as a fortnight before laying, and it was possible that others did not mob until a day or two after laying : but normally, when a bonxie began mobbing, eggs might be expected and 80 per cent of the Noss pairs began mobbing on the actual day of laying or within an interval of three days before laying. Even at this early stage the attacks might be very savage, the aggressor doing everything but actually strike me. The female of one pair, indeed, twice smacked me hard on the right ear before I moved off her mound on the day that she laid her second egg. There was much individual variation in the intensity of the attacks, and where three or four pairs were nesting very closely together a savage pair would so dominate the others that the latter would attack only diffidently or not at all, circling me impotently, uttering a deep nasal *quaa-aa*. As however, a pair kept strictly to its own mound, once eggs had been laid, they were never to be observed mobbing one another, except occasionally in the air over a breeding area. In this respect the average distance between one occupied mound and the next was fifty-eight yards, with an extreme range of from fifteen yards to one hundred and thirty yards, though, of course, the nearest occupied mound on *one* side might be as much as two hundred yards distance in the next colony; while the average distance between the mounds of the members of the small Bressay colony on the eminences around the Sand Vatn was very much greater.

There was variation, too, in the bonxie's reactions to the various types of intruders on its breeding grounds. The only birds ever mobbed were arctic skuas in adjacent territories, the raven on its infrequent visits to the Noup, and once a fulmar – though the latter was the one species that frequently swept low and unhurried over the breeding grounds. Dogs were hounded mercilessly from one territory to another with audible swinging smacks on head or back, a black dog receiving severer attention than a yellow one : the presence of a dog drew off most of the attacks from the accompanying human. A white sheep and her lamb, however, might pass without incident right through a group of bonxies sitting on eggs : but a few minutes later a second pair, also white, would be attacked when the ewe was almost treading on an incubating bonxie. The latter, however, does not trouble to rise from its eggs, merely striking and pecking at the ewe's rump, until she moves away. Even when this same bird has a week-old chick, and two ewes and their lambs approach it and its neighbour, which is incubating addled eggs thirty-two days set, neither mob the sheep, but jumping up and down, with fanning wings half-raised, as when fighting, peck at the ewes' faces or hover with wings still fanning over their rumps, pecking at their fleeces. Neither strike with either feet or wings, though a casual observation of that unusual fanning motion might lead an observer to suppose that they were actually striking with the latter.

Only one who has worked *alone* among nesting bonxies, without companions or dogs, has any conception of the potential severity of their attacks. When two or more persons were on the grounds together the concentrated mobbing of a single person was dissipated. The bonxie was quickly confused and unable to determine upon which intruder to concentrate. Mobbing might never materialise, was much less severe, and was soon abandoned. This was an important consideration to be taken into account by the naturalist, for unless the mobbing was concentrated it was often impossible to determine the mound from which the disturbed pair originated, as they merely circled overhead without, as was customary, attacking the intruder more severely as he drew nearer to nest or mound. The locating of their eggs was thus a matter of chance. On those very few occasions when I took my dogs with me on to the bonxie grounds I would be struck only once or twice all day.

While the initial attacks, and also the majority, were normally head-on, the bonxie might subsequently attack from the rear and also from the sides, to the accompaniment of a soft *kek-kek* or, in the case of the female, an anguished gullish screech. The latter cry, however, normally signified that I was in the immediate proximity of eggs or young, and coincided with very severe mobbing. In some individuals this screech degenerated into a mere squeak. The actual attempt to strike was clearly and invariably made with a three-quarter swing down of the legs at the moment of the lowest trajectory of the stoop. There was never any question of the wings or beak being used for this purpose. It was not, however, the spectacular long-range aeronauts that were the severest smackers, but those that hovered almost motionless, with particularly brazen impudence, just above one's head, dropped their legs and deliberately struck with swinging feet. When kneeling to examine one pair's exceptionally beautiful clutch of golden-stone and golden-brown eggs – huge eggs with rough coarse shells – for example, the female strikes me on the back of the head and, when I stand up, hovers above me most persistently and aggressively, with that hoarse quacking *quark*, still striking at me with her feet. As one would expect, she is a particularly bold individual, returning to her nest, thirty yards from the mound, as I leave the latter – to sit panting, though whether from the physical exertion of mobbing or from nervous excitement I am not prepared to say. Such distress was most marked after periods of mobbing, but on the other hand incubating birds suffered much inconvenience from the heat and, on a humid day with mist on the hill, sat panting on their eggs, with spiky tongue protruding from lower mandible.

This particular pair were more uniformly darkly plumaged than most, and I presumed that they were comparatively young birds. A minority of the bonxies, probably less than one quarter, bore white markings on the heads and these I presumed to be the older birds. As I got to know individuals of some pairs it appeared to me that the majority of the females were paler plumaged than their mates. Twenty-two pairs noted as especially savage, pressing home their attacks to strike, were, with one exception, among the earliest laying birds on the grounds and therefore probably among the older birds.

Day by day the number of pairs mobbing increased and by the middle of May there were some twenty-five doing so with varying degrees of severity. Pair 19, who had then been sitting for a fortnight, would put up a most impressive show. Taking full advantage of a strong north-easter the two of them hurtled down the steep of the Head at tremendous speed, one after another again and again, to brake hard with banking wings and a shrill scream of air when full upon me and zoom up sideways an inch or two from my head. By the end of the month, at the peak of ovulation, mobbing was so general and regular that I no longer recorded it unless of particular significance or severity. As soon as a number of pairs began mobbing there was a distinct stepping up of territorial tension. There was fighting when third birds alighted on mounds occupied by pairs, and there was more aerial chasing and buffeting of territorial intruders than previously.

There were two aids to indexing the current breeding history of each pair of bonxies – their possession of a territorial mound and their habit of attacking intruders approaching their mound. Given time and patience these were adequate aids to locating every egg laid. That I did not find every egg on the day it was laid was solely due to lack of time, for it was not always possible to locate the eggs by observing at what point the pair mobbed most fiercely. A few pairs did not mob at all. Others might mob me until I was near the nest and then stop mobbing : in contrast to those pairs of which one bird would attack first, but the other not until I was close to the nest. Other pairs nesting in small scattered colonies or on the outskirts of large colonies might select nesting sites forty or fifty yards from their mounds. In this respect the overall average distance of nest from mound was seventeen yards : but two pairs with no proper 'made' mound nested actually on the place where they were accustomed to stand.

Others, again, first mobbed me when they were in possession only of empty hollows – deep rounds of grasses in wet clumps of *sphagnum* moss so many feet or yards from their mound. Some pairs made three or four such hollows, none of which might be the ultimate receptacle of their eggs. This making of trial hollows was all a part of the heightened threshold of the reproductive urge – for here is one bonxie with hackles raised running at another, which has alighted on the heather after a considerable fly round, barging against it in an amorous manner and then waddling round it with head pointed to the ground : whereupon the newly arrived one walks away and settles down to 'round a nest'. The amorous bird then squats beside its fellow, evincing interest in this rounding operation; but the impulse soon passes and the two sit side by side quiescent. Similarly, on the male of another pair alighting, the female solicits him with the usual outstretched head : whereupon the male raises his wings, with two or three little jumps, and finally jumps on to her back and balances with wings waving, for two or three minutes, during which the mating is consummated a number of times. Fifteen minutes later the female again pokes round and round the male, but nothing comes of this invitation and the pair begin to round a nest, upended bill to bill, the male imitating the more vigorous and assiduous rounding of its mate. After twenty minutes of this mutually interesting work both take up position on separate mounds thirty yards apart. From time to time, however, the female is seized with the urge to rise and peck about, and after five minutes she takes a short flight and alights on a mound forty yards from the male and 'rounds' again. The next day she laid her first egg.

Thus it was that, inexperienced in these matters, I did not find the eggs of the earliest pair until 11 May, though they had been laid on or about 30 April. I was misled by this pair's habit of mobbing me from the steep of the Head as much as one hundred and fifty yards from their territorial mound. Despite their mobbing and the existence of mounds the bonxies' eggs were by no means easy to locate, and only one clutch did I find without deliberate search. Searching in widening circles round the mound was often not sufficient, and I might have to retreat to a distance and lie down. It was in this way that I discovered pair 19's eggs, after they had attacked me savagely from the Head, returning again and again to their anxious watch on the siding. After I had lain quiet for a quarter of an hour the ruddy-plumaged female made two or three brief alightings at a place only a few yards from my retreat, and I then discovered that this was their true mound, one hundred and fifty yards from the false mound they had foxed me into pegging out on the steep of the Head above! A few feet from it a hardly perceptible hollow, with a quantity of bent strewn around it, contained one golden-brown egg and one stone-brown egg. When the female flew down to the nest on my departure her mate began to tear at a gull's carcase. (Eggs were laid at forty-eight-hour intervals and the majority incubated from the first laying, though in one or two instances eggs were found cool or cold on the third day.)

On the same day I watched a pale-plumaged pair flying round and round, mobbing me only mildly, waiting to alight on their mound. For half an hour the pair flighted and alighted, flighted and alighted, before I discovered that they had a nest with two olive-brown eggs eighty yards from the mound. Again, there was much bent and *sphagnum* moss lying around, for within a few days of the beginning of incubation an untidy litter of grass and moss was commonly scratched out round the nest, which was usually situated on damp ground or on patches of *sphagnum* in the heather. Normally heather and short sward were avoided, but one pair nesting on a little flat far down the grassy siding above the Cradle Holm and two hundred and twenty yards from their nearest neighbour had a substantial nest of dead grasses; another pair nesting on short sward had a neat round plate of bent and heather for a nest; while a pair nearby had laid their eggs in a small trench in the peat. Some nests were sheltered on two or three sides by little hillocks of heather, moss, or bent; just as those few pairs nesting on flats on the steep of the Head constructed large nests of bents in the great clumps of green *juncus*.

It was a characteristic of the bonxie that while it was so confident that it would almost allow one to touch it on its mound, it was exceedingly reluctant to return to its nest while an intruder was obvious in the vicinity, and not once during the season did I flush a bonxie off its eggs. As soon as an intruder appeared every sitting bonxie would leave its eggs and take up position on its mound, until the intruder had passed on or had lain quiet for a while. Thus, on my approaching one pair, whose two yellow-brown eggs stained with black and brown blotches at their fat ends had been laid a week previously, the female, distinguished by a patch of white behind the eye, rises from her nest to attack me and is joined by her mate. I retreat twenty yards from the nest and lie down, whereupon the female alights one minute later, but takes off again and the pair display on the wing twice, before the female alights once more and settles on her eggs immediately (rising again to mob me when I depart), while the male alights on one of his two mounds and eyes me watchfully. Similarly, another pair mob me hard on the morning their first egg is laid. On my retreating, the male alights, struts about and barges his mate who, for her part, solicits him, bowed forward low and pointing her bill aganst him. Reassured by his alighting, she finally settles down on her nest, twenty yards from the mound, after the lapse of a quarter of an hour. A third pair mob me hard when I approach their mound – they had first mobbed me gently two days earlier – whereupon I retreat and lie down. Five minutes later the female *walks* up twenty yards from the heather and settles down thirteen yards from the mound. She has one warm maroon egg. This habit of walking on to the nest normally distinguished the female from the male. No matter how far away she might alight from her nest she would waddle or run to her eggs after her initial alighting, thought this might be as much as fifty yards from the nest : whereas the male flew from point to point until close beside the nest.

Not until two hours after this does the male, the darker of this pair, desert his mate and is absent for half an hour. On his return he alights by the peg on his mound and *gyangs* : but the female takes no notice of him. Again, four afternoons later, this male flies up from his resting place off the mound and gently prods up his mate from her eggs with his bill, but she opens hers aggressively at him, and after a little jump and wing raise he stands off from her and finally settles down again a couple of yards away. Other males, however, are more successful in their attempts to incubate, and I catch a glimpse of another pair changing over a couple of hundred yards away, one bird taking a hop or two forward off the nest and leaving for sea immediately. At the same time a neighbouring pair are stimulated to rise from their nest and mob me by a similar action on the part of another bird, which has just returned from sea after an hour's absence from his territory. They alight very shortly, however, arching wings and *gyang*ing together. Eight minutes later the female is back on her two eggs again, of which the first – an unusual grey-green in colour – had been laid six days earlier. Though the breeze is chilly the sun is hot and she yawns and pants. Very soon her mate relieves her on the nest, without protest on her part. After being relieved, however, she stands preening on her mound only four yards from the nest for twenty-five minutes, before she too goes away west to sea, soaring to a great height.

3. *The Gathering Hill*

The general stepping up of the emotional threshold late in May coincided with a completely new aspect of life in a bonxie colony. Before I first came into Noss my interest had been aroused by the description given me of their social display on one of the eminences at the south end of the Maiden's Paps. This, it was suggested, served the purpose of stimulating pair formation and the consummation of the mating.

There was no doubt as to the actual location of such a gathering hill : for, just as in the case of the small territorial mounds dotted about the island, so the whole flat top of one of the Paps had been trampled bare of heather and bent, leaving a sparse growth of grass and sorrel that hardly covered the peat. So, confident of the locality, I built myself a breastwork of turves in the first days of my coming, from behind which I might observe at my leisure this interesting *lek*. But day after day passed and no bonxies gathered on this eminence or anywhere else on the island at any hour of the twenty-four. There was, however, one place where a number were accustomed to gather and where up to a score might be seen at any time of the day – and also the night at high summer. This gathering place was the Loch of Pundsgeo : for though an occasional bonxie would bathe briefly in one of the little rainwater pools that pitted a great part of the island and particularly the Setter Hill flat, their main resort for this purpose was this tiny lochan, which was also visited occasionally by such small game as rock pipits, skylarks, wheatears and, infrequently, a pair of hoodies, while an inquisitive fulmar would plane round it from time to time. But it was predominantly a bonxie reserve and only once did I ever see an arctic skua bathe there. Here the bonxies would bathe and sit on the sandy sward at the edge, preening, sleeping and occasionally scrapping. Invariably drinking on first alighting, they would then bathe for five or ten minutes at a time, cleaning their bills under water in a curious way with scratching claws.

As the weeks passed and there was still no sign of any gathering of the clan I was much puzzled and chagrined. It was evident that such a gathering could not bear any relation either to pair formation or to mating, so far as the majority of pairs were concerned, for most were already in pairs, some already had eggs and many consummations of mating had already taken place on territitorial mounds. Two alternatives remained : either that the gathering when it ultimately materialised would consist of the off-duty mates of sitting birds or that it would comprise nonbreeding birds.

More than five weeks had passed since the return of the first bonxie to Noss, when, on making my way up the moor on the very cold afternoon of 4 May, I observed with some surprise that a number of bonxies were sitting together, not on the reputedly traditional gathering eminence, but on one of the middle eminences of the Paps, where there was only a little trodden ground and much untrodden heather. On approaching them two hours later I found upwards of twenty gathered on the heathery slope of the hill : twenty being the maximum at any one time, for birds were continually arriving and departing. Despite the foul weather they sat for the most part on the windward slope, facing into the north-easterly squalls of sleet. Some territorial significance seemed to be attached to individual sitting places, for every now and again a sitting bird would float upwards a foot or two, poised on the gale with hanging legs, and make as if to drop on to the next bird, when the latter would either float up likewise and make way for the other to alight or, standing up, rear its head with menacing open bill. Some pecking and exchange of blows might then follow. One bird deliberately tried to pick a fight with a number of other birds, bumping into them in that 'chest-stuck-out' way that the male of a territoried pair sometimes employed when soliciting its mate for coition, and pecking at them with reared head until it was ultimately put in its place by one of those it had attacked. For the rest, there was the familiar wing and voice display by one or two sitting birds whenever a newcomer alighted among them – they tended to sit very close together despite this intermittent undercurrent of aggressiveness among them – while the jumping or floating upwards, as if to alight on a neighbour's back, was of frequent occurrence; but by 4.15 p.m. I had still seen no sign of any set social display, nor indeed was I expecting one, in the light of their behaviour during the preceding weeks. What I did see, however, was that several of the birds were very palely plumaged and exceptionally hoary about the head and mane. At this juncture therefore it seemed possible that the gathering might be instituted by those older (and probably hoarier plumaged) mates of sitting birds, now that incubation was getting under way : but against this possibility had to be set the undoubted fact that it was extremely rare to find a pair with eggs and not find both birds present in their territory.

The gathering was still in being at 7.5 p.m., its score or so of members still sitting in a clump facing the wind – and the next morning too, despite a north-easterly gale and almost continuous and very heavy squalls of rain. On 16 May, when the gale had abated to a strong breeze, great numbers of bonxies were on the grounds between 11 a.m. and 2 p.m. and a clump of birds were to be seen sitting quietly together on the gathering hill, dispersing from time to time only to be reconstituted almost immediately. Thereafter the gathering was in perpetual being.

It was at this time that I concluded the initial pegging out of occupied mounds, attaining a maximum of 170, a figure that approximated more closely than one might have expected to the 160 pairs I had estimated that there might be before I began putting out pegs. But within a few days of the establishment of the gathering hill, I noticed that some of the mounds I had pegged were no longer occupied. At first I attributed this to the fact that some pairs occupied more than one mound and that on different days I might have pegged two or three mounds used by the same pair; but by the end of the month, when as many as thirty-five birds were to be seen at one time on the gathering hill, I was finding that there were fewer bonxies on the breeding grounds than previously. No doubt this falling off in numbers could be attributed partly to the fact that ninety per cent of the pairs were now sitting on eggs and were thus less conspicuous; but it could not wholly account for the fact that I had ultimately to pull up fifty-seven of my pegs, and it was significant that this latter figure approximated to that of the fifty-plus bonxies which might be seen on the gathering hill at one time when it reached its maximum strength early in June.

Let us consider these facts in relation to procedure on the gathering hill. Day after day a glance at the Maiden's Paps, which could be seen from almost every quarter of the island, revealed a number of bonxies, usually about thirty, sitting quietly together, always facing the wind on whatever might be the windy slope that particular day – sitting in fair weather or foul, fog or shine, except for an occasional bird standing up to arch its wings on the arrival of a newcomer, or for the customary intermittent strutting around with reared head, and for the little scraps and aggressive runs or flights at one another and at those members occupying choice sitting places. Sit quietly as they might, there was always in being that excited undercurrent of latent aggressiveness of one bird for every other. This, considering that the bonxie's normal role on the breeding grounds was to stake out possession of a private mound, was very natural. Intermittently the assembly would break up, as all its members rose and floated away, at some disturbance. Mounting and circling, soaring like buzzards for many minutes over the Paps, they might rise to a height of a thousand feet perhaps : gradually drifting away to sea, but never alighting on any territorial mound within my field of vision; nor was any newcomer ever observed to have left a mound to join those birds on the gathering hill. All through the light nights the latter was occupied : yet never throughout the day did I find more than one or perhaps two incubating pairs, and often none, that had not both birds present at the territorial mound or in the vicinity of the nest. After prolonged observation one noticed that many of the *habitués* of the hill sat in pairs and that there was sexual excitement, with a pair walking around, heads reared, bill to bill. On one occasion a male attempted a mating, with the familiar little jumps with uplifted wings around the female, endeavouring to get behind her : but the latter refused him and there was general excitement and some fighting among those present – of whom sixty or seventy per cent were always white-streaked and tawny birds with a generally ragged appearance, while even the darker birds showed some degree of white. Indeed the exceptionally pale plumage of the majority of the gathering was its most striking feature.

As, from the laying of the first egg until the fledging of the young, one or other parent (and most commonly both) was in continuous attendance either at the nest or on the mound, it was evident that those brief and infrequent intervals during which only one of the parents was present in the nesting territory allowed barely sufficient time for the absent bird to procure food or to bathe in the lochan. Therefore, those birds that sat for long periods on the gathering hill could not be members of breeding pairs, while no bonxie was ever observed either to come into the gathering hill from a breeding territory or to return to one. On the other hand there had been an apparent surplus of occupied mounds before the gathering was established, and there was a noticeable sitting in pairs on the gathering hill by many of its *habitués*. Taking into account the predominance of pale white-marked birds among them, and presuming such a plumage to denote longevity, I concluded that the gathering was composed, predominantly at any rate, of aged individuals and possibly pairs which, after returning initially to traditional mounds, had either failed to pair up or were psychologically or physiologically incapable of proceeding further with the reproductive cycle.

Certainly the gathering held no pairing or mating significance for the majority of breeding pairs. That potentially fertile birds might exist among its members was suggested by the fact that after the peak of the laying season had passed eggs were laid by three pairs – on 30 May, 11 June and 20 June respectively – on the edge or actually within that ground occupied by the gathering; while eggs were also laid by two further pairs on 6 June and 21 June within 110 yards of this area. Three of these pairs laid single eggs and all seven were abnormally coloured, belonging to the pale type with little or no dark blotching, while three were abnormally long. Four of the pairs never mobbed me – none, of course, had 'made' mounds – and three of the nests were only fifteen, twenty-one and thirty-two yards apart, constituting the densest breeding group of any. One of the three fashioned an unusual nest of heather and reindeermoss on the bare and trampled ground. A photographer put up a hide on the gathering hill on 22 June and two days later I found that this pair's eggs had been sucked by a bonxie, their shells being intact but pierced with the beakholes that were characteristic of eiders' eggs sucked by bonxies. Neither parent was present, and this was my only experience of both parents deserting the nest immediately after the loss or addling of eggs – an abnormality accounted for no doubt by the presence of the idlers in the adjacent gathering. Three of the remaining four pairs, however, succcessfully reared young.

For two months there was no change in procedure on the gathering hill, but about the middle of July the numbers there began to decrease, and on the morning and afternoon of 24 July there was a departure from normal procedure when the fifteen or twenty-five bonxies present were in a state of unprecedented restlessness, deserting the hill from time to time to sit on breeding pair 80's unusually large mound on the moor two hundred yards below. I presumed this restlessness, which coincided with the fledging of the first batch of young bonxies, to be the prelude to the permanent breaking up of the gathering preparatory to departure from the island. This state of restlessness continued for the next four days and when disturbed the members of the gathering would drift away to settle on any mound on the moor below. The big one, however, remained the favourite alternative, and at any given time some might be seen sitting on the gathering hill and others on this mound. When on the morning of 4 August there were only six birds present at the gathering hill I concluded that the majority had indeed left the island. What then was my confusion when twelve hours later I found no fewer than fifty sitting on the hill, a number considerably greater than any recorded for five or six weeks past! Thereafter thirty or thirty-five sat quietly on the hill, hardly noticeable – for they no longer settled on other mounds – until 17 August, after which day the gathering was deserted permanently. As the first bonxies normally began to appear in nonbreeding waters in Shetland in the latter half of July, I concluded that the unprecedented restlessness among the members of the gathering at this time did indeed signify its breakup, and that the sudden influx in August was composed of birds from the twenty-nine pairs that ultimately lost eggs or young, for it was in the last days of July that one or two breeding pairs abandoned their territories.

4. *Young Bonxies*

It was 4.15 p.m. on 27 May and dense sea fog swathed Noss Head, where a raven was croaking. So thick was the mist that I found it almost impossible to locate the pegged mounds of those bonxies on the Setter flat I knew so well. Suddenly, when I was groping round in the mist uncertain of my precise whereabouts, the male of pair 19 swooped down on me and I found myself close beside its nest, the bleached bedding of which was now well littered around. From the nest I heard cheeping and there, just free of its dark golden-brown shell, though the smaller end was still linked to its neck, was a wet dark-purplish nestling. (Two hours earlier I had found my first arctic skua's egg.) The nestling, which struggled vainly to rise to its feet, was surprisingly bonxie-like and, though only a central slit of its eye was open, its black beak, with diamond-shaped eggtooth, was well developed. The other egg was still intact, though the embryo cheeped from within.

From the very first hour of fracturing the shell, observable from thirty-six to eighty-five hours before it hatched, the embryo might be heard cheeping. After working for from nineteen to seventy-three hours it would succeed in forcing up a few pyramidal flakes of shell : once a sizeable hole had been made in both envelope and shell further progress was slow and the chick might rest for the next five hours. Finally the shell collapsed and the chick emerged after an incubation period of from twenty-eight to thirty-two days, though as much as twenty-six hours might elapse between the collapse of the shell and the emergence of the chick. The majority apparently hatched during the night or in the early morning, but ten were known to hatch between 8.45 a.m. and 2.45 p.m.

Though the male of this first pair to hatch out young mobbed me very severely on this occasion, his mate only *kek*ed around, standing sentinel on her mound after my departure, while he displayed the customary wariness in returning to the nest. Three-quarters of an hour later, when the nestling's eyes were fully open, revealing a dark-brown iride with a dark-blue pupil, the parents changed over on egg and nestling.

At six hours the chick is half-dry and at ten hours when it is still not quite dry, it *peeps* immediately it sights me and threatens me with its beak, with an angry little *kek-kek-kek,* half tottering as it rears up, one pale-blue foot out of the nest. A partially eaten whiting, nine inches long, lies near the nest. At twelve hours it is sleeping on the rim of its nest and *kek-kek-kek*s on my waking it : but it is an effort to hold up its head at this tender age for any length of time, the head falls forward and its sleeps with its beak buried in the ground. By this time it has dried off into a fine-haired fawn down, darker on the head. Other nestlings, however, took up to twenty-two hours to dry off.

At 1 p.m. on the second day, when the top half of the shell was still in the nest and both parents mobbed me very severely, the nestling was three or four feet out of the nest. It snapped at me and screamed when handled, reiterating a rapid *gyer, gyer,* its menacing open beak revealing a pale mauvish-pink interior. A piltock's backbone lay near the nest, while another one-day-old chick had a twelve-inch herring near it. On my retreating, the male settled on the egg, but not on the chick (which I had replaced in the nest), for the latter left the nest immediately its parent returned.

The remaining egg had still no more than a chip of shell off its top end, but twenty-four hours later this egg had also hatched, and the chick was a little way out of the nest, which still contained one eggshell, with the female brooding it. (The normal hatching interval was forty-eight hours, twenty-four hours in some cases and seventy-two hours in a few.) This chick was much darker than its bigger fellow, a dusky fawn, darker on the head, paler on the belly, with pale greyish-blue legs. Unlike those of the arctic skua, however, bonxie nestlings were remarkably uniform in colouring: though one pair hatched two velvety mole-brown chicks from dark golden-brown eggs, another pair a blackish-fawn chick from an olive-brown egg, and a third a sooty-fawn one from a dark-brown egg.

On my moving away the nestling followed me, with a 'teezing' cry. Two other chicks, less than thirty-six hours old, belonging, like this one of pair 19, to pairs with plenty of territorial space, also followed me, with a diminutive triple *kek*, apparently for the purpose of settling against my boot. The elder chick, however, continued to crouch quietly when I squatted beside it. When I sat beside the other the male parent struck me lightly on the head. On my departure this chick followed its parent around, but the latter led it to the nest before brooding it.

On the fourth afternoon, when both parents were mobbing me severely, the younger chick was nine yards from the nest and the elder was not to be found; and on the fifth afternoon, with the parents still savage, both were nine yards out, apart as always, sheltering from the rain against tussocks of grass. Another pair of the same age in a large territory were already two or three score yards apart. A few feet from pair 19's mound, were six partially or fully cleaned piltock backbones and a rabbit's leg bone, while another five-day chick had a half-eaten herring on its mound. In other territories were the skins of young rabbits, and a pair of old birds on the wing might sometimes be seen chasing a young rabbit down the hillside.

At 6.45 p.m. of pair 19 fed one of its chicks by disgorging on to the ground. Its mate eventually joined it and both assisted in finishing up the mess, before going off for a drink at a nearby pool, while the unfed chick wandered around at a little distance. In the far background two other parents were each feeding one chick, four and five days old respectively; and half an hour later another parent left its nest, where it was brooding a day old chick, to feed or to assist in feeding its three-day old chick – for I missed seeing whether its mate, now standing apart a little, provided the disgorge, as no doubt it did. The young were fed at any odd hour of the day.

On the sixth day, when only one parent of pair 19 was present at 11 a.m., one nestling was seventeen yards from the nest and the other scuttling away from its vicinity. After they had been put together and photographed first one and then the other shortly scuttled off a few yards and settled down on a clump of *sphagnum* in the shelter of a tuft of bent, panting with the heat of the sun : for even when a cold breeze was blowing the chicks evinced distress at the sun's rays, and on those infrequent comparatively hot summer days, with only a light breeze, many chicks were to be seen sitting in pools of water or on clumps of wet *sphagnum*.

After the third day two chicks of a clutch were never to be found together either in the nest or out of it, and it was unusual to find even one chick in the nest; once they had passed the tenth or fifteenth day many wandered far from the nest and mound, so that it was not only difficult to find them, but still more difficult to assign each chick to its proper nest. Hence the paramount necessity of ringing the chick as early as possible after the eighth day, when the precocious development of the 'ankle' made it possible to ring perfectly without 'overlappping' the band.

On the seventh afternoon, when the elder chick was twelve yards out and nipped my fingers hard, both parents were very savage, striking my spaniel's back with swinging smacks and knocking off my beret, which no wind could displace, when I bent down to examine the chick. For that matter, as soon as the embryo began to cheep within the egg the adults' mobbing reached its peak of intensity, and I noticed that near the mound of one pair which had a chick working away at a punctured shell, there was the carcase of a kittiwake eaten except for wings and legs; while in other territories were the beaked skull of a puffin and a dead snipe.

The elder chick was now very much bigger than its fellow, which scuttled off into the heather immediately I placed the two together : but development varied from pair to pair, and some elder chicks were only slightly bigger and more active than younger twins, despite their one or two day advantage.

By the eighth day, when both parents mobbed me very severely, striking me hard several times on the back of the head, the younger chick, now a foxy-brown in colour, was sixteen yards out : but the elder was not to be found.

The next day the latter was again missing, while the younger was crouching in a drain thirty yards from the nest. For a quarter of an hour I lay fifty yards away from this chick. Though both parents mobbed me very severely, the male hitting me repeatedly and most unpleasantly, they were as usual very wary where the chick was concerned, and not until I had retreated another fifty yards and lain down again in partial concealment behind a hillock for many minutes, did first one and then the other parent brood the chick for brief periods.

To judge by the number of fishbones the chick was still being fed on the mound, but a parent of a neighbouring pair dropped a herring from a height near its seven-day-old chick, probably disgorging from anger or nervous reaction at the unusual presence, in addition to my accustomed self, of my wife and son and the two dogs, all moving around looking for chicks.

At the end of the first week of June there were gales and heavy rains, and some well-known nestlings disappeared. One clutch of embryos lay dead in their shells with beaks protruding, though one parent still sat on them and both parents mobbed hard. Another dead chick, about five days old, appeared to have been pecked over the eye. This chick belonged to a pair in a congested area on the extreme south edge of the Setter flat, where four pairs nested in a circle whose diameter was only forty-eight yards. Here also was a dead eider duck. Rather than dead you would have deemed her crouching to escape notice, for she sat with her head bowed forward on a little bank. But her beak and the back of her head were bloody, and as I stood looking down at her I could enact the tragedy – the duck trying to run back to her nest, tripping up in the long grass and on the uneven ground from time to time, and those mad devils of bonxies, now at the height of their territorial savagery, continually striking her on the head, until weakened and bemused she was ultimately unable to rise again from her last rest and just sat there and died.

But on a calm sultry afternoon all would be quiet on the bonxie grounds, except for the songs of larks. Now and again an adult bonxie would drink from a little dub, before taking wing and sailing over the Rumble Wick cliffs or down over the Maiden's Paps to the Voe of the Mels. Yet, as we have seen before, it was the rarest thing to find a mound that had not both birds of the pair in attendance. No doubt the sight of a score or two of their fellows on the wing above their particular breeding colony would bring back those bonxies not too far distant. Even at 2.30 a.m., when flights of as many as fifteen bonxies at a time might be seen leisurely circling and planing out to sea, I would find myself still being mobbed by *pairs* of birds, notably those with young, and I could never definitely determine any mound that had not its pair present. On those occasions when the mass of the adults had been disturbed, and were on the wing over one of the colonies, the bigger chicks might be seen scuttling for cover, their pale-fawn down rendering them most conspicuous against the green hillside. When the majority of the adults had settled again the chicks would emerge from their places of concealment, perhaps to feed on slugs and other small game.

In the third week of June there was a second period of heavy rains and further casualties among those chicks in process of hatching : one pair, not fully uncurled from the embryo position, dying in a pool of water. After heavy rain had set in shortly before 11 a.m. on 18 June I noticed, an hour later, that the majority of the chicks were very wet and had not been brooded, despite the weather conditions, and I found only one pair of one-day-old and three-day-old chicks dry in their nest. Another pair about ten days old were crouching in hollows filled with water, and black slugs were in the nests and under some of the chicks. But when, after nearly three days' continuous rain, I was fearful that I should find heavy mortality among hatching chicks, I was intensely relieved to find only three dead, and on this occasion not a single wet chick was to be found, even the biggest being dry.

Throughout this period the adults were most savage and of forty pairs visited on 19 June ten were exceptionally severe. One pair, which had smacked me continuously since their chicks first hatched, were so determined and incessant in their striking that I found it beyond endurance to examine their nine- and ten-day-old chicks for more than a few minutes at a time; while another bird, with a two- or three-day-old chick and a second clambering out of the nest only half dry with a piece of shell adhering to its neck, struck me on the brow with both its feet; and a third with eggs struck me severely above the right eye. When I first went upon the bonxie grounds I had been inclined to scoff at tales of strangers to the hill beating a hasty retreat from the mobbing bonxies. I did so no longer.

Among those chicks that disappeared during the first spell of bad weather were those of pair 19, and the mobbing of this pair immediately became much less severe, though they continued to frequent their famous stand on the Head and to swoop down on me mildly until 15 June, and did not finally abandon their territory until more than two months after the loss of their young.

5. *Young Bonxies on the Wing*

By the thirteenth day the chicks' down was a much paler fawn than previously and was being shed on the scapulars, where blue quills were appearing, while the legs were now a very pale and patchy blue. Differences in development were noted among chicks of the same age, a single chick being heavier than one of a pair, though not so forward perhaps in the development of its quills.

At this age a chick belonging to a pair with a big territory might have wandered as much as eighty or ninety yards from its parents' mound, though others in small territories might be only five or six yards from their nests. One three-week-old chick, well down on the moor below the Maiden's Paps, wandered no less than two hundred yards over No-bonxie land, with its parents circling over it. When their chicks wandered to these distances the parents would mob the more fiercely as the intruder approached their mound and *not* the chick, and it was at this stage that I found an adult arctic skua lying dead near the mound of one of the fiercest pairs of bonxies with a sixteen-day-old chick.

Between the fifteenth and eighteenth day black feathers began to sprout from the blue and white quills of the chick's wings and scapulars, and it had lost much of its down, except on the head and rump. Very quiet were these dark-eyed big chicks, doing no more than peck sharply at me a few times with their powerful beaks when I handled them as they squatted head up against tufts of grass, in watery hollows, even in deep pools of water, or sheltered in little peat recesses a score of yards apart and forty yards out of their nests. It was exceptional for one to struggle when I handled it, though occasionally one would vomit up an undigested fish.

After the lapse of three weeks tail quills were prominent, the legs and enormous feet were now greyish-black, and the scapular feathers formed two large black patches on either side of a ridge of fawn down. And now, for the first time since the initial thirty-six hours after hatching some pairs, though not all, were at last associating together, and a pair of these monster nestlings might be found sitting side by side with their heads stuck into a peat bank, only nine yards distant perhaps from another pair of monsters. And there they just sat, rising occasionally to preen and take up new positions a yard apart. One pair, however, of which the elder was very much more advanced than the younger, remained 150 yards apart until they fledged.

At a month old, when both parents would still be striking me, a chick's scapulars and also its secondaries were almost completely feathered, its primaries were an inch and a half long, and it had lost most of its down except on head and belly. The bite of its great bill was strong enough to draw blood from my fingers, and the interior of the bill had changed in colour to ivory-blue and mauve.

A week later it had assumed almost full fledging plumage, with only a few wisps of down remaining on its head, though birds of the same age varied considerably in the amount of down they retained, and some twins had reversed their age status, the younger being more advanced than the elder. On the belly all were sheathed in a smooth pale copper-brown mail. On mantle and wing the majority were a dark-brown, lightly or heavily linked with copper or chestnut, and in some individuals this coppering on the back and shoulders was so heavy as to obscure the brown; while one or two wore light-yellow manes of down and had yellow throats, which gave them a curious appearance. Ten or eleven, however, out of the one hundred and fourteen ultimately fledging, bore no copper links on their upper parts, which were instead an almost uniform drab-black.

When thirty-six days old the far-wandering chick on the lower moor returned to its nest territory and I found it sitting in a drain only twenty-five yards from its parents' mound. With only a few wisps of down still adhering to its head, it seemed perfectly plumaged for flight, and it gave me great pleasure to sit beside this splendid young bonxie, whose fortunes I had followed since the day, more than two months before, that the egg had been laid. It crouched quietly by me, observing me with its fine clear eye, still dark-brown of iris and dark-blue of pupil, while its parents mobbed me, one occasionally brushing my head with its feet. But when I threw it up into the air it made no effort to fly. Two other thirty-two- and thirty-four-day-old young ones were floating a yard apart against the bank of a large pool, and the younger, after allowing me to handle it, swam quickly across to the other side of the pool. When the elder of these two ultimately fledged, the younger still swam round and round the pool, not now allowing me to catch it.* Two days later it, too, rose on to the wing at the second attempt, after first swimming across the pool. Of another pair, forty and forty-two days old, one sat on a little grassy island in a pool, while the other swam alongside. Others, again, crouched in the long swampy grass.

Another six-weeks-old chick in a smooth black plumage, faintly scalloped with a copper lacquer, with a few wisps of down on its throat, also seemed ready to fly. (Despite its sooty plumage one of its parents was an exceptionally pale-yellow-streaked tawny bird and the other a pale-streaked dark-capped bird.) When I had handled and released it, however, it just ran away, with shoulders humped and head bowed forward like a pheasant. At this age those young ones inhabiting big territories would run a great distance, and there were casualities among them : for I found one forty-day-old chick dead in a deep drain and another, much battered about the head, lay dead in another pair's territory.

The days passed, and still these enormous, perfectly plumaged young ones did not get on the wing, but sat sluggishly in their hollows. The forty-sixth day dawned and, when I was walking up the moor from the hill-dyke at 10.25 a.m. on 15 July I perceived that at long last the wanderer was flapping laboriously round on a light easterly breeze, accompanied by its parents. When mobbed by the adults of other pairs, which its parents drove off, it uttered a squeaky form of the female's screech, before making a clumsy alighting after a short flight. Though on the ground it had seemed as big as the latter, it was much inferior in size when in the air, though its wings were long in comparison with its bulk.

Five days later this fledgeling, still the only one on the wing, would get up off the ground when I was as much as a hundred yards distant. One or other of its parents was now spending longer periods away from their territory and on 18 July, when both it and the other sooty young bird were sitting in holes, only one parent was in attendance on each for the first time on record. At 10 a.m. on 20 July the latter, now also in its forty-sixth day, was sitting with its head sloping up against the wall of a drain, characteristically. After I had examined its plumage, smoothing its

*In all the studies in this book I use the term *fledge* to denote the act of first taking flight, not of assuming flight-plumage.

head and back with my hand, and admiring the smooth perfection of the pale copper mail on its underparts, it ran off and, when I approached it again, laboured off into flight as if the most natural thing in the world, though this was almost certainly its first flight. It remained on the wing quite easily for a couple of minutes, mobbed by other pairs of adults, before alighting clumsily.

A week later there were fifteen young ones on the wing, for the average fledging period proved to be forty-six days, though some fledged in forty-two days and one, slow to develop, did not get on the wing until the fifty-sixth day. Some were able to take off into immediate flight : others could only just lift themselves clear of the ground, and would scuttle along it in between flights. One such forty-six-day-old scuttler disgorged a partially digested twelve-inch fish on my approaching. Another, just able to fly, was mobbed by the gulls nesting on the seaward edge of the North Croo. You could see the parents dropping lightly on to the backs of those fledgelings that were strong on the wing, shepherding them back to their territories and forcing them down to the ground; and a pair in the small colony above the Setter *crö* evinced much anxiety when their fledgeling flew seawards. Some fledgelings on the moor might settle temporarily among the *habituées* of the gathering hill on the big mound already mentioned or on the hill itself. As soon as they fledged they adopted for the first time a standing posture, whereas previously they had, without exception, invariably sat or crouched; but in contrast to the adults, which stood four-square with head and neck at right angles to the horizontal axis of the body, the fledgelings stood with humped shoulders, and were thus distinct from the adults at any distance.

In the last days of July it became very quiet on the bonxie grounds. But on a sunny breezy morning in the first week of August, when there were sixty-four young bonxies fledged and the eldest, now three weeks fledged, was playing on the wing with one parent, there sounded from all quarters a squeaky rippling hunger cry – a cry heard only from those that had fledged. Though occasionally the cry might be uttered by one on the wing it came predominantly from those standing in ones and twos on their mounds, with or without parents : for now, for the first time, some fledgelings between fifty and seventy days old were being temporarily deserted by both parents. Hence this new cry from those deserted, this three- to seven-note reedy rippling, which bore a faint likeness to the skirling of a curlew or, more faithfully perhaps, the softer skirling of the whimbrel. Temporary desertion, however, did not imply that the adults had ceased feeding their young, for here at 10.15 a.m. is a parent disgorging to both 'her' fifty-two- and fity-four-day-old fledgelings together, after which she takes the customary drink at a dub and washes her beak. Subsequently, she is approached by another pair's fifty-four-day fledgeling, which is waving its spread wings, bowing its head, and 'rippling' : whereupon she makes a little flight away from it. Such dancing was to be observed up to the sixty-first day – that is for about a fortnight after fledging.

By the second week of August the majority of the fledgelings were to be seen alone most of the day, and as many as eleven might be lined up on and off a single mound – though here and there one might still be seen with two parents in attendance. The latter continued to mob me, though without striking, until their fledgelings were seventy days old. Only for an hour or so after sunrise, however, was there aerial chasing and mobbing by the adults in any way comparable to that of earlier days.

Between three and four weeks after fledging some young ones and their parents disappeared from their territories, and by the end of the third week of August about one third of young and old had left the island. Yet, with one exception, none of the fledgelings had ever been seen to leave the approximate vicinity of their territories, other than to circle around on the wing or alight temporarily on another mound or gathering place a few hundred yards distant. Only once was a fledgeling seen to venture out over Rumble Wick, though the old birds were continually there making abortive attacks on the gannets.

Though the last remaining fledgelings were still dancing and hunger-crying up to the middle of September and one adult, which had lost its young, was still mobbing me in its territory at that date, the bonxies had at last surrendered their six month dominance of the island's hinterland, and the few adults present during the day tended to gather in such unwonted places as the North Croo, though an occasional pair might still float over the breeding grounds with the whistling *keeyuk*. The sheep, which all through the spring and summer had grazed by day mainly on the Head and on the green holms and those coastal sidings where no bonxies nested, now ventured over the moors again at all hours;

families of hoodies were raucous over the gathering hill; and round the carcase of a rabbit on the Maiden's Paps might be seen together a swaabie, an immature herring gull, a pair of hoodies and two bonxies. Only two young bonxies remained on the Paps, where the sixty-six-day fledgeling of one pair kept company with the forty-day-old chick of another pair.

It was on 15 September that I was on the bonxie grounds for the last time, between the hours of 10.15 a.m. and 1.30 p.m. There were now only about a score of adults and young remaining on the island, but the strong west wind kept them at a great height when they rose at my approach, and I could not identify all of them. With one sixteen-day exception, however, all the young had been fledged for three weeks or more : so we may assume that the last of them would have left Noss before the end of the month*. Accompanying them presumably would be the faithful parents of a crippled fledgeling, finally deserting it at the age of one hundred and fifteen days, having watched over it and fed it for more than six weeks beyond the normal span. As far back as 7 August their then sixty-one-day-old fledgeling had broken its right wing. For a week or two after this both parents had mobbed me very fiercely, and it was perhaps significant that the only dead adult bonxie ever found on Noss was one freshly dead at this time in this pair's territory.

Though both parents were still feeding the fledgeling a month later they stooped only rarely at me and visited it only briefly, though frequently. By this time, being ninety-two days old, the latter was assuming its first winter plumage. The marked uniformity of the fledgeling dress had given way to a rich mottled chestnut, darkening to brown on the crown of the head, at the shoulders of the wings and on the primaries. On 15 September one parent was still present with the cripple and stooped at my dog – as did both parents of the youngest sixty-five-day-old fledgeling on the Maiden's Paps; but thereafter, we can only conjecture as to its fate, and as to the fate of more than one hundred other fledgelings I had ringed and which would probably not return to Noss until their third or fourth year.

Postscript

In the following New Year I received news that one of my

---

*Two young ones were still on the Island on 18 October the following year.

fledgelings had alighted exhausted on a French fishing smack off Nieuport, West Flanders, on 6 January. The skipper took it home with him and it died the next day, seven months after it had hatched from the second egg laid by one of those pairs with a look-out on the Maiden's Paps and a territory in the corrie above.

VIII

KILLERS AND PIRATES

Thus far we have observed the bonxies on their breeding grounds, but what of their *extra*territorial activities? We have seen that from the first day of their return to Noss they did not restrict these activities to the island and its adjacent waters, but passed to and fro across the Sound, going over to bathe in the big lochs of the Sand Vatn and also of Grimsetter, veering to and fro over Bressay and the waters of the Harbour. We have seen that their passing out of Noss was a cause of concern, not only to gannets and gulls, but to such diverse species as oystercatchers and eiders, rockdoves, hooded crows and starlings, though no bonxie was ever seen to display any evil intent towards any of the three latter species. Nevertheless the cause of alarm was present.

As early as 7 April, the second day of their return to Noss, I had seen a bonxie mobbing an immature swaabie over the White Hill of Bressay, though on this occasion it had appeared more a matter of one intermobbing with the other than definite piracy on the part of the bonxie; but it was not until my first day in Noss that I observed the latter in the act of obtaining food. If I ever gave the matter any previous thought I suppose that before I visited Shetland I conceived the bonxie as obtaining its food mainly from piracy on the gannets, especially on an island such as Noss, where a large colony of gannets was established on the very edge of the bonxie grounds. It was therefore with some surprise that lying on

153

the cliffs above Rumble Wick that first morning, with an occasional pair of bonxies or a solitary one flapping to and fro along the wall of cliff, I saw first one and then six of them disembowelling a kittiwake on the sea at the base of the cliffs. Two would sometimes tear at the carcase together, but for the most part there was continuous fighting among the six, and two or three at a time would rear up in the water and strike with their talons, hammering savagely at one another with their beaks and threshing with their wings. Throughout the proceedings a pair of swaabies swam around the carcase, without, however, ever venturing to touch it, and they eventually retreated when assaulted by one of the bonxies : whereupon, to my still greater surprise, a fulmar swam into the *mêlée* and pecked up the titbits floating off the carcase.

Four days after this I noticed that the bonxies were already flapping purposefully to and from the cliffs at 5 a.m.; and at 7.15 p.m. on 28 April three were again tearing at a kittiwake's carcase. When they finally drew off, satisfied, I was surprised, once more, to see a fulmar swim up and rip at the carcase, while a swaabie swam around impotently; and what was more surprising, on another bonxie approaching, the fulmar shot at it with wings busked (its feeding posture) and actually drove the bonxie away. The fulmar then returned to tear at the carcase, while two bonxies and two swaabies, besides other fulmars, swam around, awaiting his lordship's pleasure. As further evidence of its mastery this particular fulmar subsequently again chased a bonxie away from the carcase, and then two bonxies together, and then a swaabie. Finally, having finished feeding, it busked its closed wings and twice drove off a bonxie : but in this instance the latter retained final possession of the carcase, the fulmar no doubt being full-fed.

Two afternoons later I learnt more of the bonxie's methods. Every now and again, as was their way, colonies of kittiwakes would suddenly 'shoal' out and down from, and return to, the cliffs. On one such 'shoaling' I perceived that one of the bonxies continually prowling along the cliffs was dropping on top of a kittiwake and forcing it down to the water, where it began to peck it about the eyes and possibly drown it deliberately. On being joined by another, no doubt its mate, the two began ripping up the still living victim, tearing at its neck, with the customary pair of swaabies swimming around. White feathers began to float away on the water and a red dye spread outwards. On an empty stomach I felt rather sick at this butchery, before being astounded to see a fulmar swim up and chase *both* bonxies away from the carcase ! While ripping vigorously at the carcase the fulmar was disturbed by one of the swaabies which, however, was chased off by a bonxie. The fulmar then chased away the latter but, having fed well, finally lost possession to the two swaabies.

Similarly at 8 a.m. the next morning a fulmar was tearing at the carcase of what appeared to be a guillemot, with the usual bonxie and swaabie awaiting its pleasure. Subsequently fulmar and swaabie fed together, with the bonxie still waiting on. Other bonxies flew to and fro close along the cliffs, but no kittiwakes shoaled off at their passing, and it seemed that the bonxies made only chance kills during their sporadic and spontaneous shoalings. On the other hand a bonxie flapping close past the cliffs two afternoons later, twice brought off clouds of kittiwakes, but made no attempt to strike; and similar phenomena were observed the next evening.

For two weeks, then, I had watched the bonxies at their killings, but not once had one even so much as stooped at a gannet : their sole source of food had been kittiwakes – though sole source was not quite correct, for on the morning of 3 May a bonxie had harried a swaabie over Gunstie, causing it to release some object, the bonxie going down after it; and the the next day another, harrying a herring gull over the Sound, finally droppped on to the ground, knocking some feathers out of its back, when the gull surrendered a six-inch, silver-bellied piltock, which the bonxie gulped, after standing with it in its beak for a minute or so; while, on another pair harrying a herring gull into disgorging a fish, a swaabie and a hoodie were first at the place of its fall and the bonxies could do no better than alight together on the brae and arch their wings in protest : before taking off to harry another gull unsuccessfully.

By this date the earliest bonxies were beginning to incubate and henceforward their presence at the cliffs was not so constant; nor were they to be observed at all frequently with carcases of kittiwakes, for shortly before the middle of May the latter began nest building, and a ceaseless procession of them shuttled to and from the cliffs and the muddy dubs down by the hill dyke, passing either over the bonxie grounds, where they were permitted safe passage, or coastwise, hugging every indentation of the geos. During a period of bad weather prior to the eighteenth, indeed, there were no entries of any killings in my notebook, but that evening numbers of bonxies were working the cliffs and water of Rumble Wick in familiar manner, and one, in company with a swaabie, was tearing at a guillemot's carcase.

Up to the end of May I had still not witnessed any act of piracy on the continual stream of gannets alighting on the cliffs, with the sole exception of one bonxie stooping briefly at a gannet on 22 May – the day that my first gannet nestling hatched. A couple of weeks later, however, on the afternoon of 3 June, when two pairs of bonxies also had nestlings, I at last saw one harry three or four gannets in succession, tweaking the tail of one of them; but it sheered off very quickly from each victim, evidently not obtaining the proper response from a gannet carrying undigested fish. Subsequently I just missed seeing another bonxie forcing a gannet

Bonxie dropping on Gannet

to disgorge, but did see it dropping down to the water after the fish which, however, two swaabies gobbled up before the bonxie could get to the spot.

It seemed clear, then, that the bonxies did not begin to seek food from the gannets until the latter had nestlings : but what was the nature of the stimulus that initiated piracy at this juncture, and why should gannets be carrying undigested fish to the gannetry at a time when their young were, in fact, being fed on regurgitated and digested fish and not on disgorged whole fish?

After this initial day of piracy, however, there were no further instances, nor any killings of kittiwakes, which were now incubating; and though there were always bonxies circling over the Wick and flapping along the cliffs, bringing off clouds of up to two hundred puffins at a time, I witnessed no attacks on them. The presumption was that the bonxies, most of whom now had nestlings to feed, were obtaining their main source of food at the Atlantic fishing grounds of all these sea birds. On the other hand, so short were the absences of one or other of a pair of bonxies from the nest, it did not seem possible that they could reach out to any great distance from Noss.

By the fourth week of June pairs, trios, and solitary bonxies were to be seen circling and planing over the Wick and working the cliffs at all hours of the day from as early as 2.25 a.m., yet an hour might pass and I would not see even one bonxie stooping at a gannet. Not until the evening of 24 June did I see one make four abortive stoops at gannets. At 3.15 p.m. on the next afternoon there was a similar incident. For once it was fine, with only a light westerly breeze, and at 3.58 p.m. there was a second abortive attempt, and a third at 4.15 p.m., when a swaabie surprisingly seized the harrying bonxie by the tail. Five minutes later a bonxie, hotly pursued by a swaabie, forced a gannet to disgorge and may have retrieved the falling fish, though I did not actually observe this. The attack did not appear to be pressed home, the bonxie flying beside and beneath the gannet. At 4.22 p.m. there was a fifth (abortive) chase, and eight minutes later a sixth bonxie dropped on to a gannet's tail, with what result was not seen. There followed three more apparently abortive chases, the ninth a very long one. Thus in seventy-five minutes only one, possibly, of nine bonxies had been successful in its piratical attempts, and my impression was that these activities over the Wick could hardly be

considered primarily food productive, for all but a few pairs of
bonxies now had nestlings, some three or four weeks old, which
would demand a great deal of food.

Again, during an hour's observation on the late afternoon of 1
July, when for the first time for many weeks two bonxies were
tearing at a carcase – probably a guillemot's – there were three
instances of piracy. One was abortive; a second was a very long
chase, for the most part on an even keel, and so long that when the
gannet ultimately alighted on the water and submerged, the
bonxie had passed out of my field of vision; in the third instance
the bonxie apparently recovered the fish and swallowed it before
the attendant swaabie could filch it.

The next morning a bonxie was waltzing round the cliffs, as
they continued to do all and every day. Nine times did this bird
make tentative slanting stoops at those gannets continually
circling off the cliffs or coming into the Wick. Twice it struck a
gannet on the back with its feet, at which the latter looked up
inquiringly but took no stronger evasive action than to descend a
few feet. Once it upset a gannet's balance by tweaking its tail : but
though following this bird for a considerable distance ultimately
broke off the chase. Its piracy appeared to be a matter solely of
trial and error or success, the bonxie having no definite knowledge
of which gannets were carrying whole fish : while those gannets
with empty crops displayed no active fear of their persecutors.

Towards the end of the second week in July the first young
guillemots began to leave the cliffs for the sea, and at midday on
12 July six bonxies were significantly sitting on the reef at the base
of the Noup, below the great townships of guillemots, of whose
young ones they would take toll during their nightly fledging.
Though present at the Wick for two hours I only noticed one
bonxie stooping to retrieve a fish in midair disgorged by a gannet,
and part of the fish falling to the water was taken by the inevitable
pair of swaabies.

At the end of July another cycle was reached when the young
kittiwakes fledged and the bonxies were once again to be seen
ripping up carcases on the water – this time of young not adult
kittiwakes – as late as 8.15 p.m. Nor were the fledgeling
kittiwakes their only victims at this season, for on the evening of
31 July one was killing a fledgeling herring gull on the sea off
Pundsgeo, though repeatedly struck, or near-struck, by the latter's

parents. When the gull was dead the bonxie's mate then joined it in ripping off the feathers. A hundred yards away another bonxie was killing a second fledgeling gull, pecking at and then standing on its head to drown it, while balancing with raised wings. Once again, its mate waited until the gull was dead, while fulmars and tysties swam around curiously. Other bonxies were successfully harrying adult swaabies over the Bressay croftings and there was much harrying of gannets and also of lesser black-backed gulls over the Harbour.

In August fledgeling kittiwakes were the bonxies' staple food supply off Noss – though it must be remembered that the latter's young were fed almost entirely on fish – and the waters of the Wick were strewn with their corpses. As early as 3 a.m. the bonxies would be at their butchery, with fledgeling swaabies as jackals. Yet I never actually saw a young kittiwake knocked down and on the only occasion on which I saw a bonxie stoop at one, it avoided the stoop with a quick roll. Though the bonxies were continually over the Wick their harrying of gannets continued to be as sporadic and mainly unsuccessful as heretofore, and in one instance a gannet without a fish lunged up at its attacker with its beak.

Towards the end of August nearly all the fledgeling and adult kittiwakes had left the Noss cliffs, and yet another food cycle was reached when, shortly before noon on 26 August, as many as six bonxies at a time were continually working, though without result, a spiral of some 150 gannets milling over the Wick. One even pulled a feather out of a gannet's tail but, not provoking a favourable response, sheered off immediately. And then I was a witness for the first time of that incident of which I had heard so much and which had so often been recorded off Hermaness, when a bonxie suddenly and most unexpectedly seized a gannet by its wing. The latter crashed – though under full control – and shot almost flatly into and just under the surface of the sea, disgorging on emerging. Its fish, however, was captured by two other bonxies, alighting simultaneously with a swaabie, and the pirate itself made no attempt to drop down and retrieve the fish from the water.

Shortly afterwards another bonxie seized a gannet by the tip of its wing. Though this victim was not knocked off its balance, it nevertheless disgorged, and its assailant, passing immediately below it, neatly caught the fish before it had fallen more than a few feet. This incident was followed by yet another seizure of a wing tip and disgorge, when however the fish fell to the water and was retrieved by another bonxie, two others also alighting.

It was ironical that I had had to wait five months to see this manoeuvre. But what was the actual position? Nearly all the gulls, kittiwakes and auks had now left Noss. Apart from the occasional adult gull or fledgeling only the gannet remained as a potential food source. On 1 September a bonxie was attempting to kill a fledgeling herring gull on the Hill of Papilgeo, returning twice to knock the screaming juvenile on its back, but finally sheering off, distracted by two hundred milling gulls and the mobbing parent. Though large numbers of both young and old bonxies had also left the island, those that were still on the breeding grounds had big young to feed and were hungry, pressing home their attacks to the full. As gulls and kittiwakes also nested in large numbers at Hermaness, it was difficult to understand why the piracy on gannets should be intense there and not at Noss, though had I myself found time to visit this other gannetry the reason might have been apparent by comparison with conditions on Noss. However that might be, 26 August remained the one and only occasion on which I observed this wing seizing manoeuvre. The probability is that most observations at Hermaness have also been made in August when, as on Noss, the gannet is the only remaining food source. In September I observed a new technique when a bonxie, swimming with raised wings behind a gannet on Bressay Sound, constantly forced the latter down, whenever it attempted to rise from the water, itself rising from time to time to hover above it. In the end, however, the gannet was allowed to fly off. And on my last visit to Rumble Wick in the middle of the month there was the more familiar spectacle of four bonxies, one possibly a fledgeling, tearing at the carcase of a young gull, with the usual fulmar swimming nearby; and very shortly the latter flew at them with busked wings and tail spread and raised, chasing all four from the carcase! The Lord of the Seas!

IX

A STUDY OF A BREEDING COLONY OF ARCTIC SKUAS

1. *Their Homing*

It was on the afternoon of 28 April, when I was watching bonxies bathing in the Lochan of Pundsgeo, that a strange cry rang out over the Head, like, and yet not like, the yodel of a herring gull. Twice more I heard it, but still could not trace its origin. And then two couples of big dark birds, their lines as sharp-cut as those of terns, came swooping and falling headlong over the lower part of the Head. Again the cry rang out, resembling now the jubilant *wick-gewr, wick-gewr* of a kittiwake, and the first homing arctic skuas, harried by and harrying the already resident bonxies, dived down to the little Corrie of Pundsgeo. In comparison with the gigantic bonxies they appeared fine petrel-like birds with exceedingly long wings.

This was almost certainly the initial return to their breeding grounds of any of the Noss Skuas – as I shall refer to them hereafter – from wintering in the South Atlantic. One couple (pair 1) took up their position on a hillock forty-five yards south of a small peat stack in the middle of the corrie and couched down in the hot afternoon sun. They were a little shy in their new environment and when I rose from the slope of the hill seventy yards distant, to improve my observation point in relation to the angle of the sun, one of the pair made a little flight from the

161

R·A·Richardson.

Arctic Skuas.

hillock. On my lying down again, however, at a distance of fifty yards, it relaxed and drank from a drain, before settling twenty yards from its companion. This restless bird was handsomely plumaged a uniform sooty-brown except for a just perceptible darkening on the crown of its head. Its mate was a rather paler shade of brown and, with the sun shining full upon it, there was the suggestion of a cream pigment underlying the brown. Especially was this so on the nape and the sides of the neck, in contrast to the dark-brown cap.

A third bird (pair 2), another uniformly dusky one, settled on a prominent grassy mound fifty yards north of the peat stack. On the ridges on either side of the corrie, and from one hundred and fifty to two hundred yards from the peat stack, were six pairs of bonxies, and there were other pairs on the Maiden's Paps to the south. Only northwards were there no bonxies. That way the corrie shelved down to the steel-blue sea with, in the far background, the long low brown ranges of Mainland curving round to the high island of Whalsay and the long chain of the Outer Skerries, which terminated in the tall white light stack on Bound Skerry.

For a long while nothing exciting happened. Rabbits ran around the stack and a wheatear sang from its dome; the jingling bells of piping oystercatchers sounded intermittently from the green holm of Pundsgeo; the crying of kittiwakes passing endlessly upcoast never died for a second. And then, after an hour's interval, number 2 was joined by a beautiful bird with a white nape and belly. A pale greyish-brown band, barely meeting across its breast, alone marred the white expanse of its underparts. This bird was more active than the other three, which had just sat quietly, and pecked about its mossy mound. None of the four, however, displayed any apparent interest in the occasional bonxie passing over the corrie, though those bonxies on the knolls overlooking it acknowledged such passers by with the customary arching of wings.

After an hour and a half and just as I was about to approach the four more closely, for cloud was veiling the sun and rain threatened, the dusky bird of pair 1 rose and stretched its wings, spread them to preen – revealing a faint white lattice effect on the primaries – and then took off and flapped steadily east out to sea, leaving its mate still sitting on their mound. Its departure evoked a single *ayer-yah* from pair 2, though they remained sitting. This was the cry so much resembling that of the kittiwake and also recalled the kaaloo's 'bagpipes'.

A quarter of an hour later the other three also took wing. Almost immediately, however, three flighted into the corrie again, with soft *pewk*ing calls, and the two dusky individuals pitched down on the heather a score of yards apart, the white bird going out again at once.

After a ten minute interval 2 moved up on to its mound and 1 to a spot near its original alighting place – for there was no obvious mound in this bird's territory. But on its brown mate coming in five minutes later, it at once took flight : whereupon the brown bird joined 2 on its mound! Almost immediately five more (four dark ones and one white) circled over the corrie with soft *pewk-pewk* calls and that ringing *ayer-yah, ayer-yah*. The two on the ground appeared to ignore them, though one of them was the dark bird 1. The latter came down to circle close around my head, as dusky as a swift or a stormy petrel, and alighted in its territory : whereupon the dark bird 2 took wing in its turn.

The latter alighted again a quarter of an hour later, when seven skuas were wafting and swooping around the corrie and then chasing out to sea – whence five returned still in pursuit of one another, and two white and two dark birds settled amicably on pair 2's mound and one dark bird near pair 1's mound. Then they were up once more, with wild *ayer-yah, ayer-yah, ayer-yah* : to settle yet again, this time with the two white birds on pair 2's mound and three dark ones near pair 1's mound. Ten minutes later one of the three dark birds rose and alighted *between* the two white ones, without any offence being taken. But in another five minutes most of them were on the wing again, and the two white birds chased each other with characteristic upward zoom, before making off to sea with other partners, leaving behind the dusky bird 1 and its brown mate. The former was restless, for it first moved across to pair 2's untenanted mound and then, when I flushed it, rose and settled by its mate again.

At this juncture I left, after two and a half hours of watching, but returned again an hour later at 6.15 p.m., when a group of four dark birds were standing *ayer-yah*ing, with some arching of wings. Two made off at my coming, leaving pair 1 *in situ*. Subsequently, after first walking and then flying a little way from its mound, the brown bird flew back to its mate. The latter – the female, as events showed – greeted him with a high-pitched *pewk*, throwing up her bill nearly vertically; and he, bowing his head and turning up wide-open bill sideways, with wings loosened at the shoulders and tail spiked up, uttered a violent cry and nuzzled into her : whereupon she too bowed her head to him. This ceremony was enacted more quickly than I can recount and immediately afterwards they took a fly round, alighted separately and walked far apart, apparently feeding. At 6.45 p.m., when I left for the cliffs, another bird passed over the corrie and both pair 1 birds departed seaward, leaving the dark bird of pair 2 sitting alone on its mound.

In all, about a dozen skuas had visited the island on this initial day of homing. Of the dozen only three pairs had taken up what would presumably be territorial mounds – a third pair of dusky birds being present in the evening on the grassy siding above the Cradle Holm, where they were harrying members of the small colony of lesser black-backed gulls, which were then beginning to take up territories there. Pair 1 had demonstrated that they were a mated pair. Pair 2 showed every appearance of being such. No illwill, however, was shown towards other skuas visiting their mounds. Little groups of birds, indeed, took pleasure in each other's company and in pursuit on the wing.

On 29 April there was neither sight nor sound of any skuas about the island from 6.35 a.m. until 2.20 p.m., when two pairs appeared over the Pundsgeo corrie, but made off again immediately; and I saw no more of them up to 5 p.m., when I left.

At 6 p.m. the next evening, however, both pairs 1 and 2 were sitting on their mounds and another pair (3) had taken up their position fifty yards west of the peat stack. Of this pair one was dusky and the other a rather darker brown than the male of pair 1, the brown shading into pale grey on neck and throat. Very shortly four more came playing over the corrie with their customary cries. Very dark and sharp were their silhouettes against the heavy grey sky on this evening of light rain. At their noisy coming the male of pair 1 stood up and answered them with the customary *ayer-yah*. But after this brief surge of feeling both pairs 1 and 2 walked quietly about their territories, occasionally chasing insects with little runs and leaps, as a wagtail might do. Then pair 2 took a little fly round and, on alighting again, the

Arctic Skuas

white male circled round its mate with spiny tail elevated. On a third bird joining them, however, the three stood together with heads thrown back and *ayer-yah*ed, their wide-open bills revealing a pinkish-white interior.

Meanwhile three others were stooping at a bonxie on the North Croo, beyond the ridge on the north side of the corrie (though none had paid any heed to my dogs), and I heard a new cry, a musical *yeh-yeh-wow*, and remembered Edmund Selous's description long before my time :

> 'Oh, that cry, that wild, wild cry, that music of the winds, the clouds, the drifting rain and mist – like them, free as them, voicing their freedom, making their spirit articulate! ... Let it live for ever in the memory of him who has sat on the great Ness-side, on the dividing-line of sea and sky, and heard it pealing so clearly, so cheerily, so gladly wild, so wildly, madly glad. So let it come to him again in his own soul's music, scudding with the clouds, driving with the driving mists, ringing out like *the wild bells to the cold sky*. And never let that sky be blue that it sings to, unless in pale, moist patches, drowning amidst water clouds; and never let there be a sun, to be called one, but only a glint and a gleaming, a storming of stormy light, a wet beam flung on a rain-cloud.'

Pairs 1 and 2 were still present at 6.40 p.m. and it was possible that they, and perhaps other pairs, passed the night in their territories, for I heard their cries at 4 a.m. the next morning, and a quarter of an hour later found both in the corrie, besides other pairs on the North Croo, and as many as seven together would come crying over the corrie, continually going to and from the sea.

By the afternoon of 3 May, when both pairs 1 and 2 had third dusky birds with them on their mounds, the skuas were returning in numbers to their breeding grounds, at least sixteen being present. When I went out of Noss in the evening a dark pair rose from Ullins Water, that little lochan beside the road in the dip between the Ander and the Ward. To this freshwater lochan the skuas had been accustomed to repair from Noss, for the purpose of bathing, from time out of memory. And the next evening, when there may have been a score of pairs in Noss, a pair of white birds were bathing there, dipping and rearing heads and breasts, with frequent *pewks,* and lying on their sides, white bellies turned up. On subsequent days as many as eight might be seen bathing at one time and pairs would be going out of Noss, Ullins-ward, as late as 9.30 p.m.

At the end of a week's residence on the island there was a raising of the threshold of territorial awareness among the skuas. On the male of pair 1 joining pair 2 in their territory, but off their mound, on the evening of 5 May, for instance, and all three pointing their beaks to heaven with the wonted joyful *ayer-yah,* its mate immediately mobbed the white male of pair 2, which retreated therewith to its mound. (As it happened these were the only pairs present on the island at this hour.) Again, when a brown bird alighted midway between the mounds of these two pairs the next morning it was harried by one bird from each pair : while a dusky stranger subsequently alighting beside pair 2 was driven away solely by the two throwing up their heads and *ayer-yah*ing. But for the most part pairs 1, 2 and 3 were quiet, sitting or standing about in pairs or solitary, rising from time to time to fly round after others of their fellows. When, however, a bonxie crossed the corrie, pair 1 broke into a chorus of *yeh-yeh-wow*s — the cry associated with the aggressive impulse — and rising for a short flight, alighted on another of their several mounds; while on two pairs suddenly leaving the corrie the cry of the peregrine was heard immediately after their departure.

These three pairs, together with that pair above the Cradle

Holm and a white couple in the south-west corner of the moor at the head of the Voe of the Mels,* were still the only pairs to be seen regularly at their territories – though some nights at any rate they passed out at sea, for there were no skuas on the island between 9.30 p.m. and 12.15 a.m. on 10 May. Though all were in possession of regular territories, so far as area was concerned, none except pair 2 used the same mound at every alighting, but stood indiscriminately on any slight eminence within the territorial area : the reason being that pair 2's territory alone included a salient hillock, a well-developed mound trodden flat into grass and moss comparable to those of the heavier bonxies.

By 10 May, however, two more pairs, 18 (both brown) and 39 (dusky brown), had taken up territories at the extreme south and north ends of the corrie; and morning and evening now there was wonderfully swift aerial chasing by twos and threes over their territories, with lightning sharp turns, stoops, and sixty-foot vertical climbs, to the ringing *ayer-yah, ayer-yah* : but at midday hardly a pair or even a solitary bird was to be found on the island.

Ten days later another pair (4) had taken up their position west of pair 3. Of this pair one was dusky and the other brown with paler underparts and a distinctly yellowish neck ring much lighter in colour than the necks of those brown birds already noted. In addition a seventh pair (5) had established themselves one hundred yards north-east of the peat stack. One of these was a white bird – probably that second white bird present on 28 April – and the other, like 4, a yellow-necked bird. This new white bird and pair 1 intermobbed over the corrie at break-neck speed with rush and 'scrap' of wings, to the accompaniment of that incessant tern-like *pewk* and sometimes the ringing *ayer-yah*. Even when the pair alighted on their mound the white bird continued to mob them, forcing them to bow their heads – at which indignity the two, standing side by side, lifted their heads, with the customary protest; and it also mobbed all other birds present in the corrie, while its mate stood on the peat stack. After all had settled down once more on their mounds, but were as yet a little uneasy at my newly arrived presence, I could hear a quieter form of the aggressive *yeh-yeh-wow*. But tension was unprecedentedly high among all the skuas present, the entrance into the corrie of any newcomer being the signal for a general aerial interharrying. The

*A pair of white birds have occupied this territory for at least twelve years.

cause of this raising of the emotional threshold became apparent when at 12.40 p.m. the male of pair 4 after *yup-yup-yup*-ing, while his mate pointed her bill to the ground, jumped on and off her back three times and finally mated with her, at which she turned her head up to him, screeching. A number of other pairs were also to be observed mating in various parts of the island on this twenty-third day of residence, including those solitary pairs which, nesting among gulls or bonxies hundreds of yards from the nearest neighbours of their own species, lacked any social stimulus.

At this stage one or other member of those pairs that had taken up territories were probably present in these at all hours of the twenty-four; but except for an occasional song from a lark it was quiet in the corrie at 8 p.m. on the calm evening of 23 May, with the sun still well up a little west of north after a perfect summer day – though banks of fog and cloud resting on the Ward were a reminder of a chill easterly air. Shortly after my arrival, however, l became aware that the paler bird of brown pair 18 was uttering a strange mewing cry, as if in pain, while bowed forward almost vertically. Evidently the urge to round a nest was upon her, and after a little of this anticking the male made his way to her, and I heard a thin whistling note, resembling the tystie's penny-whistle piping. This apparently excited the male of pair 1 in the adjacent territory, for he flew up and mobbed the couple persistently, and for several minutes the peace was broken by persistent *ayer-yah*ing and *pewk*ing, as the three mobbed and flighted round and round. Ten minutes earlier this disturber of the peace himself had mated five times, to all appearances at the female's invitation, as she bowed forward a little, pecking at the ground; while, on the male of pair 3 running to his mate, the two got together excitedly, head to head, and the latter bowing forward and turning up her bill to him, solicited him to feed her. This he did, disgorging some morsel on to the ground, which she picked up. Having swallowed it she pivoted around on her breast before him with spread tail elevated. Then, after a fly round, she solicited him again, and he disgorged a second time in a different place. (Courtship feeding continued as late as the ninth day after eggs had been laid and it was also observed in a nonbreeding pair.) All the pairs in the corrie – at least nine being present – displayed every intention of staying in for the night, as they sat on their mounds, or walked and ran around chasing insects; and they were still present at 10.30 p.m., when the Maiden's Paps were swathed in mist.

By 25 May I had twenty-five territorial mounds pegged and numbered and there were between thirty and thirty-five pairs of skuas present on the island. Their mounds were very much more difficult to locate than those of most of the bonxies, because of the already noted absence of salient hillocks and their habit of pitching down anywhere in a territory, and also because of their shyer nature, which led to their taking flight and indulging in aerial pursuit at the least disturbance – though once I had settled down near a territory or colony they would perform their antics without concern at a distance of no more than thirty-five yards.

During the last week of May two nonbreeding pairs, 7 and 28 (the first pair brown and white and the second both brown), had established themselves in the corrie east and west of the peat stack, and on 17 June another brown and white nonbreeding pair (29) took up position in the extreme north of the corrie well down towards the sea. There were thus now ten pairs of skuas in the corrie, their territories covering an area of about seven acres, with maximum axes of two hundred and fifty yards by two hundred and forty yards : while the average distance between the mounds of the breeding pairs was seventy-five yards, with a range of from forty yards to one hundred and ten yards.

Finally, by the end of June, when the last of the nonbreeding pairs had taken up territories on the island, the skuas' total strength was thirty-seven and a half pairs, of which thirty-one were breeding pairs, and six and a half nonbreeding – the half pair being a solitary bird which, after associating with an isolated pair west of the Setter *crö* on 24 June, subsequently occupied a territory east of the *crö* for a few days, but failed to acquire a mate.

The thirty-seven and a half pairs had distributed themselves in two main colonies – one in the Corrie of Pundsgeo, the other on the moor south and east of the hill dyke. There was an extension from the latter colony on to the North Croo, and there were isolated single pairs at Setter, on the moor immediately below the Maiden's Paps, on the sidings above the Feadda Ness and the Cradle Holm, and at the east corner of Rumble Wick. There were fifteen pairs in the second main colony, that on the moor, two of them nonbreeding. This colony covered an area of about sixteen acres with maximum axes of three hundred and eighty yards by three hundred and thirty yards, the average distance between the mounds of breeding pairs being sixty-eight yards, with a range of from thirty to one hundred yards. Thus each pair occupied rather more than one acre, compared with the seven-tenths of an acre to each pair in the Pundsgeo colony. Excluding isolated pairs the total area within the skuas' sphere of influence amounted to about one hundred acres, though, as we have seen, the bonxies had driven wedges into the west moor North Croo colony and extension and also between the Croo and the Pundsgeo corrie.

2. *Young Skuas*

On the afternoon of 27 May the scene in the Corrie of Pundsgeo was one of great animation, with any number from one to ten skuas in the air at a time harrying the westbound stream of kittiwakes, which were passing down to the Voe of the Mels in quest of building material. As many as eight skuas might be harrying a single kittiwake, striking at it with their feet, as it twisted and turned with agonised *zoo-oo-oo*. The mobbing of bonxies was also persistent, and there was a continual chorus of *ayer-yah* and a circling and rushing at breakneck speed of these giant 'swifts' low over the corrie. Yet hitherto they had ignored the constant passage of kittiwakes over their territories. What was the cause of this unprecedented excitement at the end of their first month of residence?

I had not been five minutes in the corrie before I perceived that the dusky female of pair 2 was behaving in a strange manner, 'sitting back' on her tail and thrashing partially spread wings unstably, to the accompaniment of an abnormal wheezing cry. Presuming this curious behaviour to indicate that she had eggs I walked towards her mound to find them, but could not. A quarter of an hour later, when I was still searching for her nest, she displayed again. The spreading of the primaries, drooping to the ground on either side of her, revealed the two long white quill stripes which, in flight, formed a thin white margin to the front edge of the wing. Though, by her displaying again, I supposed myself to be close to the nest its whereabouts still eluded me, and it was not until the third attempt ten minutes later that I found one warm egg on a little round of dead bents in the thick herbage nineteen yards from her mound. The round of bents was just laid flat on the ground and no attempt had been made to scoop out a hollow as the bonxie normally did. The egg — very small in comparison with the latter's — was a dark olive-brown heavily mottled with brown and dark-brown blotches.

The next morning she had laid a second similarly marked egg. She was still the only Pundsgeo bird with an egg, though the male of a pair on the west moor had mobbed one of my dogs — the first to do so — while his mate displayed in the curious manner already described, but I was unable to find their nest. Though the Pundsgeo corrie pairs were quiet on this morning of thick mist there was great activity on the moor, with those bonxies on the southern edge of the skua colony mobbing me and the skuas harrying them, playing with them as they pleased, with their marvellously swift flight, and striking them with their feet with tremendous and audible force, without the bonxies retaliating.

On the evening of the 30 May, I observed that the male of pair 1 was waving spread wings to the accompaniment of a chittering *ik-ik-ik* : but he did not return to a nest the while I leant up against the peat stack; so, eventually, I circled his pegged mound in widening rounds and found one pale-olive egg on a few wisps of bent ten yards off the mound. And though neither of pair 18 in the adjacent territory displayed, I very quickly located a single olive egg belonging to them on a little mat of dead bents thirteeen yards from their mound. As I hurried Gungstiewards, after nine hours on the hill, two screaming pairs on the moor were falling about with waving wings, and I happened by chance on two dull-olive eggs lying on the bare sward of a little ridge eleven yards from their mound — twenty-five yards off the mound being the maximum distance from it that any pair laid their eggs. It was evidently high time that I was ascertaining the precise stage reached by all the pairs, and, after intensive search the next day, I located a further six clutches, including a pale olive-green egg, with a blurred brown zone, belonging to pair 3.

I was surprised to find that pairs 1 and 18 still had only one cold egg apiece on the morning of 1 June and both females were absent. Pairs 2 and 3, however, had laid theirs on consecutive days and pair 39 on the first and third days. Though pair 3's eggs were cool the female displayed, running crouched along the ground, with an incessant *jig-jig-jig*. In the afternoon both pair 1 were present and their egg was warm, though neither displayed. I found ultimately that the second egg might be laid on the second, third, or fourth day : though only pairs 1 and 18 allowed the maximum interval of seventy-two hours to elapse between the laying of their two eggs. The male skuas were more often out at sea than present in their territories, but they did a certain amount of incubating : the changeover on the nest being conducted without ceremony.

A fortnight elapsed. Then on 17 June I found that one of pair 2's eggs were just perceptibly fractured, and the next day the fracture, though still slight, extended half way round the top of the egg. Two days after this there was a small hole in the shell and a cheeping chick was working away within. Though both parents were present they neither displayed nor mobbed me, but stood quietly on their mound. Five hours later the diameter of the hole had increased from half to three-quarters of an inch and the egg had turned over, with the hole to the ground.

On the morning of 21 June, about ninety hours after the first fracturing and on the twenty-sixth day of incubation, the chick had hatched, and on the bents, just free of its shell, its purplish hair barely covering its raw pink skin, was the nestling. Its fellow was working at a half-inch hole in the other egg. Again, both parents were present and the female displayed slightly, but I was not subjected to any mobbing until I had examined the nestling, and had retreated forty yards, when the white male attacked me once.

The next afternoon the other chick had also hatched on the twenty-sixth day, less than forty hours after the first fracture, and had nearly dried off into a velvety blackish-brown down of a peculiarly silky mole-like texture. (The period of hatching to drying off in the one instance recorded precisely proved to be thirteen hours.) Its irides, like those of the bonxie nestlings, were brown with dark-blue pupils; its gape was pale-pink; its legs and feet palest pinkish-blue. By this time its fellow nestling was two feet out of the nest, and both parents were again present, the female displaying only slightly, as on the previous occasion.

By 24 June, when both nestlings were seven yards out of the nest, no marked increase or disparity in their size was noticeable : whereas the three-day-old nestling of another pair was very much bigger than its imperfectly dry fellow. The latter pecked repeatedly at the elder and gripped it by the bill when I placed the two together in the nest : just as all these skua nestlings, in contrast to those of the bonxies, pecked at my fingers, while one almost ready to fly would first peck at my fingers and then, with characteristic confusion, at its own carpal joints. This morning pair 1's first nestling (also hatched on the twenty-sixth day, twenty-five to twenty-six days being the normal incubation period) had already moved towards the edge of its nest, though only three parts dried, and the female mobbed me, as she had been doing since 8 June. Twenty-four hours later this nestling was under a bank four yards out of the nest : but the second chick did not hatch until 27 June – an interval complementary to the seventy-two hours that had elapsed between the laying of the two eggs.

As soon as a skua nestling gained sufficient strength its main objective was to get out of the nest and run away from its fellow, and thirty-six hours after the first had hatched the two nestlings were never to be found together in the nest. On 26 June indeed, I rescued one pair's three-day-old nestling from a burrow halfway down the far side of a drain two feet wide, while the female mobbed me.

By 1 July pair 2's younger nestling, now ten days old, was twenty-seven yards away from the nest and its elder fellow was not to be found. The sooty female sat unconcerned on her mound, while I hunted around, for when their young hatched some of the adults became much more confident, allowing me to approach to within eight yards of them without betraying uneasiness. The female of pair 1, however, and both pair 5, whose young one had hatched on 23 June, continued to mob me directly I approached their territories. Once the nestlings reached the age of ten days I had the greatest difficulty in finding them in their lairs in the long grass, and to keep track of them it was essential that they should be ringed as soon as possible after the ninth day, by which age the 'ankle' was of a size to retain the rings without overlapping. Moreover 80 per cent of the casualties among young occurred in this first ten days after hatching. Such evidence as there was suggested that this mortality – thirty per cent of the total hatch – was caused mainly by the adult skuas themselves attacking those nestlings of neighbouring pairs wandering into their territories which, as we have seen, were very crowded in the two main colonies. On 4 July, for instance, the older of pair 39's nestlings – a six-day-old chick – had wandered into pair 2's territory and lay dead by the latter's mound, seventy-five yards from its own nest; and previous to this on 29 June, when neither of another pair of adults on the west moor were present in their territory, I found that their elder nine-day nestling had been killed by pecks on the side of the head, though this territory was far removed from those of any bonxies – which in any case were never permitted to alight in the skuas' territories. Where, however, the latter were adjacent to those of the bonxies, then there was a tendency for the parents to attract the young outwards from the bonxie territories. It was possible that both nestlings of one pair on the North Croo were killed by a bonxie whose big nestling had strayed near their territory : while those of another pair on the Croo may have succumbed to a lesser black-backed gull which also had chicks there. On the other hand a third pair, whose isolated territory was adjacent to that earlier mentioned savage bonxie, reared both their young successfully.

It has been noted that both parents of one pair were absent from their territory when their elder chick was nine days old. In marked contrast to the behaviour of the bonxies the majority of the skuas began to desert their young temporarily about the tenth day, one pair indeed deserting theirs for a short interval as early as the fourth day. There were, however, exceptions to this practice, for the females of pairs 1 and 2 were never observed by me to leave their territories during the hours of daylight, though their mates put in only intermittent and brief appearances.

On the evening of 8 July I watched the female of pair 2 feed her two young, about forty yards apart, disgorging on to the ground to them, while the male sat on his mound. She then went out to sea and did not return for the next hour. On her departure the two young ones started walking about, taking no notice, however, of the white male sitting on the mound in full view of them. Though they were one hundred and fifty yards distant from me I could see the rings on their legs flashing in the evening sun. After ten minutes' exercise both went into cover, though the elder made a brief appearance a quarter of an hour later. On my return nearly two hours after this, the female was back again.

Three evenings later the male of pair 3 arrived from sea and, alighting on his mound, circled with little paces about his mate in courting posture with head stretched out low to the ground. Both then flew a little way to (as I supposed) drink from a drain, and on their return a young one approached them : whereupon both flew to it and the male, with that same courting posture, brought up a thin silver fish which the younger one took from his bill, dropped, picked up from the ground, and swallowed. The female took an active interest in the proceedings, during which they were persistently mobbed by adjacent pair 4. The latter, having lost their first clutch of eggs, were now completing the incubation of a second clutch – olive in colour like the first but of a rather duller pigment with heavy brown blotching – in a new 'nest' twenty-five yards from their first one. On 15 July this pair triumphantly hatched one velvety blackish-brown chick, but on 7 August the latter was dead near pair 1's mound.

3. *Fledgelings and Pirates*

On the fine calm night of 15 July I was making my way along the sea edge of the North Croo, bound for the guillemots' cliffs, when I saw the first young skua on the wing in slow flapping flight. With golden-chestnut head, mane and breast gleaming in the evening sun it was a breathtakingly beautiful bird in its first flight plumage, which bore not the slightest resemblance to any of the adult phases and for which none of the prefledging plumages had prepared me. This unseasonable fledgeling belonged to a pair of whose territory I had been aware since the earliest days, but whose eggs – they being one of the nondisplaying pairs – I had never had time to find on the Croo's shorn plantain pasture devoid of landmark, though these must have been laid more than a week earlier than any in the Pundsgeo colony. Mobbed by other pairs of adults on the Croo, at which the one parent present stooped, the fledgeling threw up a fish in midair, the disgorge being caught by one of its assailants, and alighted clumsily. Two days later it was quite strong on the wing. On this day, 17 July, the island was entombed in its thickest sea-fog, and there was a great chorus of *ayer-yah*ing in the Pundsgeo corrie in the afternoon, with that swift chase of urgent wings I recalled from other foggy days.

By 20 July, pair 2's younger chick also seemed all set for its first flight. In contrast to the golden fledgeling this was a dark-brown bird with copper coloured underparts and ivory-blue legs paling off into an ivory-white patch at the base of the black webbed feet. But it was the next afternoon, on the thirtieth day after hatching, that it first rose on the wing as I approached its territory and, after a seventy-five-yard flight across the corrie, tumbled on to its head on alighting. It still, however, preferred walking to flight and on my retreating walked around for long distances. Forty minutes later both young ones of this pair were walking about on pair 39's ridge attended by the female, while the male sat on his mound, tern-like, stern and spiky tail projecting in a long upward slant. On this rare summer day, with wisps of fog cloud clinging to the Noup, I could make out the bright rings on the chick's legs at a distance of two hundred and fifty yards, and the elder chick shone a glossy black, much blacker than its sooty parent. After drinking twice, ten minutes later the male went out to sea – returning after forty minutes – and when I subsequently approached the elder chick it, too, took wing (on the thirty-first day) with less effort than the younger, and also made a seventy-five-yard flight with a good alighting, followed by a two-minute flight round the corrie, terminating in a partial tumble.

On the moor a uniformly dark-brown fledgeling was sitting *upright* beside its crouching and still unfledged younger fellow, a black bird with a tawny mane and throat and copper underparts. As soon as the young skua got on the wing, but not before – and the average fledging period was twenty-nine to thirty days, with extremes of twenty-seven and thirty-three days – it assumed this upright posture when sitting, in contrast to the crouching posture to which it adhered consistently throughout the prefledging stage, even when fully feathered. Similarly, it was only during the last week before fledging that pairs of young were to be found sitting together.

By 25 July both pair 2's fledgelings were strong on the wing on the fifth day after fledging, even twisting and turning a little in flight, and when the male parent took wing from his mound the elder fledgeling flew after him and solicited him with the same antic as the courting adult; but I could not see whether it was fed or not though, as the parent subsequently drank, it probably was. On the male returning to his mound the fledgeling harried its fellow, swooping up vertically and hovering above it like an adult, striking it with its feet. After this exhibition it again solicited its parent; whereupon the latter flew away to sea and the fledgeling took its place on the mound. The male returned after an absence of twenty minutes and this time disgorged a fat silver sandeel to the fledgeling, which it picked up and swallowed, after which its parent flew down to a drain for the customary drink.

The next morning both fledgelings were sitting on the mound with the female, who however went out to sea a quarter of an hour later. For the first time for many weeks the female of pair 1 was also absent – though she returned very shortly after my arrival – and parents of other fledgelings came and went at frequent intervals. Now that the latter were between four and five weeks old the parents raised no objection on finding fledgelings of other pairs associating with their own young in their territories and even sitting on their mounds. On the other hand two casualties occurred during this earliest stage of the fledging : pair 5's single fledgeling and pair 1's younger one disappearing. The chances were that they had been killed by those bonxies with territories on the east ridge, up to which it was their custom to fly from time to time; for I had previously noticed one of the North Croo fledgelings, just on the wing, being mobbed by both bonxies and lesser black-backs, and on alighting close beside me it disgorged two fish, one of which it swallowed again. Another fledgeling had a feather knocked out of it by the swinging feet of a bonxie. When, however, the latter fledgeling had been on the wing for fifteen days it itself mobbed an adult of its own kind, while another ten-day fledgeling mobbed a bonxie in company with its parent, and a second fledgeling of the same age was sufficiently confident to mob an adult lesser black-back and ten days later to mob a young bonxie.

There were days in the first week of August when all was quiet in the Corrie of Pundsgeo morning and evening. Few adults were present and they did not mob me. There were none of the recent aerial pursuits and the cries now came from the fledgelings, which at the age of five or six weeks, occasionally *ayer-yah*ed squeakily or *yeh-wow*ed thinly. But the cry most frequently heard and directly associated with the long absences of both parents was a new cry on the island – an incessant hunger cry, an unforgettable plaintive mewing *wiv-wiv-wiv-wiv-wow*, which came from those groups of four or five fledgelings gathered together for company on one pair's mound, or moving from mound to mound without interference from the few adults present. This new cry had been anticipated by a single nestling which, on the fourth day after hatching, had uttered a reedy little rippling note, additional to the normal squeak.

Their parents were, however, still feeding the fledgelings and at 5 p.m. on 7 August, when for the first time both pair 1 were absent, the male of pair 2 fed both his young.

Where did the skuas obtain their food supplies? Until the third week in June when, it will be recalled, the earliest nestlings were just hatching, Noss provided no answer to this question. Occasionally one would glide leisurely out over Rumble Wick and on 3 June one harried a herring gull over the Sound. But that was all. It seemed that they must obtain their food at the source – that is, at the fishing grounds of the gulls and kittiwakes off the west coast of Shetland : for the latter were not yet returning to Noss with food for young. Much harrying of kittiwakes and also terns took place in the sea area a couple of miles or so north of Noss, though only homeward bound kittiwakes were harried, despite the fact that the latter tended to fly at a greater height than those outwardbound from Noss.

By the third week in June, however, both skuas and bonxies were to be seen circling and planing over Rumble Wick at all hours of the day : yet it was not until the afternoon of 21 June that between 12.45 p.m. and 2 p.m. I for the first time saw guillemots twice chased by skuas and once forced down on to the waters of the Wick. This was also the first day that I was able to make out a guillemot carrying fish and the first day that I saw puffins bringing up transparent grey fry to their nesting burries. Interesting that the pirate and his victims should all hatch out their young at the same date!

Four afternoons later at 3.15 p.m. a skua, darting into the cliffs from several hundred yards out in the Wick, forced down a guillemot with a clearly perceived fish but made no attempt to descend to the latter on its submerging. Five minutes later a second guillemot was forced down in a nose dive, with what result I could not see. The speed of these pursuits was terrific, complicated to follow, and often ultimately lost below the overhang of the cliffs. Moreover the field of activity was too vast to be covered by binoculars. One had first to spot a likely looking skua with the naked eye and then put up the binoculars at the appropriate moment. Even so, these sharp cut dark skuas were exceedingly difficult to keep in view against the steel-blue and grey sea. At 3.24 p.m. there was another apparently unsuccessful force down of a guillemot and half an hour later yet another after a chase right into the cliffs, followed by two more.

On the afternoon of 1 July there were more of these apparently abortive chases, the victim twice escaping by diving, after being chased along the surface of the water by, in one instance, two skuas. Never once, however, was a skua seen to stoop and retrieve a fish either in midair or from the water, though in one instance a gannet made one of those beautiful flat dives into the glass-green waters of the Wick and retreived a fish dropped by a guillemot forced down by a pirate. One could only presume that piracy at the deepsea fishing grounds was very much more productive than off Noss. Were it not so, it would be difficult to understand how the adult skua or bonxie could secure enough food for itself, let alone for its young. Two evenings later, for instance, a skua chased a tern (also fishing for young) over the Nesti Voe without result, another harried a lesser black-back unsuccessfully, and though I witnessed many chases of guillemots (and of a puffin on 6 July) all were abortive or the result obscured by the cliffs; and on 12 July I distinctly saw a guillemot, forced down to the water, retain its fish. Pursuits of guillemots continued until 31 July, when there were very few of them still on the wing in Rumble Wick, and there was one pursuit of a fledgeling kittiwake over the Nesti Voe; but not once throughout the season did I observe a skua actually rob successfully any species of bird except fledgelings of its own kind!

Throughout the second week in August, in contrast to the first week, large numbers of adults were present and noisy on the breeding grounds at all hours of the day, and as early as 3.25 a.m. on 8 August there was a general chorus of *ayeh-yah, ayeh-yah* over the moor from birds gliding with decurved wings, like joy-flighting redshanks, or standing with heads thrown back. Once again I heard that high rush of wings and saw those incredibly swift stoops and anglings of pairs chasing in rhythmic flight. With a sudden renewal of territorial emotion the female of pair 1 stooped at me, brushing my hair with her feet. At sunrise, nearly two hours later, there were more aerial pursuits and mobbing of bonxies than there had been for some weeks. Ten minutes after sunrise the first fledgeling was fed, after dancing for a short space before its parent and waving extended wings, hollowed so that the closed primary tips touched the ground. This dancing was identical with the feigning display of the incubating or brooding adults and also with the hunger dance of the young bonxie.

What was the significance of this sudden raising of the emotional threshold? On 11 August I noticed that the Cradle Holm fledgeling, now eight weeks old, was missing, and though large numbers of adults were again present next day more fledgelings were absent, while those present were sitting about anywhere and were continually on the move from one territory to another. That earliest missing fledgeling was present again on 13 August but, even as I drew near, it left its one parent on the ground and taking wing, flew out over Rumble Wick. Ignoring two adults returning Nosswards from sea it glided a great way out over the Wick, before making a brief stoop at a kittiwake, after which I lost sight of it. On the same day another fledgeling, ten days younger, circled widely out over the Voe of the Mels from its territory outside the hill dyke and stooped at a young herring gull, while one of the Pundsgeo fledgelings chased a rockpipit down in a geo. Complementary to these excursions was the fact that the hunger cry was now only occasionally heard, and when pair 3's two fledgelings, neither of them quite eight weeks old, danced frenziedly with wavering wings before one parent, the latter moved away from them and ultimately flew out to sea. It was evident, then, that between the seventh and eighth weeks the parents stopped bringing food to the young and the latter began hunting their own food, foraging ever farther afield. With only their own food to seek the adults were thus able to spend much of their time on the breeding grounds.

On the morning of 17 August I noticed that the numbers of both adults and young were fewer than for the past nine days, and that evening there were no fledgelings on the North Croo. The next day a fledgeling accompanied by one parent was bathing at Ullins Water, and by 21 August all the adults and young on the North Croo and most of those on the moor had left the island for good, when eight or nine weeks old and from three and a half to five weeks after fledging. On 22 August fledgeling 18, now eight weeks old, was still uttering its hunger cry to its parent flying above it, but by the end of the month all the Pundsgeo colony had left the corrie, parents and young leaving together. The only fledgelings then remaining on the island were two on the west moor. These two, both singles, had not hatched until 5 and 6 July;

but they, too, left on 5 or 6 September. Thereafter no skuas were seen on Noss, though the previous autumns two had been present as late as 10 September.

Of the seven nonbreeding pairs, one pair and also the unmated bird occupied their territories for a few days only after their initial return in June, but the remaining five pairs were more or less regular attendants from late May or June until the middle of August, at which date those breeding pairs that had previously lost eggs or young began to disappear. In the middle of July up to seven of these nonbreeding or unsuccessful breeding birds might be seen in a little group on or near a nonbreeding pair's mound far down in the north corner of the west moor. They did not, however, do anything exciting and this was the only form of sociality recalling the big gathering of nonbreeding bonxies.

In addition to these nonbreeding residents the island was visited by one or two immature-plumaged birds, and on the evening of 23 June one such bird was attempting to associate with various of the breeding birds – I noted it with five different pairs in the space of two hours. This was a white-phase bird with a pure white nape, but with greyish-white bars and mottling on its belly and the underside of its wings, and with dark bars across the white patch on the upper part of its tail, of which the central streamers were as yet only half as long as those of the adult birds. On 28 August this bird was present all day, teaming up first with one pair and then with another : sometimes tolerated, sometimes driven off. But after this I saw no more immature birds until 4 August, when two white-phase birds – one of which stayed until 10 August – were associating with the Pundsgeo colony.

4. *Attack in Defence and Injury-Feigning*

The peculiar antics of a skua, either male or female, when its eggs or young were approached by a human being – but so far as my observation went, no other animal – depended, I found, upon the precise mental and emotional reactions of a particular individual to such a situation. The skua's 'injury-feigning' display very obviously had no conscious luring-away purpose and showed every evidence of being induced by shock to the nervous system, which in the more extreme cases apparently resulted in a temporary, partial paralysis resembling that induced in the rabbit by the hunting stoat. Such display was naturally never indulged in by

Arctic Skua injury-feigning.

any of the nonbreeding birds, even though some of them occupied territories from May until August : for no bird displayed until the day it laid its first egg. Display might continue, however, for seven days after the loss of a clutch, and in the case of one pair there was both display and mobbing until the seventeenth day after the loss of a clutch. Possibly this indicated a second laying, though no eggs were found and no young reared.

Fifteen pairs – except where otherwise indicated the term *pair* in this chapter signifies one or other of two birds of a pair – displayed on the day the first egg was laid and a further five pairs at some stage during incubation. Five others, however, did not display until their chicks hatched and one not until its chick was fledged – when it would do so at a distance of one-hundred yards from me. This pair continued to display extravagantly for a fortnight after the young one was on the wing, and display might continue as late as the twenty-first day after fledging. Three pairs did not display at any time, though they mobbed me when their chicks hatched, and it was not without significance that these were the three pairs whose eggs I was never able to find. One pair was never observed either to display or mob.

No factor, except the psychological, would seem to account for the many exceptions to the rule. And just as there was this variation in displaying and not displaying from one pair to another, so there was variation in the degree and frequency of display. Pair 2, for instance, which was one of the pairs I watched most often, displayed only three times to my knowledge throughout the season – on the day the first egg was laid; on the day the first egg was fractured (about ninety hours before the chick hatched); and on the day the first egg hatched, when one of the pair, the male, mobbed me on the only occasion throughout the season.

Another pair displayed only once, on the seventh day after its young had fledged, when it alighted on the Voe of the Mels and displayed on the water! Another (39) displayed only once or twice, after its chicks hatched, *teey*ing and dancing up and down with flapping wings only fifteen yards from me when I ringed its twelve-day-old chick. This pair also mobbed me once only throughout the season, though persistently mobbing other adults from their territorial ridge when the latter attempted to drink from a pool on the ridge. Finally, one pair displayed once only, on the day their single egg was fractured – though the shell was not punctured until seven days after this and the chick did not hatch until the eighth day!

In contrast pair 5, both male and female, displayed extensively and also mobbed me severely throughout the season, while two other pairs, though displaying extravagantly throughout, never once mobbed me. As a general rule it could be taken that when a skua displayed it had eggs and when it mobbed it had young. Fourteen pairs, however, never mobbed me : among the seventeen pairs that did there was the same variation in severity and intensity from one pair to another as there was in display. Seven pairs mobbed me during incubation – two as early as the third day – though the majority of these did not begin to do so until the eleventh day, which was the first day I was struck on the head. One pair mobbed me once only, the day their egg was fractured (seventy-two hours before the chick was hatched); two pairs not until a day or two before their young fledged; and seven pairs from the first days after their chicks hatched. The majority mobbed me on some occasions, but not others : but there were certain pairs, among them 1, 5 and 3, which were inveterate mobbers right through the season, once they had begun, and they were also liable to display violently. Pair 3 was striking me from the thirteenth day of incubation but, generally speaking, mobbing was most intense during the first ten days after the chicks hatched, and tended to decrease in severity once the young were on the wing – though pair 1, as we have seen, stooped mildly at me on the thirteenth day of fledging. The latter, the most severe mobber of them all, did not actually strike me until the day her first chick hatched, though she had been mobbing me since the fifth day of incubation.

Again, the psychological factor seemed to be the only one accounting for all the variations in the frequency of mobbing and its degree of severity : though it was probable that in the crowded territories of Pundsgeo corrie the exceptional fierceness of pairs 5, 3 and 1 may have subdued the remaining pairs. When mobbing me or other pairs of skuas the three pairs would range over the territories of their fellows, dominating the situation – though this did not prohibit pair 18 from being very severe on that pair of bonxies a hundred yards south of them – while an isolated pair would mob me more than fifty yards distant from their mound. Similarly, one bird of a pair – invariably the female – was much more severe in its mobbing than its mate. The male of pair 1, indeeed, may never have mobbed me throughout the season; and while both birds of a pair would display, the female was again the most persistent and extravagant in her antics.

In addition to the variations in the frequency and intensity of both display and mobbing there were also variations in the pattern of both. As we have noted, the first bird I saw display, the female of pair 2, leant backwards in a broken-bodied manner on its tail, threshing spread wings on the heather, to the accompaniment of a *teez*ing cry. The female of pair 1 substituted the more normal *ik-ik-ik* or *jig-jig-jig* for this wheezing note. Pair 3 shuffled along the ground with wings drooping from the shoulders – all these on the day the first egg was laid.

On the second day 3 *jig-jig*ed incessantly – running crouched along the ground; while the female of another pair staggered about with waving wings fully extended and primaries curving to the ground, twenty-five yards from her mound, and her mate tore at the heather with his beak. He did this again on the day the first egg was fractured, while on the day the first chick hatched the female danced up and down in an extravagant manner.

On the third day of the incubation period the female of pair 5 hopped about, cheeping, with expanded wings and also mobbed me; and by the ninth day she was mobbing me severely, with a sudden, almost perpendicular stoop and a swish of dropping feet, attacking me from the front as much as from back or side.

On the fourth day the female of one pair *yeh-wow*ed, while waving wings only slightly; and both birds of another pair waved wings and fell about (but did nothing the next day); while the female of a third pair uttered a hissing scream when I touched her eggs, and fell about extravagantly within fifteen yards of me, wings rocking to one side or the other. Eight days later she showed every sign of being in a state of shock, as she rocked about, leaning sideways on stiff unflexed legs, allowing herself to be blown about by the wind, hissing and screaming the while.

It was on the fourth day, too, that one of a pair on the North Croo waved only slightly extended wings, but mobbed me, with legs hanging perpendicularly – very delicately in comparison with the mobbing bonxie. Nine days later, after both had displayed together with waving wings and a peculiar twisting of spread tails from side to side, the female mobbed me the most severely of any at that time. With legs hanging perpendicularly (which one did not observe in the bonxie) and striking at me with her feet, to the accompaniment of an incessant *pewk, pewk*, she missed my head by a hair's breadth again and again. On my retreating the pair proceeded to peck holes in a pair of oystercatchers' eggs.

On this day pair 3 also struck me for the first time on the back and sides of the head. The next day both the North Croo pair again displayed and mobbed me very severely, hitting me on the back of the head, *yeh-yeh-wow*ing continuously. But on the fifteenth day, when only the male was present, the latter did not mob me, attacking instead two ewes and lambs when they were close to the nest and smacking the lambs' rumps with his feet. Dogs, sheep and bonxies were targets invariably taking precedence over the human. Sheep, however, were not always mobbed, for there were occasions when a pair would ignore sheep only a yard or two away from their eggs.

It was on the fifteenth day that the female of pair 1 mobbed me for the first time with a devastatingly fierce stoop and a near-miss when I ducked my head, and a week later she was striking at me with her feet – the invariable weapon of both skuas and bonxies – with the vicious swish of a whiplash. Her mobbing was no less severe after the young hatched and on the eighteenth day after hatching she was hitting the stick, which I was now compelled to hold above my head by way of protection, with tremendous force, without apparently causing herself any inconvenience, while the male sat quietly by on their mound. Four days before the young fledged she actually knocked the stick out of my hand with a terrific dunt : but this only quietened her for a few minutes, and she was subsequently successful in striking my head despite the waving stick. At this time of the fledging the Corrie of Punsgeo was a lively spot by day, for in addition to the severe attacks of pairs 5 and 1, the male of pair 3 mobbed me very severely after feeding his young, and I could hear the sound of the blows that one of pair 18 was inflicting on the back of her bonxie neighbour. Yet at 9 p.m. I could walk right across the corrie without a single attempt at mobbing by any of the pairs.

The female of pair 1 was the bird I feared more than any other skua or bonxie on the island. From the time that she first began mobbing me on 9 June she never gave me one day's peace until 26 July when, her young being fledged, she was absent for the first time from her territory; and she continued to mob me sporadically and less violently until 8 August, when her fledgelings had been on the wing for seventeen days. Throughout this period her attacks were continuous so long as I was within fifty yards of her mound. Stooping at me head on, on my first approaching, she would smack my head in passing, swoop up almost vertically, turn, stoop, and smack me from behind : pass on, swoop up, turn, stoop and smack me head on; and continue to do so indefinitely, with an occasional side attack thrown in by way of variation. She never drew blood with those small stinging feet of hers, but the cumulative effect of stinging smack after smack on head and ears was intolerable physically, while even more intolerable was the nervous suspense of waiting for the severe blow that would inevitably follow that menacing whipcrack of feet swung down with incredible force – sufficient to lift a beret clean off one's head. To spend more than a minute or two in search of her crouching young was a torment.

R.A.Richardson.

Gannet about to fly.

X

A STUDY OF A BREEDING COLONY OF GANNETS

1. *Life in a Gannetry*

From that grassy promontory at the south corner of Rumble Wick
I could look down and directly across at some hundreds of gannets
nesting on the back wall of cliff, from a score or two of feet above
the waters of the Wick to within a few feet of the cliff top, which
at this point reached a height of three-hundred and fifty feet. The
nearest half-dozen pairs were on a level with my eye, only thirty
feet distant, and nested nearest to the cliff top of any gannets on
the island. In the dead ground below the overhang of my
observation post were more gannets, but all those nesting on the
back wall could be observed from the observation post (O.P.)
except for a few pairs in dead ground in the upper portions of a
central recess of flattened 'stalls', which shelved backward and
upwards, tier on tier, into the cliff.

Along the upper limits of the gannetry, where there were no
gannets' nests, occasional fulmars occupied niches under slabs of
rock and vomited over any gannets alighting nearby, causing them
to depart again immediately; while, thinly interspersed among the
even rows and tiers of gannets and squeezed into the cells with
which the weathered sandstone was honeycombed in places, were
a few kittiwakes. Here and there a small township of guillemots
huddled up on a platform in an angle of the cliffs. Others were

189

packed tightly a dozen together among the gannets, where the latter were nesting less evenly, and there were even solitary pairs shrinking up against the cliff wall between the nest drums of two pairs of gannets. Their humming *oo-oo* was an amusing and familiar accompaniment to every untoward movement on my part or the rustling in the breeze of the leaves of my big notebook. What sharp eyes they had, bowing their heads in mutual unease at my appearance no matter how far their township from the cliff top.

Photographs illustrated how great had been the reduction in the numbers of guillemots in this gannetry in the past fifteen years or so, complementary to the increase in gannets – not that there had ever been any active persecution on the part of the latter. Those remaining little groups of guillemots huddled up within beak range of sitting gannets, but the latter did no more than nip a restless guillemot very gently with their bills, infrequently; nor did the threat of that potentially dangerous beak deter these diminutive neighbours from fighting incessantly, driving one another hard up against the gannets' nest drums, nor from mating beneath a gannet's very beak. In the hurlyburly of one gannet being turned off a ledge by another an adjacent pair of guillemots, which had just mated, would be shocked into such characteristic mental confusion that they would fight severely, before realising their error. If a gannet, which had not yet laid, left her nest temporarily the chances were that one of the neighbouring guillemots would take possession of it immediately, retreating on the owner's return.

The infiltration of the gannets had been peaceful, but none the less inexorable, mainly because of their size, the bulky nature of their nests and the relatively small space of a foot or so between the nest drums – a space covered by the lunge of one sitting gannet at another, in which a pair of guillemots might stand or even walk quietly about, but in which a resident group was not tolerated.

Each pair of gannets was in possession of a nest drum, or merely a territory on the bare rock, a foot or so from its neighbours on either side and above and below, except at the outer limits of the gannetry and in those places where a sheer slab of cliff contained perhaps only one small shelf or honeycomb cell with room for only a single pair of these huge 'boobies'.

These beautiful 'boobies', sitting each in its place with black primaries crossed, tern-like, over snowy mantles, were now at the end of April at various stages of the breeding cycle. Some two-thirds of them had big nest drums raised on previous years' foundations, which were so concreted to the rock and whitened with the excrement of both gannets and guillemots that it was impossible to distinguish where rock ended and nest began. On top of the drum perhaps might be an impressive round pile of dead grasses, nine inches deep, with fresh green grass surmounting the whole structure. But little new material appeared to have been added to the permanent structure of these big ancestral drums.

Other pairs had no drums and only rudimentary nests, their occupants sitting rather on raised lumps of less weathered sand-stone than on nest stuff comprising a wisp of dead grass or a white feather or two – which some swimming birds were retrieving at the base of the cliffs, shooting through the water after them, with wings loosened a little at the shoulders and primaries crossed over their tails. Nevertheless, material was continually being brought up to both rudimentary and drum nests.

Besides gathering material from the sidings and from the reefs and waters of the Wick the gannets flew many miles to the shores of Mainland in search of tangle; and when one was sailing well out to sea off Bressay they might be seen coming up in ones and twos with huge beakfuls of bladder weed from farther north than the binoculars could pick up.

Another source of supply was contained in the gannetry itself, where a regular feature of nest building was the filching of material from other gannets' nests – not those, of course, of incubating birds, which never left their eggs unattended for a second, day or night, but from those of pairs which had not yet laid and which were in perpetual process of building and losing nests. It was clear that those old-established pairs with ancestral nest drums, or at least the foundations of drums, must hold a considerable breeding advantage over the younger pairs. On their initial return to the gannetry – and no doubt more often than not to the same nest drum – late in January or early in February they would have substantial nests on which to sit, and would tend to sit more assiduously than younger birds, so that it would matter little whether fresh material was accumulated on the top of the old drums or not : whereas it seemed to some extent a matter of chance whether pairs returning to or prospecting bare ledge sites ultimately succeeded in retaining an adequate proportion of the material they collected, or filched from other vestigial nests, to form a nest; and what actually happened was that these later-laying birds did not accumulate any permanent nest structure until such time as they laid their eggs and sat perpetually – at which juncture the material continually brought up by their mates became a permanent addition to the nest, being no longer subject to the incessant depredations of other building gannets. It might be true to say that no pair of gannets ever succeeded in building a nest until after incubation began.

The difficulties which these later-laying pairs had to contend with in their endeavours to establish any sort of permanent nest foundation were exemplified by those pairs on that top ledge immediately opposite my O.P. Now, on 25 April there were four pairs. Pair 1 at its north end, with an egg on a nest composed entirely of white feathers was, however, the only pair with a permanent nest, though not an ancestral drum; and my attention was drawn to another gannet filching an enormous beakful of nest stuff, including feathers, from an unoccupied vestigial nest (5) farther along the ledge. With this it flew out into the Wick, returned to the robbed nest again, flew out again and finally returned to another unoccupied vestigial nest immediately adjacent to pair 1's and some thirty feet from the robbed nest. Here it deposited its beakful of stuff and sat on it. Subsequently this bird (2) filched more beakfuls from pair 3's unoccupied nest, adjacent to it on the south side : but, on itself going off later, its own nest was robbed by a bird from another part of the gannetry – and so it went on.

By 27 April for instance, pair 2 had acquired some green thrift, three white feathers and a stick of dead thistle. Almost immediately after my arrival in the morning, however, neighbour 3 filched that attractive thrift and flew off with it : but in the evening 2 was again robbing 3's nest. A morning or two later, however, the male of pair 2 made no attempt to prevent 3, which had just arrived with nesting material, from taking in addition an enormous beakful of material from *his* nest. On the contrary he flew off! Whereupon 3, having filched a second beakful, also flew off! (In those places where I refer specifically to male or female it must be understood that they are identified by the act of mating or by some physical peculiarity.)

It was apparent that the fashioning of a nest was to a greater or lesser degree fortuitous, and a gannet alighting without nesting-stuff at an unconstructed nest would seize up a beakful of stuff lying nearby on the ledge, as if to consummate a forgotten, but now remembered, mission : just as 6, a pale-headed bird, alighting empty-billed at its solitary niche above and north of pair 1, characteristically, at the moment of alighting, seized in one motion with the braking of its feet on the ledge a beakful of stuff from its own nest, which it began to arrange. While, on one bird of another pair without a nest bringing up a big bunch of seaweed, neither partner appeared to know what to do with it, and it was ultimately purloined by a bird sitting on a nest below. In another instance one male bird alighting with a small billful of stuff deposited it on an empty place on a ledge, not without difficulty in ridding its break of it, then picked up a fragment and hopping along the ledge to a bird with almost no nest, deposited it there and subsequently mated with her.

There was mandibulating by sitting birds of the nesting material brought up by their mates and, when 2 was standing fiddling with some stuff it had filched from pair 3's nest, both of pair 1 were encouraged to begin fiddling with their nest, the pale-headed male twisting his head affectionately over his mate's head in order to do so. Then the two played lovingly with a beakful of green stuff, before the female took it ultimately from her mate's upstretched beak and the two together bowed down with it to the nest, where the female arranged it delicately. A bird sitting on a big nest drum would continually fiddle with little bits of disturbed nest stuff, mandibulating them precisely inwards to the egg with a curiously vibratory movement of the just-parted tips of its beak − that grey-blue, black-lined daggerbill which, distended in a yawn, revealed a black interior; and when pair 4, a late-laying pair on the north side of the gannetry, ultimately settled down to incubation, the sitting bird was continually digging into the rampart of its new nest of seaweed and then raising its head and shaking its bill.

The bringing up of nesting material and its idle mandibulating by the incubating bird were not only almost the sole direct acts of nest building, but also provided the major stimulus maintaining that tempo of high activity and vocal expression which while crescending and diminishing in intensity, never wholly slackened for more than a few seconds at a time during the hours of daylight. In April most of the gannets would be sleeping at 5 a.m., with few coming up to the ledges, and there would be little noise in the gannetry. Not for another half hour is the first nest stuff brought up, and it is an hour before the first mating takes place.

By 4.30 p.m. there are signs that another busy day is drawing to a close, and the last bird has plucked its billful of grasses from the sidings of the West Noup. An hour and a half later, when ninety per cent of those present on the nesting ledges are single birds, several are beginning to sleep and only their orange crowns and napes can be seen above beaks buried in scapulars. At 6.15 p.m., however, some are still bringing up seaweed from more distant sources, and when I leave the gannetry three quarters of an hour later, with the sun pretty low in the west, the tempo of activity and vocal refrain has not materially decreased.

The effect of stepping back a yard or two from the cliff-edge dyke is startling. Instantaneously and incredibly all visual, aural and olfactory evidence that tens of thousands of sea birds are nesting immediately below me is gone. All that remains of the tumult is the cawing of fulmars high up on the West Noup; and as I go down the boggy hill into the westering sunlight, through that other world of skua-held hinterland, I hear all around, instead, the *kyee-ek* of protesting bonxies and the 'creaking' of snipe twisting up at my feet.

On returning at 9.45 p.m., however, the gannetry is almost completely quiet, with half its inmates sleeping with heads buried so deeply in parted wings that their foreheads are hidden, and only five birds are on the wing in the Wick at one time. An hour later all are on the cliffs and most are sleeping, though from time to time a sitting bird gets up, with a quiet *urrah*, to flap its wings and wag its tail, or to arrange its egg. An occasional outburst comes from the guillemots and kittiwakes, a fulmar caws, and an oystercatcher pipes from the siding above the Cradle Holm.

At 11 p.m. on a May night, when the wind is blowing distinctly warm off the sea, it is still light enough to pick out the white heads of kittiwakes sixty yards away with the naked eye and (with binoculars) to see the white bellies of the more distant guillemots. Herring gulls and an occasional dusky bonxie are the last birds on the wing before 11 p.m., though half an hour later occasional kittiwakes are still circling out from the lower parts of the cliffs and their *kit-kit* is to be heard frequently, penetrating the sullen roar and surge of the cold relentless sea. Then for a while – a long while it seems, though it lasts only from 11.30 p.m. to 12.45 a.m. – the lonely night knows only the wretched being huddled for warmth in the lee of the cliff dyke and the winking beams of distant lighthouses. The night grows neither appreciably darker nor lighter, and none of the sleeping sea fowl show any reaction to the beam of my torch playing upon them. At 12.45 a.m., however, a faint red glow is perceptible east of the Noup, and I hear the crying of unseen herring gulls and swaabies over the Wick. Ten minutes later larks begin to twitter over the bonxie grounds and the Head. By 1.15 a.m. it is distinctly lighter, for I can make out the faint grey outline of the southern hills of Mainland, but the gannets are still sleeping and the gannetry is dead silent. At 1.30 a.m., the first fulmars and kittiwakes are on the wing, and a quarter of an hour later, when I can see to write my notes without the aid of a torch, the gannets waken at last, after more than two hours' total inactivity, and the first one leaves the cliffs, and a second two minutes later. By 1.50 a.m. most are stirring on the ledges, and at 2 a.m. there is a brief display of affection between a pair without a nest (and a mating twenty minutes later), for some nonbreeding birds also spend the night in the gannetry. At 2.10 a.m. roosting birds are leaving the cliffs at regular intervals and twenty-six leave the gannetry between 1.45 a.m. and 2.30 a.m. : but it is not until the latter hour that the first alighting bird arrives. By this time I can bear the cold of the stiff on-cliff dawn wind no longer and, rising with difficulty from my four-hour couch on the bare rock, I am forced to leave the gannetry when the tempo of activity is still low.

As early as 2.10 a.m., however, a gannet standing alone on its nest drum, or one of a pair, might be seen to display with those antics that occurred from minute to minute throughout the hours of daylight. After first wagging its head the displaying bird then bowed forward, turning its head sideways in the same motion to, or under, one or other of its wings. These were either 'hung' open, cormorantwise, with primaries closed, or loosened at the shoulders, and depressed – so loosely perhaps as to rest on the ledge – with the black primaries crossed, like open scissors, over the upper part of the tail, whose spine-like point was spiked upwards. Thereupon, as likely as not, an adjacent pair would briefly enact the same ceremony. The head wagging antic, which was often coupled with the pretence of picking up nest stuff, was continually indulged in : just as the head-bowing-to-wing antic might also be coupled with the pretence or actual picking up of stuff and also with the waving of it : no matter whether it was a ceremony between a pair of birds or the antic of a solitary bird. One might be seen bowing its head incessantly, first under its left wing, tilting up its tail with every bow, and then under its right wing. And just as the bowing of one bird or pair would stimulate an immediate neighbour to bow, so six solitary birds sitting on a row of nests would have spasms, either together or one after another, of bowing under primary-crossed wings. Nor was the antic confined to nesting birds, for a solitary gannet alighting on a ledge devoid of nests would stand on its edge, wings fully open – though not of course stretched to their full span – tilt its tail up and down and bow forward two or three times.

When a pair wingbowed together, the ceremony very often culminated in the two stretching up their heads, wagging them, and then fencing bills lovingly. This fencing and clashing of bills might be extremely vigorous – as might the fondling of heads, when one bird crossed its head over the other's neck – and might continue without a break for a minute or more, with constant crescendos in the tempo and violence of the clashing, as one partner stimulated the other should the latter display any slackening of enthusiasm. In between two such bouts of fencing one of the pair might, though infrequently, elevate its bill vertically, with mandibles parted and throat pulsing tremulously, while its blue eyelids were almost closed over the pale grey-blue eye disks with their tiny black pupils. So, too, infrequently, a solitary incubating bird would indulge in this curious, perhaps cooling throat pulsing – which was also a peculiarity of the nesting cormorant – without a second's break for several minutes, until perhaps it was interrupted by stuff falling from a nest above. Similarly the head wagging, and often the twining of heads, might also continue for several minutes without a break and might lead ultimately to a mating or attempted mating, as might also the arrival of one partner with nesting material – the act providing the most frequent stimulus to mating.

The mating was initiated by the male taking a firm beak hold of his mate's head : an alighting bird, indeed, normally gripped its mate by the nape. It might even fly direct to its mate's ochre-coloured head, gripping it before its own feet were on the ledge, or alight with one foot on its mate's back. Either method might lead to the mating or to that extremely vigorous and prolonged clashing of bills and fondling of heads. Thus, when the male of pair 2 came up to alight he did so with such a direct lunge at and grip of his mate's head that he appeared to be, rather, a rightful owner returning to find his nest being robbed than a fond husband. Nevertheless he subsequently mated with her, flew off, returned with the same vicious lunge and trod her for the second time in ten minutes. Having failed on another occasion, however, to consummate a mating, he became extremely violent in his grip of her head and finally pushed her off the ledge! This contrasted with the behaviour of another newly united pair, who were preening one another's heads and throats with the utmost delicacy, and with a third pair, the male of whom was preening the tips of his mate's primaries – at which she gripped his bill in hers more tightly than he altogether enjoyed. One could, indeed, never be quite certain initially whether a bird without a nest gripping another by the head and then standing on its back was about to mate, as one supposed, or in actual fact was only manoeuvring to push it off the ledge. If it was with the intention of mating then, having obtained his beak hold, the male would proceed to paddle about on his mate's back, balancing with waving wings – while she continually shook her head – until such time as he had secured a good grip on the folds of skin he pulled up with his beak; just as the cock fulmar continually rubbed his beak across his mate's brow and beak while treading her and might begin to do this again after the mating had been consummated, until, pecking her too roughly, she would throw him off.

When the mating had been consummated the male gannet might fly direct from his mate's back to sea – though not, perhaps, without first performing the special antic that usually, but not invariably, preceded a gannet's departure from its nesting ledge – or he might merely step off her back, when a mutual clashing of bills would follow; while the mating of a pair without a nest might be followed by mutual head wagging and beak pointing. The departure antic in no way resembled any of those antics already described, and is worth special consideration in as much as the gannet did not normally fly direct from its nesting place like any other sea bird. When the impulse to leave its ledge took it, the gannet seemed to pass into a trance-like state and would begin to paddle about the ledge very slowly, lifting its feet only just clear of the rock and gradually straining up beak, head and neck vertically, while at the same time slightly busking closed wings, inflating its chest, and elevating its stern or, alternatively, depressing the spiny tail stiffly. Once this unique posture had been assumed the bird might continue to paddle around in an attitude of intense concentration for several seconds and sometimes as long as a full minute, totally oblivious of the surrounding tumult, before approaching the edge of the ledge. At this point it would bow forward, with neck still upstretched and tail tilted, but wings now loosened a little at the shoulders – or, alternatively, with head and tail depressed – and finally launch forth in flight in this looped-up manner, expelling as it did so a sighing *woo-or-er,* not dissimilar from, though louder than, the sigh of a kittiwake when it zoomed down and out from the cliff face. On a calm sunny morning this departure note sounded like the last sigh of a departing spirit and reflected the disembodied antic of departure, as with an S-shaped kink in its neck, head still being stretched up vertically, and with spiny tail now depressed, the great white bird floated feebly off into space – a most humorous caricature.

As in the case of so many avian antics this curious departure antic of the gannet was occasionally, though by no means so frequently as the peculiar antics of other species, provoked by the wrong stimulus. Thus, a gannet wishing to relieve its incubating partner on the nest might begin to assume the departure antic, and one such bird pushed its mate violently aside when the latter was too slow in removing itself from the nest. With similar confusion the mate of one nesting bird performed this antic after shoving a non-nesting bird off its ledge, while another did so before flying to a different ledge on being threatened by the rightful occupant. At 7.15 p.m. on 27 April, the female of pair 2 arrived at the nesting ledge and there was an audible brittle clashing of sabre bills between the two and a smoothing of one's head down the other's, to the customary vocal accompaniment, which continued without a pause for two minutes and intermittently and less violently subsequently – the female being the more violent of the two – though at this date they had not a scrap of nest stuff. Half an hour later the male performed the departure antic, but did not leave, clashing bills with his mate instead, and after more strained anticking waved wings twice, but still did not leave. Similarly, on another occasion, after one of this pair had assumed the antic for a full minute its mate nibbled its taut, vertically stretched throat delicately. This led to a mutual and gentle billing and in the end it was the mate that left – returning again in another half-minute. On 10 May both the pair went through the ceremony, but this led, not to their departure, but to one of the two paddling along the ledge and concluding with a gleeful run and hop forward to seize a huge beakful of stuff from pair 3's nest and return with it to its mate! This pirating was repeated and then a minute or two later further anticking did finally lead to this bird's departure, while its mate arranged her latest foundations. Of another pair, which had changed places on their nest, the relieved bird departed with the customary sighing *oo-oo-oo*, but returned in two minutes and mated, proving to be the male – the absence of any nest was no bar to mating – whereupon the female left after thirty seconds, but returned again in another thirty seconds, leaving once more after a similar period.

And throughout these antics of birds continually departing, of others alighting, and yet others displaying, came from the gannetry that incessant vocal refrain, broken only at second intervals and continually renewed by every new alighting, continually crescending with every wave of bowing and every clashing of bills – that harsh repetitive *gurrah-gurrah-gurrah*, with the accent on the *gurr*, pitched somewhat higher than the similar greeting cry of a bird coming up to alight, when the *gurrah* was abbreviated almost to a monosyllable and slowed up, with the accent on the *rah*. Since the cry was emitted through closed bill it was extremely difficult to tie down the refrain to any particular bird amid the general tumult. Nor was the refrain limited to those gannets on the ledges, for one coming in from the Wick to alight, planing up at great speed to the cliff face and then braking, with tail depressed vertically, would begin *gurrah*ing when still a hundred yards or so from the cliff face; and there was a constant chorus from that off-cliff stream of not-immediately-alighting gannets, which were in perpetual process of coming up to the cliffs, passing along their front, falling away again and circling out into the Wick : for the number of alighting birds was only a small percentage of those circling off the cliffs at any one time, and there was a constant falling away from the cliffs of unsuccessful or undecided potential alighters – great white attenuate hawkmoths drooping at head and tail. Despite this constant traffic of birds alighting and departing and others planing along the face of the cliff in a continuous stream, only once did I witness a partial collision.

A nonterritoried gannet purposing to alight at some spot in the crowded gannetry, but able to locate only a mere crevice in the face of the cliff, might find itself suspended almost in midair, while hanging on to the lower mandible of a bird sitting on a nest at the edge of the ledge above, and scrabbling with its claws for purchase on the cliff face : for there was much aggressiveness among the occupants of a gannetry, both between neighbouring pairs and against solitary nonterritoried birds alighting on unoccupied sites between two nest drums. The latter were ejected by threatening beak lunges or pushed off the ledge by the actual pressure of a beak hold. On the other hand a bird alighting on a ledge containing no nests, had no difficulty in forcing off any nonbreeding occupants. Incubating birds, however, never left their nests for combat and this was restricted to the savage lunging and actual beak gripping of one sitting neighbour by its adjacent fellow, whether on the same ledge or on those ledges immediately above and below : while neighbours might tweak the two combatants' tails, which were spread in diamond-shaped fans in their efforts to push the other off its nest. The endurance and sustained powers of pressure of two combatants were hardly credible. For twenty minutes, and longer for all I knew, I on one occasion watched two gannets without nests locked together, beak in beak, and one, or both, had blood on them. In this contest I saw that the prime object of the beak hold was to push the rival off the ledge, and it was apparent that tremendous pressure was exerted. Very gradually, but relentlessly, first one combatant and then the other would force back the head of its rival to, one would have thought, breaking point, or would twist it round over its back – maximum pressure being obtained by pressing half-open or even fully expanded wings and depressed fan-spread tail against the cliff face. Every now and again one of the two would shake its beak violently in order to obtain a better grip, and this might give its rival the opportunity to exert pressure in its turn and force back the other's head : but never once were the beaks unlocked. With a fresh and bitterly cold updraught blowing it was too cold to await the outcome, and I was forced to leave my O.P. temporarily after half an hour, when beak was still locked in beak : it ended some time in the next half hour. But generally a gannetry was a remarkably peaceful community, and acts of aggression between neighbouring pairs were for the most part limited to occasional menacing beak lunges, tip meeting tip from outstretched necks at the halfway point between two nest drums; this double stretch governed the territorial space between every pair of nest drums and accounted for those ordered rows so characteristic of a gannetry.

With a strong wind or breeze from south or east causing a stiff draught up the cliffs the circling gannets had the greatest difficulty in alighting, and had to float-drop on to their ledges at right angles. With the updraught so strong that I would be thrown off my balance from time to time on the landward side of the cliff dyke, the gannets would give a marvellous display of aerobatics, and fulmars and herring gulls performed the most extravagant actions with wings and tails, all soft curves and no rigidity, just above or below the cliff top : while high overhead, hundreds of feet above the Noup, hovered the falcon peregrine on seemingly motionless wings. On such breezy days there was a continual circling of birds round the Wick and sideways along the cliffs, and an idly circling whirlpool of sea fowl off Puffin Holm might contain gannets, bonxies, arctic skuas, kittiwakes, fulmars, herring gulls and swaabies. In the evening great numbers of gannets, fulmars and kittiwakes would soar over the Wick at scores or hundreds of feet, and pairs of bonxies would wheel like buzzards in overlapping circles out to sea. Such aeronautics were not to be confused with the milling out of a cloud of inquisitive gannets on those infrequent occasions when a yacht sailed into Rumble Wick or a tramp steamer or Norwegian shark boat chugged close past the Noup, and five hundred gannets would circle off the cliff and plummet in the boat's wake; while on a calmer day after a gale the sea would be dotted with solitary swimming gannets almost as far as the eye could reach.

2. *Nine Weeks A'Growing*

By the end of the third week in April two thirds of the pairs in my
gannetry had eggs and the majority, though not all, of those pairs
with nest drums appeared to have laid : some eggs being stained
brown by a few days' incubation; but I could only make out two
drumless nests with eggs, of which one was that nest composed
entirely of white feathers belonging to pair 1. There was much
billing of the egg inwards by those incubating to their black feet,
with their curious pale-green veins. I observed that one webbed
foot was not placed on top of the other over the egg when
incubating, as traditionally stated, but after first placing one foot
along one side of the ridiculously small egg, the other foot was
then placed along the other side, overlapping its fellow; this
operation might take quite a while before the bird finally sank
down on to its feet. From time to time one would rise to flap its
wings and then rearrange its egg.

Incubating birds sat for long periods without being relieved by
their mates, a bird here and there becoming heavily stained with
green excrement voided by those sitting above. The operation of
relief was seldom seen except in the early morning, and the
alighting rate was at its maximum in the three hours after sunrise.
On being relieved the sitting bird might fly directly out to sea or
might delay its departure for anything up to three minutes,
clashing bills or fondling heads with its mate; this would be
followed by the appropriate antic preceding departure, after which
it might circle off the cliffs for the few minutes that it could be
distinguished among the throng of its fellows. As no birds with big
nest drums ever left their eggs unattended none of the latter were
ever lost and the percentage of infertile eggs was apparently
extremely small : but losses occurred among pairs with new
drumless nests. All these rudimentary nests were situated on the
outside ledges of the gannetry. On 22 April for example, pair 1's
nest of feathers was the only nest on the ledge which contained no
foundations from previous years. We may surmise with some
confidence that these outer ledges in a gannetry were occupied,
predominantly at any rate, by the younger adults. Certainly the
female of pair 1 behaved like one unused to incubating. She never
performed any of the various ceremonies and antics of display and
courtship perpetually indulged in by the vast majority of the
members of the gannetry, whether solitary or in pairs – though

her abnormality might be attributed to the absence of stimulating neighbours above and for some distance below her, to the irregular attendance of the three other pairs without nests on her ledge, and to the long absences of her mate, a very pale-headed bird, who was not seen at the nest until 27 April and was only observed on five occasions thereafter throughout the season. His absence was naturally most felt in the early morning, the most popular hour for relief, and at this hour she would leave her egg unattended and make fifteen-minute flights round the Wick — which no other gannet ever did — returning with a pathetically brief *urrah* and no display antic to stand over her egg, without covering it with her feet, for long periods. Though bitterly disappointed I was not, therefore, surprised to find on 28 April, when the male alone was present, that this pair had lost their egg, filched no doubt by a gull during one of the sitting bird's intermittent absences.

Pair 2 were bringing up nesting material on 25 April (and no doubt previously) and began and lost many nests between that date and 13 May, finally laying an egg sometime between 25 and 29 May on a wretched jumble of feathers, dead stalks of angelica and other flotsam. The egg was already stained on 30 May and the next day I noticed the pair changing over.

Pair 3 had a rudimentary nest on 25 April and probably laid on 11 May. As, however, the male visited the nest very infrequently — 23 May being the only occasion on which I noted both birds present — and the female sat very tightly, I did not actually see their egg until 1 June, by which date they had acquired a big nest.

The fourth pair of birds on this ledge (pair 5) were first noted on 23 May. By 7 June their permanent nest comprised one feather and on 24 June one bird was still sitting and sleeping on the bare rock! They laid no egg and this was possibly an unmated birds, for I never saw two birds at the 'nest'.

Finally, the pale-headed partner of pair 6 first occupied its solitary niche above pair 1 on 6 May and by 10 May she had a fair-sized new nest of dead grasses and greenstuff. All this day and for at least five days subsequently she did not budge an inch or raise herself from her nest during long periods of observation, sitting in an attitude abnormal for an incubating gannet with fully erect head. I presumed that she laid during this period of intensive sitting, but I was never able to catch a glimpse of her egg. Then on

19 May my observations at the gannetry suffered a second mortifying setback, when two companions stood too far out on my O.P. Their sudden appearance proved too much for the nerves of this peculiar bird and she flew off her egg. Immediately, a herring gull (whose kind I had hardly noticed about this end of the Wick previously) appeared from nowhere, seized the egg and flew off with it almost before I had realised that the felonious act was being perpetrated. Thus, I had lost my two closest observation nests with eggs. The pale-headed bird – a mate was only once observed, on 7 May – continued to visit the nest until 23 May, but was not seen thereafter.

Meanwhile, for a week after the loss of their egg pair 1's attendances were very brief and their nest was filched piecemeal. By 8 May, however, they had gathered together quite a good nest again. Attention has already been drawn to the peculiarities identifying this pair, and on 30 May I was astounded to see, on her rising from the throat-pulsing attitude, after I had been watching for an hour, that the female was sitting on a second egg, together with a guillemot's egg which must have rolled into the nest. This second egg must have been laid about 14 May, seventeen days after the loss of the first, though from that day to this I had never had the slightest suspicion that she was sitting on anything except an empty nest. She continued to incubate the guillemot's egg until some date between 14 and 19 June, and on 20 June the nest was provided with fresh greenstuff for the last time.

Here and there a guillemot might be seen sitting on her egg up against the cliff wall and within beak range of two sitting gannets. To the already heavy losses among eggs, due to the carelessness and nervousness of sitting birds usual in a guillemot colony, were added those further losses due to alighting gannets, especially nonterritoried birds, which knocked sitting guillemots off the cliffs, and to the many eggs that rolled within range of sitting gannets, where the restless endearments of a pair of guillemots were not tolerated for any length of time, though the gannets did not deliberately peck these guillemots' eggs that rolled their way. So long as the guillemots sat quietly all was well, but the excitement aroused by the arrival of its mate was likely to result in the shifting of the egg to a point where the gannet would not tolerate even a quiet guillemot.

As I thought it possible that the earliest pairs might have laid at the end of March, I began to scrutinise the gannetry very closely, early in May, for evidence of hatching, and it was with some excitement that shortly after the middle of the month I was able to make out that one of the drum nests, on a broad ledge just above the sea and far down below me, contained a naked and minute greyish-black squab with a grizzled white head. With eyes still closed it lay spreadeagled helplessly flat on the drum, which still contained the shell. It was, however, the last days of May before chicks were hatching in any numbers; and not until at least a dozen had hatched was there any circumstantial evidence as to their presence. At this point, the percentage of couples of adults present at nests in the control area at any given time began to rise steeply.

Meanwhile the parents (pair 7) of this first chick, whose egg must have been laid in the first day or two of April, bowed together triumphantly under 'hung' wings, or 'throat-pulsed' in an ecstatic rapture, or clashed bills exuberantly and fondled heads continuously; until the newly arrived parent began to preen the chick, while the much-stained sitting bird performed the departure antic. (By the time it was a couple of weeks old and growing very rapidly into its 'puff' of woolly white down, with black 'lores' and beak, the chick would also 'throat-pulse'.) But the chick was a magnet, and after five minutes of 'anticking' the brooding bird settled down on it again. Though the newly arrived parent had twice opened its bill suggestively, the chick had not solicited food from it, as I had expected it would. A quarter of an hour later the brooding bird got off the chick again, anticked and departed : to return in three-quarters of an hour, when there was more preening of the chick and fondling of heads between the pair; but four minutes later she anticked and left again, returning this time immediately. Once again the chick was not fed. While it *might* be fed by the newly arrived parent, subsequent events showed that the act of feeding was not specially related to the returning of one parent from the sea – a routine that aroused no response in the chick – nor with any special hour of the day, feeding taking place as late as 9 p.m. In actual fact it was more often fed – though even so infrequently – at any odd time by the brooding parent.

Feeding took place from the earliest stages and a chick not yet free from the hinder part of its shell, and still wet and black except for its grizzled head, would be fed by its parent regurgitating, at which the chick would peck inside the latter's lower mandible. When older the chick thrust up its head into its parent's gape, commonly five or even six times in the space of a couple of minutes, while the parent swallowed back and regurgitated after every two or three feeds. When the latter drew up its head to swallow or broke off the operation and began bowing, the chick would point up its bill at the other's, to stimulate further feeding. Such importunity, however, was not always effective, for on one fourteen-day-old chick biting its parent's bill the latter ignored it and continued to play with a feather. Occasionally there was a hitch in the procedure. After much importunity, for instance, one chick was fed three times, but then twice failed to put its bill into its parent's gape, though successful at a sixth attempt. Nor was feeding confined to one parent : for nestling 8 was first fed by its most recently arrived parent and then fed five times by its much-stained brooding parent – a solid white residue remaining on the parent's beak after the feeding. After this the latter subsequently made two further abortive attempts to regurgitate again. Five minutes later, however, it fed the nestling a seventh time, when the other clean-plumaged mate left after an earlier period of anticking.

No regular fishing took place off Noss. After a gale gannets might be seen plunging into the Voe of the Mels for piltocks, or surface fishing for fry off Setter, with much excited croaking, in company perhaps with a school of porpoises and a basking shark; but their main fishing grounds were no doubt among the herrings twenty or thirty miles out to sea. As early as 5.45 a.m. scores were to be seen coming up from the south into Rumble Wick in rhythmic flights, six or nine at a time, before each at its journey's end wheeled off to its own special cliff or continued on round the Noup to the gannetries on the north side. I never saw a gannet cross the island from sea to sea, though one morning I found one standing on the green outside the hill dyke, unable to get airborne : but it had disappeared by the evening.

By the time the nestlings were a fortnight or so old their parents no longer brooded them and they passed their days in a comatose condition, sleeping with heads stretched full length down the wall of the nest drum – a characteristic posture – or curled up with head turned round to belly. Seeing a big nestling laid out motionless, or lying curled up on its side, fouled to the very beak with ordure, one's first impression was that it was dead, and I suffered one or two shocks in this way. After long observation, however, with the aid of binoculars, it was apparent that a membrane was nictitating slowly and intermittently three-quarters of the way across the 'dark-blue' eye and up again : but this was the sole evidence that the young one was alive. When one such comatose nestling raised its head, after several minutes' inertia, it was severely pecked on the front part of its head by the adjacent pair of adults : whereupon it cowered its head round for some considerable time, before beginning to preen. Here was a possible cause of mortality among the bigger nestlings, when their bulky size tended to result in their 'overflowing' into a neighbouring pair's beak territory : though, in actual fact, probabaly only one big nestling in the control area met its death in this way, when at the age of about forty days, pair 7's chick – the oldest in the gannetry, older by four or five days than any other and by a month than half of its fellows : was lying stretched out in that peculiar comatose way, while its parents bowed to one another. In this instance, however, this did indicate death and ten days later its carcase had been almost trodden into the nest drum, at which one or both parents were still in constant attendance.

By the end of the third week in June, when some sixty-five chicks in white down were obvious in the control area and the eldest surviving were three weeks old, the latter woke up a little, preened themselves, twiddled feathers lying about the nest, or played with their parents' beaks or with nest stuff with them. Up to this age they had been preened by their parents, sometimes by both at the relieving hour – which was still predominantly in the early morning – and a curious incident occurred when one of two parents mandibulated a grey squab quite severely across the head and neck, possibly to turn it beneath the brooding bird, which stabbed its mate mildly. But still more curious was the fate of a nestling kittiwake on the outer edge of a nest in a row of cells between two layers of gannets : for as its other parent alighted the nestling tumbled off and fell twenty feet, to land beside a sitting gannet. The latter mandibulated rather than pecked this waif, and after a minute or two the nestling crept under the gannet, which had either an egg or a very young squab, and after a few minutes of uneasy pecking beneath her and settling herself, she brooded

Gannet with large chick on nest-drum.

the strange nestling! The latter, however, was never seen again.

At the end of June, when about one hundred white chicks could be seen in the control area, the eldest were of a size with their parents and seemed bulkier because of the great bloom of white down which enveloped them, though black tail points were now showing. They were spry enough to peer over the edge of the nesting ledge at the sea so far below, ignoring, in their interest, their parents' bowing ceremony. A week later they had learnt to sleep standing on dark-grey feet with heads tucked back into their black scapulars. The latter were now becoming prominent and were followed before the end of the sixth week by neat black and white wing secondaries and short black tails. At seven weeks scapulars, wings and tail were almost free of down and the head was beginning to blacken; and it was at this season – towards the middle of July – that after heavy rain a number of well-advanced dark juveniles became prominent in the çontrol area : for heavy rain produced a striking transformation in the gannetry, as did the departure of the ledge-fouling guillemots, which was just beginning. The cliffs, with most of the guano distemper washed off them by the rain, appeared much closer in perspective and therefore higher and of more gigantic proportions, and all *exposed* nests, chicks and adults were very wet and dirty, the nests appearing once more as drums rather than amorphous hummocks of rock; but whereas those chicks still in full down were so wet and muddy that they were difficult to distinguish against the muddy ledges and drums, those that had shed a great part of their down, appearing a mottled grey in dry weather, now stood out very blackly. The former were in a truly dreadful dishevelled state of bedraggled down, which was now scattered all about the ledges. This state, together with their infestation by lice, probably caused them much irritation, and they preened continually, shaking out clouds of down, which settled on the ledges and floated very slowly to the top of the cliffs like thistledown : for they, and to a much greater degree the older black young, passed minutes together flapping their wings vigorously, clipping a parent on either side round the head, causing them to bow. The black juveniles were now assuming adult manners, and one might be observed with its beak locked savagely in its parent's, while another even stabbed at an adjacent brooding adult, and a third lunged mildly at its parent's head. They also had a trick of standing with heads elevated perfectly vertical without, however, the customary pulsing of the throat. At eight weeks they were completely black when wet, and when dry and in places sheltered from the voiding of those above, a mottled grey — magnificent birds in a breeding greenshank's plumage of dark or pale grey, speckled or striped with white, smooth diver-like heads hachured in white.

At nine weeks, that is, in the second week of August, when there were some one hundred and forty chicks in the control area, the oldest were completely feathered and showed a tendency to wander a foot or two from their nest drums, disappearing temporarily behind protuberances in the cliffs, reappearing again after an hour or so. This tendency resulted in a further, though small, mortality. One fell on to a ledge below its own and lay on its back all day between two drums, paddling feebly with its feet in the air, and died during the night; a second floated dead at the base of the cliffs; a third, still with down on its head, fell on to the reef at the base of the Noup and survived for two or three days, sleeping for the most part with head tucked back into scapulars, before it disappeared. At this time, too, one among many hundred parents would fly off its nest drum and leave an eight- or nine-week young one unattended for a minute or two – the first time the nest drum had been left unattended for a second by one or other of the parents since the egg had been laid four months earlier!

3. *The Young Go Down to Sea*

The circumstances attending the departure of the young gannets for sea were somewhat obscure and it was perhaps that event on Noss I was most anxious to watch. The previous year I had found thousands of adults still on the cliffs in September, when they outnumbered the young by something like twenty to one. However, as the first young had hatched shortly after the middle of May this year, I could expect them to begin fledging – that is to say to begin going down to the sea – in either the first or last weeks of August, though it seemed to be generally agreed that it was exceptional for any to fledge before September. Taking no chances, I began to watch out for any parents deserting young as early as the middle of July.

But the days passed and no parents deserted their young. Weeks passed, and still one or both parents were in daily attendance on every young one, and I saw no change in the daily routine. Then, on 10 August, when the oldest were entering upon their twelfth week, I noticed that pair 8's young one had disappeared, seventy-six to seventy-nine days after hatching, though both parents were present and one was sitting on the nest drum; but though I watched more closely than ever, thenceforward, nothing further materialised until 14 August. At 12.45 p.m. that day a rorqual whale breached at no great distance off Puffin Holm, affording a brief glimpse of white belly, shark-like underjaw, and enormous tail flukes. Fastening my binoculars on the place where it had sounded again, what was my astonishment to perceive a young gannet on the sea east of the Cradle Holm. Though flapping its wings and threshing them on the water it was unable to lift itself into the air and drifted south west with the tide. No adults were with it.

A few minutes later I perceived a second fledgeling on the water south of Puffin Holm. Three adults were near it and one 'attacked' it – at which one of the other two drove off the latter, lunging at it with open beak; but then first one and then the other of these two also 'attacked' the fledgeling, persistently flapping forward and alighting on its tail to peck at its head. They finally abandoned it, however, and flew off, leaving it like the other fledgeling to drift away alone, southwards. Were these its parents? If so, their manners were peculiar, though not dissimilar from those of the alighting adult greeting its mate with a savage grip of her head.

The days passed and I was still unsuccessful in observing any of the fledgelings in the act of leaving their ledges. At 8.40 p.m. on 16 August, for instance, one was on the water on the north side of the Noup; and at 12.15 p.m. on 17 August there was another off Puffin Holm. An hour later a second was close into the Rumble Wick cliffs but, though I presumed it must have come down quite recently, no adults were with it, as was also the case with the other two. Seven minutes later, however, two adults landed on the water near it, but the fledgeling swam hurriedly away from them, its tail awash. On a third adult also landing, one of the other two threatened it, whereupon both the assaulted bird and the attacker passed into the departure antic, in so far as they were able to raise their heads from the swimming position, and the aggressor subsequently bowed its head to 'scissored' wings with some difficulty, before all three flew off. At 1.25 p.m., when the morning sun was already off the Rumble Wick cliffs and at the hour of high water, a third fledgeling swam out from the base of the cliffs; and a quarter of an hour later I perceived a fourth in the north corner of the Wick.

Though a second known young one belonging to pair 9 had also disappeared, about eleven weeks after hatching, and the number of young in the control area had decreased by five or ten, I had not, up to now, been able to observe any signs of one preparing to take this momentous step; and, as I had expected, not one of those on the cliffs had been deserted by its parents, every visible young one, and *also* every drum deserted by a fledgeling, having one or both parents present. On the contrary, the percentage of adult couples present in the control area at any time had never been previously exceeded and the total number of adults present had only once been exceeded – on 26 July.

At 1.45 p.m., however, I caught a glimpse out of the corner of my eye of a young one flapping vigorously, in characteristic high-standing posture, on a ledge overlooking the sea, and saw it suddenly launch forth and fly steadily and evenly some three hundred yards out into the Wick, gradually descending to make a good alighting on the water. Its departure was too sudden for me to mark the drum from which it had originated, but apparently no adults took any notice of its departure and none visited it on the water. Five minutes later I was again taken unawares – it was almost impossible to keep one's eye on every one of some scores of potential fledgelings – when another launched forth from a lower ledge, descending after a flight of only forty yards to a sound, though foaming, alighting. Again I was unable to mark its nest drum, but no adults accompanied it or subsequently visited it. Thereafter, no more more young went down within my field of vision and by 3 p.m. very few were exercising their wings, in contrast to the period 12 noon to 2 p.m., and many were sleeping. The period of tension had passed.

The next morning I was at the O.P. by 3.10 a.m. At this hour there was quite a lot of light in the Wick, gathered from the yellowing east, and one or two gannets and also fulmars were on the wing, though there was as yet little noise coming from the gannetry. By 3.30 a.m., however, when it was light enough to write easily, most of the adults and young were waking, though there was little activity among the latter; but five minutes later four or five were flapping hard. At 3.50 a.m., half an hour before sunrise, the gannetry was in full uproar, though only a score of adults were on the wing in the Wick, and I noticed that a black young one and white-headed one, both without parents, were joined by one and two parents respectively; and then a deplorable scene occurred when an immature-plumaged parent with a little black barring edging its secondaries – the only parent thus plumaged in the control area – attempted to mate with its black young one and when unsuccessful, characteristically seized it violently by the head and attempted, initially, to push it off the ledge, while the young one resisted, with tail spread and wings loosened at the shoulders, as stubbornly as a female adult would have done in a similar case. After a minute or more the parent's confusion passed, and it resumed normal parental behaviour towards its offspring. This, however, was not the first such lapse in the control area. On 12 July a single parent had attempted as late as 9.45 p.m. to mate with a big white chick – one in its third or fourth week; and on the afternoon of 26 July the male of a pair with a white chick had also attempted to mate with it, while the female stood by enacting the departure antic! Matings of breeding pairs had ceased as long ago as the second week in May, though a pair with a large white chick had an abortive mating as late as 28 June, the male striking savagely at the female when she attempted to clash bills after he had got off her back, though they subsequently preened one another. With that exception there had occasionally been matings of non-territoried pairs only, up to the end of June, and one thereafter by a pair with a nest drum, but no chick, on 17 August.

By 4.50 a.m. no young ones had left their ledges, most were quiet, and none were to be seen on the sea. It was clear that the early morning hours were not those stimulating departure. When I returned six hours later, however, two were down on the water – they appeared dark-brownish on a dull day from the cliff top – and every now and again a pair of adults or a single bird would alight by one of the two and make vicious lunges at its head. At these, it being a calm day, I could hear the fledgeling's guttural, yet falsetto, *crr-eek, crr-eek* (comparable to the adult's *arrg*) – a cry that had been heard in the gannetry only during the past week or so since the fledging had begun.

At 12.20 p.m. a third fledgeling appeared on the water below my gannetry, and ten minutes later a white-headed bird also appeared there : that is one in all probability not more than nine weeks old at the most, though no doubt some young gannets might be slower than others in attaining their fledging plumage, as in the case of bonxies.

At the end of the first week of fledging there were obvious gaps in the ranks of the young in the control area, some seventeen per cent having gone down. There was, however, no decrease in the ranks of the adults, and all those nest drums from which young had fledged were occupied at all hours of the twenty-four by one or both parents, including both of pair 7, whose young one had now been dead for seven weeks!

At noon on 21 August, when another known young one belonging to pair 8 had left between twelve and thirteen weeks after hatching, I saw a fledgeling make a flight of some five hundred yards. Again, I missed the instant of its take off, but no adults accompanied it. No more went down until 12.45 p.m., when a whitish-headed bird appeared on the water; and after that no more within my field of vision up to 3.5 p.m., though for an hour or more one stood looking out to sea intently, incessantly exercising its wings. This was a rather uncommon spectacle, for only those young ones due to fledge within the subsequent twenty four hours or so *faced* the sea during wing exercises, the others religiously flapping with backs to the sea. (By 10 a.m. the next morning this bird had disappeared.) Only one other young one displayed any sign of responding to the urge to go down to the sea, straying three feet from its nest drum, to the complete unconcern of its parents – which commonly paid no heed to their young wandering into the territories of adjacent pairs; but after peering over the edge of the cliff, loosening its wings at the shoulders from time to time suggestively, it ultimately returned to its drum after an absence of an hour or so.

Thus, far, apart from witnessing intermittent visits by one or more adults to three or four of those fledgelings on the sea, I had obtained no direct evidence as to what part, if any, the parents played at the actual moment of the young one's departure, though it was becoming increasingly probable that these visiting adults were not the fledgelings' parents. At 1 p.m. on 22 August however, I noticed a young one standing, with loosened wings, away from its drum and looking out to sea in the customary intent way. It was difficult to believe that these young gannets were mental vacuums when they stood concentrating for long periods on the world beyond the cliffs. But even as I entered in my notebook the detail that, while this young one was looking out to sea its parent was unconcernedly tossing up nesting material, the former slipped away two hundred yards out into the Wick, its parent to all outward appearances completely unaware of its departure and making no pause in its tossing up of nesting stuff!

At 10 a.m. the next morning there were two fledgelings on the sea. There were also two on the sea at 1.5 p.m. on 25 August and a quarter of an hour later I saw two more go down one after the other. The first made a flight of some five hundred yards and the second was still flying strongly, flapping and gliding, about one thousand yards out from the cliffs, when it was forced down by a bonxie – at which juncture an adult gannet suddenly appeared and landed just behind the fledgeling: whereupon the bonxie sheered off. At 1.27 p.m. I lost another strong flyer in sea mist beyond the Noup after an unfinished flight on a controlled half circle. Some of the young ones fledging at this date – when about thirty per cent had gone down – were probably older and stronger on the wing than some of the earlier ones. At 1.40 p.m. a fourth alighted after a flight of only one hundred yards and was subsequently 'attacked' by an adult. At 3.5 p.m. a fifth made a flight of some three hundred yards; and at 2.13 p.m. a sixth leapt off its drum with half-spread wings, somewhat unsteadily, before gaining its equilibrium with wings fully spread : but by this time the mist was too thick for me to follow its flight to the end. As in the earlier instance, however, its parent continued to fiddle with nest stuff, without any sign of awareness that its young one – which it had tended unremittingly, first in the egg and then as a nestling, for some eighteen weeks – had, in a second of time, vanished from its ken.

Half an hour later, however, a young one attempting to take flight from one of the ledges in the central recess of my gannetry landed beside a nest drum nearer to the edge of the cliff. The occupant of the drum and its own young one unexpectedly caressed the newcomer quite gently, the young one persistently mandibulating its fellow's beak and head. On this occasion the newcomer's parent followed it down, threatening the other parent, but pecking its own young one on the head! Very shortly, however, it significantly abandoned the latter and returned to its own drum : while its young one, ignoring its fellow's attentions, except for hunching itself as flatly as possible against the rock, proceeded to concentrate intently on the sea below. Similarly, at 2.50 p.m., another young one twice stumbled into an adjacent pair's territory, but twice retreated to its own nest. In this instance its parent ignored its activities throughout, including its ultimate successful fledging flight.

By 9.55 a.m. the next morning the first wanderer had disappeared, no doubt taking flight some time after I left the cliff the previous afternoon : for no fledgelings were to be seen on the sea, though one was 'concentrating', and none went down up to 10.25 a.m. An hour and a half later, however, there was one in the Wick and two more off Puffin Holm, and at 12.5 p.m. I saw one make a long flight of six hundred to seven hundred yards, curving southwards out beyond the Holm. At 12.35 p.m. a second actually lifted in the air a little after its take off from the cliff, a manoeuvre causing it to rock dangerously, before it succeeded in straightening out and descending to a good splash landing some two hundred and fifty yards off the cliffs.

By September some sixty per cent of the young had gone down, and on 7 September one fledgeling was on the sea at 11.30 a.m., but none went down during the next hour and a half and none were 'concentrating' or exercising their wings facing seawards. At 2 p.m. one made an eight–hundred-yard flight southwards, alighting with the usual splash landing a few yards from two adults which, however, ignored it. No more went down up to 2.45 p.m., when three were visible on the sea, and though the thirty-two young still unfledged in the control area were livelier than earlier in the morning, there was not a tithe of the wing exercising there had been in August. It was the rule rather than the exception for these remaining young to belong to groups of nests. Ten of the thirty-two, for example, were close together – on or beside their own drums of course – on a broad upper ledge just below pair 1's ledge : while large areas of the control block contained no young at all. Though there was still no decrease in the numbers of adults, the percentage of couples present in the control area at any one time had dropped considerably since the third week in August.

On 9 September one fledgeling was on the sea at 11.0 a.m., but none left the ledges after that up to 2.15 p.m., though several stood looking out to sea or peered over the edge of the cliff, loosening their wings from time to time. One of the latter would probably have gone down, had it not been for the arrival of an adult on a ledge immediately below it. This upset its concentration : whereupon it clambered up to its parents on the drum and began preening. I noted with interest that there was now more building activity among the adults than there had been for some weeks past. At least three pairs were actively constructing nests and a dozen birds at a time were picking up feathers and seaweed on the water below. Almost certainly one of those bringing up weed to its mate belonged to a pair whose young one had fledged. This 'nest building' had continued right through the season among all classes of gannets, and even those with black young had been bringing up feathers or clumps of weed or grass, which the latter assisted in spreading about the nest drum, toying and tugging at it with their parents and passing much of their time in billing the stuff under their breasts in the manner of the sitting adult : just as at an earlier stage, when the chicks were in white down, enormous beakfuls of bladdercampion and other greenstuff were being brought up to the ledges and strewn around, very often over the backs of the young ones.

On 15 September when there were westerly squalls of rain, a fledgeling was down at 12.5 p.m., quite close under the cliffs. It threshed its wings repeatedly on the water, trying to lift itself into the air, as they all did. Another appeared at the base of the cliffs, where a third was standing asleep on the reef platform, at 12.40 p.m. : but none went down during this, my last, half-hour at the gannetry. The fledging had now lasted for more than five weeks, more than eighty per cent of the young in the control area had fledged, and only twenty-four individuals (including two still in three-parts white down) remained. Of these, seven were clustered together on that above-mentioned ledge, with two more nearby, and there were other groupings. And still there were no *noticeable* gaps in the ranks of the adults, with the single exception of pair 7, which had been absent on 9 September though one had been standing on the nest drum on 7 September, seventy-three days after the decease of their chick and about six months from the beginning of incubation! One of this pair, however, presumably the male, had been absent since 17 August, as had also one of pair 8. The total number of adults present, however, had never been materially higher and at least one bird was present at all known nests, other than pair 7's.

Pair 1 had successfully hatched their second egg on 2 July; but thirty-seven days later when this, an undersized nestling was only about a quarter of the size of its parent, the latter grew restive and left it alone for a quarter of an hour at 5.12 a.m.; this day was the last one on which I observed the male at the nest for more than a month. At 11.45 a.m. on 14 August the female again left the chick for three minutes. Two days later the latter, the smallest in the gannetry, had (not unexpectedly) disappeared when little more than six weeks old. On 18 August the female flew up time and again to her nest hollow, 'anticking' pathetically, very briefly and, as one would say, dejectedly. By 22 August the nest had practically disappeared : nevertheless the male was present as late as 15 September.

Pair 2, who had laid their egg between 25 May and 30 May were even less successful, for by 18 July their egg was addled after fifty to fifty-five days' incubation. Both, however, were still 'sitting', mainly standing, on the egg on 28 July, and even changed over on 7 August, the last time the male was noticed. On 16 August the egg was finally smashed after seventy-nine to eighty-one days' incubation, and by 22 August this nest, too, had almost disappeared. The female, however, was present on 15 September.

Pair 3 were more successful and hatched their chick in the last days of June. By 21 August when the nestling was between seven and eight weeks old and when I noted the male for the last time, this female was also beginning to desert the chick temporarily : but mother and young one were still present on 15 September, when the latter was not less than eleven weeks old.

Pair 5 had never got as far as laying an egg, and on 5 August the only bird ever seen of this 'pair' began to desert the nesting site intermittently, though still present on 15 September.

Pair 4, whose chick had hatched in forty-nine or fifty days, lost the latter when it was about a week old. Both parents were present the next day, but thereafter only one. This bird was deserting the nest temporarily on 28 July but, like the others, was still visiting it on 15 September.

The earliest fledgeling had abandoned its nest drum on 10 August : but had pair 7's chick lived it would have fledged as early as the last days of July or the first days of August – for the fledging period appeared to be of the order of ten to twelve weeks. My only surviving young one, pair 3's, whose hatching date was known was, as we have seen, still on the ledge, fully feathered, at the age of seventy-eight to eighty-one days : though its parent, being one of those with a rudimentary nest on the uppermost ledge had, abnormally, begun to desert it for intervals of half a minute or a minute at a time (caressing it briefly and lightly on the head on her return) as early as the fifty-third to fifty-sixth day. This unusual behaviour was probably due to the irregular attendances of the male, of whose presence I had no record after 21 August. The young one was one of those slow to develop, retaining some down on its head and much on its thighs as late as the tenth week.

Of approximately one hundred and sixteen young that fledged fourteen had been seen to take off from the cliffs. In no case did the parents accompany them and in three instances, when the fledgeling's nest drum was also observed, the parent was apparently unaware of, or indifferent to, its offspring's departure.

In addition twenty-eight fledgelings had been noted on the waters of the Wick or farther afield – most of which probably came from gannetries outside the control area. Only five were approached by adults when on the water, and these had either treated them in the peculiar manner described or had left them alone. None had been seen to *take off* from the cliffs before 12 noon or after 3.5 p.m., but others had been seen on the sea as early as 10 a.m. and as late as 8.40 p.m. The main departure hours were those between 12 noon and 2.15 p.m., and no associations could be traced between the actual fledging hour and the state of the tide or the weather : but there was a notable raising of the emotional threshold in the form of wing exercising and 'concentration', during this period. All on alighting had drifted gradually southwards to sea, though some of those making only short flights probably remained in Wick waters overnight.

Throughout the fledging period none had ever been seen on the wing off Noss – nor, for that matter, off Shetland since gannets first began breeding there – after their initial take off flight. This suggested that an interval elapsed between the initial departure from the nesting ledge and their true fledging – that is, the ability to rise off the sea and fly; this was consistent with the interval that elapsed between the earliest departures from Noss in the second week of August and the first appearance of fledgelings on the wing off the coast of Aberdeenshire in the first week of September.

All the evidence went to suggest that those adults visiting fledgelings on the water were not parents, but inquisitive strangers. It would, in any case, be difficult to explain how the parent birds, of which one or other, or both, of every pair were still present at the abandoned nests at every hour of the twenty-four, could, during their intervals away from the cliffs, locate their young several miles off Noss. I will anticipate the objection that I had no evidence that it was the original parents or pairs that were still frequenting the abandoned nests after the fledging of their young, by pointing out that, as I was actually counting more *occupied* nests in September, *when eighty per cent of the young had left*, than at any previous time, it would be necessary to replace the parents of these eighty per cent by nonbreeding birds – if it be held that the latter are the new occupants of abandoned nests.

There were no Shetland records of adult gannets feeding young ones at sea, as there would almost certainly have been, did this occur, considering the far-reaching activities of fishermen off Shetland and the unusually keen interest of Shetlanders generally in birds : so the interval before the true fledging must be presumed one of starvation. The question then arose as to whether the nestling was fed up to the hour of its departure. As already pointed out the feeding of the young was never at any time the frequent spectacle that one might have expected it to be. All that could be said was that I never observed a fully feathered young one in the act of being fed, though those with down only on the head were, and that I saw only one act of feeding after 21 August – to one of a pair of 'twins', fully feathered except for a big patch on its head – though of course there must have been other instances among the less advanced young. (It was not until the end of July that I realised that one pair in the control area, and two pairs outside it, had successfully reared twins or were at any rate feeding two young apiece.) Nor did I ever see black young ones importune returning parents for food, as they constantly did in the 'black and white' stage – which suggested, incidentally, that it was not hunger that was the stimulus leading to departure. It was fair to presume, therefore, that feeding ceased about the end of the ninth week and about ten days before the young took off : while to this period must be added the further starvation period between take off and true fledging.

Early in October, when the oldest fledgeling had been nearly two months off the cliffs and when the youngest were just going down to the sea, the bulk of the adults also left the cliffs for good, after regular attendance for six months or more.* The most remarkable feature of their departure was that it was *not* brought about by the fledging of their young which in some instances must, as we have seen, have antedated this by as much as two months, during which time they had been in regular attendance at the abandoned nest drums!

Normally ninety-nine per cent of the gannets left Shetland waters early in October, but in some autumns immense shoals of sillock, the young of the saithe, attracted a proportion of the adult gannets to winter, with as many as five hundred at a time diving for saithe in Lerwick Harbour and more at other points around

---

* The following summer the gannetries were deserted by 18 October, though gannets were on the wing off Noss again as early as 19 December.

Shetland, and continuing to do so until the middle of February, when the earliest pairs would be thinking about visiting the gannetries on Noss again. It is interesting to note that these wintering birds do not roost on the Noss cliffs, but fly straight out to sea just before dusk, returning to the harbour at daybreak.

Postscript

The following summer the Shetland naturalist, Theo Kay, conducted further investigations into the young gannet's post-fledging activities. On 24 August he took his yacht, the *Soldian*, around Noss. Let him continue the account in his letters to me :

'We went first to the cliffs and found three young ones between the Cradle Holm and the Noup and within a couple of hundred yards of the cliffs. We then motored – the wind was very light from the north – about four miles east and zigzagged to about five miles south of the Noup. Roughly speaking, we covered twenty square miles and within this area we saw twenty-five young. *None* of these could fly. When we approached to within twenty or thirty feet they spread their wings and flapped away from us over the surface. The flapping was a feeble attempt to get on the wing and after six to eight flaps the attempt was given up and either the bird turned on us, with beak in the air, or it continued to paddle away from us. A shrill cry was made when the bird was excitedly trying to get away from us, shriller and not so strident as the *kirr, kirr* of the adult. This was the behaviour in every instance. When covering this area of water I could see that we might have gone right through it and not seen a single young one. They are spaced widely apart, perhaps more than half a mile on the average, and a good look out has to be kept to pick them out. All were paddling slowly to the south-east and south. I am convinced that every one was completely on its own. Not the slightest attention was paid to them by passing adults. A feature of some interest was that every now and then they exercised their wings as is done at the nest. This was an aid to us in picking them up on the water.'

Three days later Kay made a further expedition :

'Today we counted, within an area perhaps a little smaller than on the 24th, fifteen young ones : a difference being that six of these were discovered roughly east of the Noup, the others being south-east and south. There was a breeze from the south.) Two of those seen today, while at a distance from us and undisturbed, made deliberate attempts to get on the wing by making about a dozen flaps over the water. The attempts did not succeed – as was also the case with three young fulmars – but the efforts were much better than the ones they subsequently made when trying to escape from us. It may be surmised from this that given a few more days of wing exercising, a further loss of fat and a fresh wind, they would very likely be able to get on the wing, although perhaps not to fly very far.

On 12 September Kay went out again, leaving Lerwick at 10 a.m. and returning at 7 p.m. :

'The day was favourable, as I wanted to see what effect a breeze had on the young birds; a south-west gale was forecast but did not materialise fully until my return. We passed the Bard Head a mile off, steering SE., and proceeded six miles before turning N. and NW. to the Noup. The water was very dark except for the broken tops to the seas and it was difficult to pick out dark objects. No young birds were seen in this area, nothing but an occasional adult gannet, a few fulmars and a sprinkling of puffins, adults in little groups and young birds always singly. On getting to the cliffs I found a full house of adult gannets but fewer young ones than I had expected. There were no youngsters below or near the cliffs, but I had an idea I would find some east from the Noup, owing the to wind direction, and proceeded out that way. About a mile off I came on one, and half a mile farther another, and that was the total for the day. By approaching these birds from leeward I gave them every chance to get on the wing from off the tops of the seas with the strong wind blowing, but they merely lapped to windward and collapsed exactly as they had done with a calm. Very clearly these young birds cannot fly under any weather conditions until they have been at sea for a time and are tuned up. By that time they are away from Shetland. I am absolutely convinced that the young gannets are quite on their own. A parent could never find a youngster after it had drifted all night in a heavy sea and a gale of wind.'

XI

NIGHTS WITH NORTHERN GUILLEMOTS

There was one dramatic feature of life in a guillemot colony I had always longed to see again since those memorable nights on Lundy – the fledging of the chicks. Noss guillemots differed from those of more southerly British stations in belonging to the Northern race with markedly darker plumage, and also in the high proportion of bridled variants among them. Like kittiwakes and puffins, they returned to their breeding cliffs on Noss considerably later than they did to Lundy or the Farnes, and it was 28 April before I first noted a full house on the cliffs – as late as 7.15 p.m. – and again on 29 and 30 April. After this there was the customary week when only a few hundreds were present until 7 and 8 May, and a second week of small numbers up to 16 May. Subsequently, considerable numbers were always present, reaching a peak on 2 June, when most appeared to be sitting on eggs, which were first evident on 22 May.

On 21 June I observed the first adults bringing up fish to the nesting ledges, and a tremendous *arrg, arrg* of jubilation from a row of fifteen guillemots on one ledge in my gannetry would herald the arrival of one of their fellows with a disproportionately undersized tinfoil fish, and seriously disrupt my concentration on counting gannets! None, however, of those bringing up fish appeared to have young, and though by 25 June they were being much persecuted by arctic skuas, it was not until the end of the month that I could make out any young on the ledges, and 2 July before I began to hear their faint twittering *quew-ee, quew-ee.*

Occasional strings of adults, up to twenty-five strong, had first been noticeable returning from their northern fishing-grounds, often at a considerable height and sometimes spear-headed by a puffin, in the opening days of June when incubation was approaching its peak. The earliest fishers would arrive at Noss at 4 a.m., when those roosting or incubating had been sleeping for some three hours, the first of the latter leaving the cliffs twenty minutes later. By July many strings and small disintegrated clouds of fishers would still be coming into the island as late as 9 p.m., and at midday they would be approaching the north Noup at the rate of two thousand an hour. In the middle of the month this figure had risen to four thousand three hundred an hour, and at 7.50 p.m. on a calm dull evening a young guillemot was standing alone in a cell in the honeycombed sandstone of Puffin Goe *without* its parents. I knew then that the fledging was about to begin. For an hour after this, however, there was neither check nor abatement in the customary surge and fall of raucous uproar from the thousands of guillemots on the Noup; but at 8.45 p.m. I detected a change in the cadence of the uproar and, casting around for the meaning of this saw that a great stream of guillemots was pressing into Rumble Wick in a turmoil of excitement, every individual uttering an incessant and explosive *airr-rr-gg, airr-rr-gg.* The calling down of the young had begun and these were their last nights on the cliffs. Once again, after the lapse of seven years, I heard that haunting *queewee, queewee, queewee* peculiar to big chick guillemots ready to go down to the sea; and with the light growing dim at 9 p.m. the calling of the adults on the water became continuous. Half an hour later the wheezing pipe of young razorbills was also to be heard. By 10 p.m. it was becoming dusk, but strings of guillemots, all carrying fish, were still coming in high from the north, and at 10.30 p.m. when it was so dusk as to be difficult to take notes, many adults were still calling from the water and their young were still noisy on the cliffs. The latter, however, were mainly the younger chicks, with their distinctive piping *coo-ee* : the main hour of departure for the older ones had passed and the lone chick had disappeared from its cell.

Three nights later, when strings of fishers were coming in to the island at the rate of 4,500 an hour, I could hear other adults calling off Pundsgeo at 7.30 p.m., and an hour later one or two chicks were swimming with their parents off the south face of the Noup, where the tumult was almost overwhelming in its volume. On a broad reef at the base of the cliff twenty-four swaabies and thirty-five herring gulls stood waiting. The up-draught was too strong in Rumble Wick, however, for me to watch profitably, so I moved down to the shelter of Puffin Geo, where I found fifteeen adults on the water below the cliffs and a chick swimming away with one parent, who fought savagely with other adults, before the two of them ultimately swam out of the geo and away to sea. Two more chicks, diving as they went, got away with one parent apiece at 8.45 p.m. and 8.50 p.m., and at 9.10 p.m. a chick and its parent alighted on the water together. Meanwhile single adults were continually flying down from the ledges and then flighting up again and banging against the cliffs. By 9.30 p.m., however, excitement was on the wane in this geo and only one chick could be seen standing without its parents.

Though the light was dim by 10.15 p.m. – the sky being overcast in the south and west – several adults and some young continued to call off the Noup until my departure at 11 p.m., when the tumult was subsiding.

By 17 July the *queewee, queewee* of half a dozen older chicks standing alone was to be heard above the ceaseless twittering *cooee* of the younger ones as early as 4.10 p.m., when two or three adults were already calling from the water in Puffin Geo – and this despite a blazing sun there, the remainder of the island being entombed in fog. Five minutes later a chick appeared on the water with one parent, but they made no attempt to go away to sea, swimming about the base of the cliffs instead, with the customary bevy of curious adults crowding round to examine the fledgeling. They were still in the geo half an hour after this, and as no more chicks had come down and none were calling, their descent may have been accidental – though by this time a herring gull had taken up its stand in the geo and a dozen swaabies were waiting below the Noup.

At the end of the first week of fledging there was an appreciable decrease in the numbers of adults in Puffin Geo and also on the north face of the Noup, and on 19 July half a dozen adults were calling from the cauldron of surf seething at the base of the cliffs at the entrance to Puffin Geo as early as 2.45 p.m., when a similar number of chicks were standing alone on the ledges. But activity in the townships was still at a peak and at 6.30 p.m. as many as eighty strings of homing fishers were in view off the north coast at one time. At 7.15 p.m. however, all was quiet in the north coast geos, and it was 8.15 p.m. before the older chicks began to call in Puffin Geo and the first two adults appeared on the water. Five minutes later, when many single adults were dropping from the cliffs and plunging into the boiling green and white surf at their base, the herring gull alighted on its favourite ledge. At 8.40 p.m. I caught a glimpse of one chick dropping into the cauldron and racing at incredible speed over the surge, lifting itself with raised wing arms well out of the water, to its parent waiting on the edge of the surf; and away to sea they went straightway in noisy triumph – in contrast to that earlier afternoon pair. The gull did not see this fledgeling and left ten minutes later. Judging by the inactivity of those of its fellows below the Noup very few young guillemots were leaving their ledges on this stormy foggy night.

For some days we had been waiting for wind and swell to abate in order to take the yacht *Soldian* into Rumble Wick and moor her under the great townships of guillemots on the south face of the Noup. Theo Kay had indeed lain there all night on the 10th, but though five young ones had come down from the ledges before 10 p.m. none had parents waiting for them on the water and all were gobbled up by gulls : so they were probably accidental tumblers. On the evening of the 21st, however, I saw the *Soldian* round the Bard Head in a sudden deluge of westerly rain and at 6 p.m. she sailed into the Nesti Voe to take me aboard.

By 6.30 p.m., when we were off the Cradle Holm, one or two young guillemots were already on the sea and masses of adults were calling off the south face of the Noup. We lay off the north face first, and before we realised what was happening there was a plop in the water right alongside the yacht and a fledgeling bobbed up. It must have come down from a great height for though we were more than fifty yards from the cliffs it appeared to drop vertically into the sea. Only when one was in a boat immediately below the overhang of the Noup did one begin to appreciate its towering height and gigantic proportions.

The numbers of young coming down from the cliffs began to

accelerate at 7.45 p.m., and at 8.30 p.m. we moved round to the south face in Rumble Wick, where from the beginning of the fledging there had always been the maximum of tumult and where, at a guess, ten thousand guillemots might be seen on the ledges at any one time. An hour later the operation was at its peak on a now comparatively calm evening with slight misty rain and a gently rocking swell, after the succession of stormy nights. During the past two hours we had seen about one hundred and ninety young guillemots come down from the cliffs. Initially, quite a number had come down without parents, either to find the latter on the sea at the base of the cliffs, or to swim around the yacht calling incessantly : but when the rate of descent quickened the great majority were escorted down by one parent and a few by both parents.

Between 9.30 p.m. and 10.10 p.m., when a further one hundred and sixty came down from the south face at the rate of four every minute, the *tempo* of the operation, its excitement and complexity, the ceaseless tumult, surpassed all telling; the figure of one hundred and sixty was a minimum estimate, for there were periods during these forty minutes when fledgelings were coming down all along the face of the Noup more quickly than I could record them. They tumbled off those long ledges, hundreds of feet from end to end, immediately above the sea. They dropped from higher ledges, plopping into the sea all round the yacht. They floated down from the topmost shelves and platforms three or four hundred feet above us, with the young one in the lead and the parent a foot or two above it, either braking hard, with wings and webbed feet spread wide, when close above the mast, or passing high above it to alight with a plop or a soft splash.

One in every ten or twelve fledgelings was escorted by both parents, on either side and a little above it. Ninety-nine out of every hundred alighted within fifty yards of the cliffs, but at least one fledgeling and two parents made a splendid flight, alighting some three hundred yards out from the cliffs, and there were a few other flights approaching this distance, including those of one or two razorbills, of whom five or six with one parent apiece came down close by the yacht. It was very difficult to pinpoint one fledgeling out of hundreds actually leaving its ledge on these tremendous cliffs towering vertically above the yacht to a height where their remote tops were wreathed in mist : but some of those on the lower ledges could be seen, as well remembered on Lundy, peeping over the edge for long periods, then being brooded in the parent's little tent of sheltering wings, and then bowing forward again to peer over, before it ultimately did (or did not) take the plunge with a little leap out into space – and quite a number of those that came down were small black-headed chicks only about ten days old, and distinct from their grey-headed and white-cheeked elders brothers. The desperate adventurer was followed immediately by its parent who, however, would keep above it throughout its swift fluttering flight down, on wing-converts only, at an incline of about twenty-two and a half degrees out of the vertical. The fledgelings appeared to have a certain steerage control, for not one hit the yacht, though scores alighted within a few feet or yards of it. Alighting on one side of the yacht, they might dive and surface on its other side, and one diving directly down under the yacht was not seen to surface again. They came up perfectly dry from their initial and often prolonged submersion, but continual diving soon wetted them, settling them down by the stern. One or two of those who came down without parents from a great height did not submerge on alighting, but swam around us with breasts raised high out of the water. In this attitude their white bellies gleamed dazzlingly white, possibly significantly so, in the grey evening light – too significantly, for the majority of all of these orphans were snapped up by the waiting gulls.

Never ceasing for a second was the harsh *arrg, arrg* of those parents following their young down on the wing, crazy with excitement, and often our first warning of a pair coming down was the raucous alarum of a parent whose chick was heading straight for the mast. Continuous was the *queewee, queewee* of those solitary fledgelings advertising their presence on the water while looking for their parents, and one young razorbill cried his sad *psee-ee-ee* vainly around the yacht for a long while. Meanwhile the swaabies took a dreadful toll of those fledgelings swimming out to sea, mainly of those unescorted by parents, picking them off the water and bolting them whole, though nearby adult guillemots would shoot through the water threateningly at a swooping swaabie, cawing furiously. A curious incident occurred when a gannet picked up one fledgeling and refused to surrender it to a swaabie also seizing it, obstinately pressing his head down in to the water and threshing his wings. Six bonxies took their toll from a reef platform at the south corner of the Noup, on to which many fledgelings fell from ledges above. Though unharmed by their fall the majority of the latter soon fell victims to bonxies or gulls. An accidentally fallen young gannet also stood forlornly on this shelf at the edge of the surf, ultimately tucking its white head back into its scapulars and seeking peace in sleep. I had seen it fall from the Noup that afternoon, when it lay apparently stunned, though later recovering.

At a guess, perhaps three-quarters of the chicks that fledged this night got safely away to sea with their parents, though it had to be remembered that this was only a very small percentage of the potential, for egg losses in a community of guillemots were commonly very heavy, and it was doubtful whether ten per cent of those nesting actually in gannetries even hatched chicks.

The multitudes of guillemots continually crossing and criss-crossing the Wick at all heights above the mast, the tumultuous din, the minute to minute expectation of yet another pair or trio dropping down to the mast, together made these three hours the most amazing of a naturalist's life. The passing of a rorqual whale cartwheeling close by the Noup went almost unheeded.

At 10.10 p.m. when the light was very dim, we reluctantly hauled up our light anchor and stood away for home, though there was still no slackening in the rate of descent and no appreciable diminution could be observed in the numbers of guillemots in the serried rows and massed townships on the face of the cliff above. All the way down the north coast as far as the Whiggie Geo there were fledgelings on the water and adults calling, before we ultimately passed into a strange quiet, and a smooth passage home to Noss Sound, with only silent flights of kittiwakes returning from bathing and puffins running over the sea before us, threshing the water with their wings. It was 10.45 p.m. when I was put ashore in the dinghy at Gungstie and the yacht, with its cabin brightly lit in the near darkness, stood out to sea again for Score Head and Bressay Sound.